Ecocriticism and Turkey

Environmental Cultures Series

Series Editors:
Greg Garrard, University of British Columbia, Canada
Richard Kerridge, Bath Spa University, UK
Editorial Board:
Frances Bellarsi, Université Libre de Bruxelles, Belgium
Mandy Bloomfield, Plymouth University, UK
Lily Chen, Shanghai Normal University, China
Christa Grewe-Volpp, University of Mannheim, Germany
Stephanie LeMenager, University of Oregon, USA
Timothy Morton, Rice University, USA
Pablo Mukherjee, University of Warwick, UK

Bloomsbury's *Environmental Cultures* series makes available to students and scholars at all levels the latest cutting-edge research on the diverse ways in which culture has responded to the age of environmental crisis. Publishing ambitious and innovative literary ecocriticism that crosses disciplines, national boundaries, and media, books in the series explore and test the challenges of ecocriticism to conventional forms of cultural study.

Titles available:
Anthropocene Realism, John Thieme
Bodies of Water, Astrida Neimanis
Cities and Wetlands, Rod Giblett
Civil Rights and the Environment in African-American Literature, 1895–1941, John Claborn
Climate Change Scepticism, Greg Garrard, George Handley, Axel Goodbody, and Stephanie Posthumus
Climate Crisis and the 21st-Century British Novel, Astrid Bracke
Cognitive Ecopoetics, Sharon Lattig
Colonialism, Culture, Whales, Graham Huggan
Concrete and Plastic, Kylie Crane
Contemporary Fiction and Climate Uncertainty, Marco Caracciolo
Digital Vision and Ecological Aesthetic, Lisa FitzGerald

Doing Animal Studies with Androids, Aliens, and Ghosts, David P. Rando
Ecocollapse Fiction and Cultures of Human Extinction, Sarah E. McFarland
Ecocriticism and Italy, Serenella Iovino
Ecospectrality, Laura A. White
Environmental Cultures in Soviet East Europe, Anna Barcz
Fuel, Heidi C. M. Scott
Imagining the Plains of Latin America, Axel Pérez Trujillo Diniz
Literature as Cultural Ecology, Hubert Zapf
Reading Underwater Wreckage, Killian Quigley
The Living World, Samantha Walton
Nerd Ecology, Anthony Lioi
The New Nature Writing, Jos Smith
The New Poetics of Climate Change, Matthew Griffiths
Radical Animism, Jemma Deer
Reclaiming Romanticism, Kate Rigby
Teaching Environmental Writing, Isabel Galleymore
This Contentious Storm, Jennifer Mae Hamilton
The Tree Climbing Cure, Andy Brown
Weathering Shakespeare, Evelyn O'Malley

Ecocriticism and Turkey

Meliz Ergin

BLOOMSBURY ACADEMIC
LONDON • NEW YORK • OXFORD • NEW DELHI • SYDNEY

BLOOMSBURY ACADEMIC
Bloomsbury Publishing Plc, 50 Bedford Square, London, WC1B 3DP, UK
Bloomsbury Publishing Inc, 1359 Broadway, New York, NY 10018, USA
Bloomsbury Publishing Ireland, 29 Earlsfort Terrace, Dublin 2, D02 AY28, Ireland

BLOOMSBURY, BLOOMSBURY ACADEMIC and the Diana logo are trademarks of
Bloomsbury Publishing Plc

First published in Great Britain 2024
This paperback edition published 2026

Copyright © Meliz Ergin, 2024

Meliz Ergin has asserted her right under the Copyright, Designs and Patents Act,
1988, to be identified as Author of this work.

For legal purposes the Acknowledgments on p. xi constitute an extension
of this copyright page.

Cover design: Burge Agency
Cover image: Cameron Dutch/Alamy Stock Photo

All rights reserved. No part of this publication may be: i) reproduced or transmitted in any form, electronic or mechanical, including photocopying, recording or by means of any information storage or retrieval system without prior permission in writing from the publishers; or ii) used or reproduced in any way for the training, development or operation of artificial intelligence (AI) technologies, including generative AI technologies. The rights holders expressly reserve this publication from the text and data mining exception as per Article 4(3) of the Digital Single Market Directive (EU) 2019/790.

Bloomsbury Publishing Plc does not have any control over, or responsibility for, any third-party websites referred to or in this book. All internet addresses given in this book were correct at the time of going to press. The author and publisher regret any inconvenience caused if addresses have changed or sites have ceased to exist, but can accept no responsibility for any such changes.

A catalogue record for this book is available from the British Library.

Library of Congress Cataloging-in-Publication Data
Names: Ergin, Meliz, author.
Title: Ecocriticism and Turkey / Meliz Ergin, Koç University, Turkey.
Description: London; New York : Bloomsbury Academic, 2024. |
Series: Environmental cultures; vol 32 | Includes bibliographical references and index.
Identifiers: LCCN 2023055217 (print) | LCCN 2023055218 (ebook) |
ISBN 9781350125773 (hardback) | ISBN 9781350470224 (paperback) |
ISBN 9781350125780 (pdf) | ISBN 9781350125797 (ebook)
Subjects: LCSH: Nature in literature. | Ecology in literature. |
Turkish literature–20th century–History and criticism. | Turkish literature–21st
century–History and criticism. | Ecocriticism–Turkey. | LCGFT: Literary criticism.
Classification: LCC PL210.N38 E74 2024 (print) | LCC PL210.N38 (ebook) |
DDC 894/.3509360904–dc23/eng/20240317
LC record available at https://lccn.loc.gov/2023055217
LC ebook record available at https://lccn.loc.gov/2023055218

HB: 978-1-3501-2577-3
PB: 978-1-3504-7022-4
ePDF: 978-1-3501-2578-0
eBook: 978-1-3501-2579-7

Series: Environmental Cultures

Typeset by Newgen KnowledgeWorks Pvt. Ltd., Chennai, India

For product safety related questions contact productsafety@bloomsbury.com

To find out more about our authors and books visit www.bloomsbury.com
and sign up for our newsletters.

Kızıma ve anneme

Contents

Acknowledgments	xi
Introduction	1
1 Sea	**7**
A Land Afloat: Surrounded by Water	7
From Fishing to Diving: Life above and below the Water	10
Marine Pollution: Urbanization, Industry, Infrastructure	17
Blue Anatolian Mediterraneanism	23
Mare Plasticum: The Mediterranean Plastisphere	35
2 Climate	**45**
Anthropogenic Change, Accountability, and Belatedness	45
Vulnerable Lands: Anatolia before the Climate Debate	47
Warming Climate: Contributing Factors and Impacts	54
Land Degradation, Shamanism, and Mythopoesis	60
Climate, Temporality, and Ecodystopia	69
3 Routes	**89**
Movement, Environment, and Politics	89
On Foot: Nomads, Rural Walkers, Drifters	91
Taking to the Mountains: *Mecbur, Eşkiya, Âşık*	99
Topographies of Exile	106
Migrating down the World's Throat	114
4 Animals	**125**
Writing the More-Than-Human	125
Alterity, Representation, and Violence	128
Eating and Being Eaten: Unnameable Bodies, Liminal Beings	137
Poetics of Illegibility: Reading Like an Entomologist	142

    Humanimal Embodiment and Poetic Transformation   150
    Echopoetic Journeys and Entangled Species   156

Works Cited   167
Index   187

Acknowledgments

I am indebted to the series editors Greg Garrard and Richard Kerridge for supporting this project from the start. Greg challenged me to explore my ideas in their initial form and offered invaluable comments on the manuscript. Serpil Oppermann offered me support and encouragement in the early stages. Michelle Niemann's questions and acute insights made the book ever more readable. Colleagues and friends kindly read fragments and offered feedback.

My deepest gratitude, as always, is to my family. My mother Semra, my father Oğuz, and my brother Haluk embrace me with their unparalleled wisdom, generosity, and impeccable sense of humor. I am extraordinarily fortunate to have them in my life. Thanks to my niece Ece for writing an exemplary eco-story many moons ago.

I am grateful to my husband Baler, a most wonderful companion who offers his unwavering love and support in all my ventures.

Most importantly, my special thanks go to my brilliant daughter and favorite playmate, Nil. *You are infinitely more luminous than life.* May this book be a celebration of the incomparable joy you brought into my life, your spirited explorations outdoors, and the beautiful drawings you leave on my desk for inspiration.

Parts of this manuscript were presented at national and international conferences. I would like to extend my sincere thanks to all the organizers who offered me the opportunity to share my work. A different version of a fragment from Chapter 4 was published as "Writing and Animal(ity) in Contemporary Turkish Fiction" in *Turkish Ecocriticism: From Neolithic to Contemporary Timescapes*, edited by Serpil Oppermann and Sinan Akıllı (Lanham: Lexington, 2021). An earlier version of the essay on climate fiction in Chapter 2 was published as "Ecodystopia and Climate Temporality: Oya Baydar's *Köpekli Çocuklar Gecesi*" in *ISLE: Interdisciplinary Studies in Literature and Environment* (May 2022).

Introduction

At the convergence of two continents—Europe and Asia—lies Turkey, surrounded by the Black Sea in the north, the Aegean Sea in the west, and the Mediterranean Sea in the south. In the northwestern part of the country, there is the inland Sea of Marmara, which is connected to the Black Sea via the İstanbul Strait (Bosphorus) and to the Aegean and Mediterranean seas via the Çanakkale Strait (Dardanelles). These waterways divide Turkey into two parts: Anatolia and Thrace. Most of the Turkish territory is in Anatolia, the broad peninsula that is part of the Asian continent. Across from it is Thrace, a smaller territory that is part of the European continent. Turkey has a diverse terrain, comprising dense forests in the Black Sea Region,[1] coastlines along the Aegean and Mediterranean seas, and a vast plateau in Central Anatolia, which is hemmed in by two parallel mountain ranges, the Northern Anatolian Mountains to the north and the Taurus Mountains to the south.

Brief geographic descriptions, such as this one, often serve a similar purpose to maps incorporated into books: both help readers understand spatial relations in an unfamiliar territory. Yet such broad depictions are only the beginning of any story, whose complexity truly reveals itself when we take a closer look at the diversity and constant transformation of the ecological and cultural landscapes that constitute a region. A close-up view reveals that Turkey comprises a vast and varied natural environment, continually evolving through interactions among social, biological, political, chemical, and economic forces. *Ecocriticism and Turkey* sheds light on these interactions with the goal of addressing the literary and cultural dimensions of environmental change in contemporary Turkey.

Throughout history, Turkey experienced myriad transformations. Yet the pressures on the natural environment have perhaps never been so immense as today. When coupled with socioeconomic issues, the impact of anthropogenic change to the environment is so drastic that capturing its pace becomes an arduous undertaking. Some lakes we are accustomed to seeing on the maps of

Turkey are no longer there due to climate-induced droughts, some forests are no longer in place due to massive fires and mining activities, and some historic cities we once could not imagine this country without have been destroyed due to earthquakes and construction negligence.

What role can literature assume in responding to these ongoing transformations? We are in dire need of creative narratives that help us comprehend the magnitude and irreversibility of the changes shaping the planet and remind us of our complicity in their emergence. We need a dynamic map that shows the movement of pollutants through the environment, the increasing impact of the climate crisis, the pace of species extinction, and the scale of environmental migrations—along with a million red dots that read: "You are here." I suggest that literature can be our dynamic map, our network of red dots. It is a compelling medium for elucidating environmental decay and tracing its connection to human culpability, while inspiring hope and collective action.

Literary scholars in Turkey started participating in global ecocritical debates in the early 2000s. A significant landmark was the publication of *The Future of Ecocriticism: New Horizons* (2011), edited by Serpil Oppermann, Ufuk Özdağ, Nevin Özkan, and Scott Slovic. In addition to articles from Turkish and other international authors, the book also includes a roundtable discussion among the editors about the future of ecocriticism as an emerging field in Turkey. In the following years, two more books of Turkish ecocritical scholarship were published: *Ekoeleştiri: Çevre ve Edebiyat* (2012) (Ecocriticism: Environment and Literature), edited by Serpil Oppermann, and *Çevreci Eleştiriye Giriş: Doğa, Kültür, Edebiyat* (2014) (Introduction to Environmental Criticism: Nature, Culture, Literature), authored by Ufuk Özdağ. While these books provided the initial momentum for ecocritical research in Turkey, Oppermann acted as a catalyst in creating a dialogue between Turkish and international ecocritical circles through her academic activities and publications.

Over the past decade, several works published in English placed Turkish literary criticism within the larger debate regarding environmental issues and world literatures. These include *The Ecopoetics of Entanglement in Contemporary Turkish and American Literatures* (Ergin 2017); *Animals, Plants, and Landscapes: An Ecology of Turkish Literature and Film* (Gürses and Howison 2019); *Animals and the Environment in Turkish Culture: Ecocriticism and Transnational Literature* (Fortuny 2019); *Anadolu Turnaları: Biyoloji, Kültür, Koruma/Anatolian Cranes: Biology, Culture, Conservation* (Özdağ and Gökalp Alpaslan 2019); *Turkish Ecocriticism: From Neolithic to Contemporary Timescapes* (Oppermann and Akıllı 2021); and *Shamanism in the Contemporary*

Novel: Stories Beyond Nature-Culture Divide (Öğüt Yazıcıoğlu 2022). In addition to literary and cultural analyses, many of these scholars offered new theoretical perspectives on ecocriticism. Özdağ's work on restoration ecocriticism (Özdağ 2009), Oppermann's contribution to material ecocriticism (Iovino and Oppermann 2014), my engagement with deconstructive ecocriticism (Ergin 2017), and Öğüt Yazıcıoğlu's examination of Indigenous epistemologies (Öğüt Yazıcıoğlu 2022) are a few examples of contributions to ecocritical theory.

These publications consist primarily of edited volumes and monographs with specific themes. In contrast, *Ecocriticism and Turkey* intends to contribute to the existing scholarship by being the first monograph to offer a wide-ranging overview of ecocritical issues in Turkey. Admittedly, Turkey comprises such a vast constellation of ecosystems, cultures, and languages that it is nearly impossible to do an exhaustive study. Despite this inherent challenge, the book engages with as many different contexts and methods for thinking about literary and environmental cultures that are available to the author. Following an expanding trajectory, it takes readers on various journeys from the coasts of the Aegean Sea to the mountains of Eastern Anatolia. Each chapter converses with both renowned writers from the twentieth century to shed new light on familiar material and a new generation of writers from the twenty-first century to capture fresh perspectives. In addition to including various literary genres, the study also incorporates diverse voices—Rum, Kurdish, Armenian, and Laz—in the discussion. The scope of the project is further enriched by an interdisciplinary inquiry that brings literature into dialogue with climate science, political history, underwater photography, and bioart. While taking a regionally specific approach, the book also keeps an eye on planetary ecological change and remains in conversation with the theoretical debates within and outside of Turkey.

Ecocriticism and Turkey comprises four thematically organized chapters: "Sea," "Climate," "Routes," and "Animals." Each chapter responds to a series of issues that I consider urgent or understudied. Although the book stands on four distinct pillars, common threads run throughout the chapters and create dialogues that continue over the course of the book: neoliberal pressures on the natural environment (Chapters 1 and 2), natural and cultural diversity (Chapters 1 and 3), land and politics (Chapters 2 and 3), animal life (Chapters 1 and 4), and seascapes and (trans)nationalism (Chapters 1 and 3). Through these interwoven dialogues, the book aspires to present a riveting portrayal of the ecological and cultural texture of Turkey.

The first chapter, "Sea," focuses on marine environments and cultures to set the tone for the entire book—shifting our attention from nationalist conceptions of land and fixed borders to multidirectional flows across porous boundaries. I approach the four seas in and around Turkey both as products of cultural imagination and as unique ecosystems under constant transformation. Over two sections that focus on the Sea of Marmara and the Black Sea, and two sections on the Aegean and Mediterranean seas, I investigate both the cultural and material significance of the sea. Diverse elements come into play and lead the discussion in many directions, including fishing excursions, interspecies encounters, underwater explorations, marine pollution, mytho-historical accounts, exile narratives, and speculative biology projects. Presenting large bodies of water as both natural and cultural sites, this chapter offers a comprehensive portrait of the myriad implications of living on a land surrounded by sea on three sides.

The second chapter, "Climate," moves away from the coastal areas and toward inland Anatolia to tackle the climate crisis. I argue that time has become a central issue in climate debates due to the sense of urgency evoked by extreme weather events. Consequently, this chapter focuses on the various dimensions of the relationship between climate and temporality. I begin by revisiting the rural narratives of Anatolian authors, who were the first to discuss such problems as water scarcity and proneness to desertification in the 1960s, prior to contemporary claims that the earth is rapidly deteriorating due to the climate crisis. I then provide an overview of the climate-induced changes in Anatolia over the past few decades, addressing the contributing factors and key vulnerabilities. Next, the chapter turns to contemporary examples of climate fiction that move through time as they contemplate issues like environmental degradation, intergenerational accountability, and climate mobility to call attention to the tension between taking timely versus belated action.

The third chapter, "Routes," continues to remain located in Anatolia but traces the continuum between movement, environment, and politics. It examines the myriad ways that humans navigate remote mountains, valleys, deserts, and seas to show how politics reinscribes the natural environment. I combine the analysis of fictional and autobiographical narratives to explore different forms of human mobility, including Armenian and Middle Eastern communities in the discussion. Mapping human movement in multiple directions and for various motives—following the footsteps of nomads, rural walkers, itinerant poet-singers, outlaws, exiled populations, and migrants—I investigate how the relationship between environment and politics is continually redefined to reveal the permeable boundary between them.

The fourth chapter, "Animals," examines human-animal encounters in contemporary literature to question the relationship between writing and animal life. It asks whether it is possible to use language as a medium for writing about animals without erasing nonhuman alterity and gradually moves from a critique of animal representation to a discussion of the poetics of illegibility. I begin by historicizing the presence of street animals in Turkey as a way to consider the precarity of animal existence. I analyze selected novels to expose various forms of physical and representational violence that animals are subjected to in life and in text. Next, I study contemporary tales that elaborate on the question of liminality to complicate the human/animal divide. The remaining three sections engage with poetry—exploring such motifs as bodily *poiesis*, humanimal embodiment, and echopoetics—to underscore poetry's potential for preserving the diversity of the more-than-human world.

The writers that have inspired the analyses in this book place equal emphasis on catastrophe and hope in the face of environmental disruptions and uncertain futures. While tackling difficult issues, they also avoid falling into the litany of despair. They look critically upon the present to look ahead toward a better future and place our interest in literature as a resource of hope. In her ecopoetic manifesto, contemporary author Latife Tekin notes that a writer's role is to keep alive the hope that life can be lived differently. She then invites us to imagine another, far more lively, version of the existing world: "Dünyanın bir ikizi olmalı … biri tükenmeye yüz tutmuşken, öteki canlılık saçıyor" (2009: 125–6; The world must have a double … while this one is on the verge of extinction, the double radiates vitality).[2] A poetic tool for fueling our aspirations and contemplating our culpabilities, the radiant other planet acts as a much needed reminder that we can choose to inhabit the earth differently.

Notes

1 Geographically, Turkey is divided into seven regions: the Aegean Region, the Black Sea Region, the Central Anatolian Region, the Eastern Anatolian Region, the Marmara Region, the Mediterranean Region, and the Southeastern Anatolian Region.

2 Please note that when I discuss a Turkish work, which has been translated into English, I only quote from the English translation. If the work is not translated, I both include the original quotation in Turkish and provide my English translation in parentheses.

1

Sea

A Land Afloat: Surrounded by Water

When we imagine a country, we primarily think of land. The sea, however, is a defining feature of Turkey's geography. With a coastline of more than eight thousand kilometers, Turkey appears on the map like a piece of land floating on water. It is surrounded by the Black Sea in the north, the Aegean Sea in the west, and the Mediterranean Sea in the south. Additionally, the inland Sea of Marmara in Northwestern Turkey is connected to these three seas and acts as a biological corridor and genetic pool ("Marmara" 2021) that allows all of these bodies of water to interact with one another. The four seas are also connected to various rivers that run throughout the land and create a dynamic geography marked by multidirectional flow, circulation, and permeation across porous boundaries.

This chapter investigates a series of questions set in motion by water, starting with an exploration of how Turkey's dynamic aquatic geography is portrayed in literature. I begin with the premise that there is a vast body of work, which presents the sea as a backdrop for various stories about the human condition. Writers gaze at the sea from the glimmering surface and use it as a setting for improbable love stories,[1] difficult separations,[2] and quests for freedom.[3] In these narratives, where the ever-changing seascape mirrors the various hues of human experience, it is often the cultural symbolism of the sea that is placed to the foreground. In contrast, literatures that evoke the material reality of the sea, by addressing the biodiversity of marine ecosystems or the impact of human-induced activities on underwater environments, are relatively limited in number and scope. In addition to fishing narratives that call attention to life on the water, a handful of prominent authors, such as Yaşar Kemal, have written about marine habitats and their accelerated degradation, but they are the exception rather than the norm. Consequently, Turkish ecocriticism tends to engage with the same authors and issues when there is more room, in both literary and critical production, for exploring water ecologies with a focus on the cultural *as well as* the material significance of the sea.

The goal of this study is to address the need to reconsider the sea as both symbol and substance. I approach the four seas in and around Turkey both as products of cultural imagination and as unique ecosystems under constant transformation. For example, when writing about the Mediterranean and Aegean seas, I do not merely discuss how they have been idealized for their mythological and historical significance but also examine the impact of plastic pollution on marine environments. Presenting the seas in Turkey as "naturalcultural" (Haraway 2016: 40) sites, this chapter offers a comprehensive portrayal of the various implications of living on a land surrounded by water on three sides.

The natural and the cultural are often entangled, and this entanglement has both positive and negative implications. One of the positive implications is that due to the mobility of water, the seas have afforded humanity greater opportunity for travel than the land, playing an instrumental role in the development of civilizations. The Mediterranean Sea, for example, served as the conduit that made migration, trade, and cultural exchange possible. Bordered by twenty-two countries across three continents, it historically acted as an important crossroad, where diverse civilizations came together and formed a rich cultural tapestry. However, negative implications include the adverse effects of societal engagements with the sea. One example is marine tourism, which pollutes the sea immensely by generating large amounts of plastic waste and other litter. Since the flow of waste is not easy to contain, the damage often begins in one particular sea and gradually impacts the other seas in the vicinity. Seen in this light, water is a powerful medium for both desired and undesired motion.

In the following pages, I pose a set of questions that variously highlight the cultural and material significance of the sea: What kinds of (un)desired flows take place across different bodies of water and between terrestrial and marine ecosystems? How does the sea (dis)connect various lands, cultures, and species? How do cultural narratives about the sea differ from narratives that emphasize its material reality? In what ways does thinking about water challenge existing political and nationalist discourses? How does a reconsideration of land-sea entanglements contribute to marine preservation efforts? These questions provide a framework for my discussion, which comprises four geographically organized sections: two sections on the Sea of Marmara and the Black Sea, and two sections on the Aegean and Mediterranean seas.

The first section examines the culture of fishing in the Sea of Marmara and the Black Sea. I analyze fishing narratives produced between the 1950s and 1980s to argue that they were among the first to give visibility to life on the water and to pay attention to water as substance. However, these narratives depicted the sea primarily as a source of sustenance, thus providing a limited portrayal of the marine environment. The later emergence of underwater videography and photography in the 1980s both complemented and complicated literary portrayals of the sea by allowing the audience to visually access, and grow curious about, life below the water. I discuss how these visual media played a significant role in marine preservation efforts by shedding light on marine biodiversity. The second section continues the examination of underwater environments, but it pays close attention to material transits between land and sea. It investigates the sources of land-based marine pollution in the Sea of Marmara and the Black Sea. I address the environmental repercussions of industrial activity as well as urban development and infrastructure projects and tease out the reflections of these issues in contemporary literature.

Sections three and four shift the focus to the interconnected Aegean and Mediterranean seas. The third section investigates how these two seas were variously construed as homogeneous sites of national identity and impure cultural crossroads. I first address the legacy of Blue Anatolianism, a literary-historicist movement that emerged in Turkey in the 1960s. I then turn to other authors such as Sait Faik Abasıyanık and Yani Vlastos, whose portrayals of sea cultures present an alternative to the vision of Blue Anatolianists. The fourth section demonstrates that the Aegean and Mediterranean seas, once praised by Blue Anatolianists for their historical significance, are now awash in plastic. Utilizing a new materialist lens, this section elaborates on the role of plastic and other waste matter in permeating and transforming marine environments. I use examples of contemporary film and speculative bioart to analyze material flows across land and sea.

Concentrating on marine environments and cultures, this chapter shifts our attention from fixed borders to multidirectional flows across permeable boundaries. Destabilizing the "terrestrial ontology of bounded zones" (Steinberg and Peters 2015: 253), water evokes a constant interplay between terrestrial and marine habitats, northern and southern seascapes, and nation and transnation. I thus approach the four seas in and around Turkey as points of convergence and divergence among various ecosystems, cultures, and species.

From Fishing to Diving: Life above and below the Water

The Bosphorus, which connects the Sea of Marmara to the Black Sea, is a narrow strait that runs through İstanbul and divides the city in two: the European side and the Asian side. Due to this unique feature, the strait and the Bosphorus Bridge that spans the strait have historically held symbolic significance for (dis)connecting the many easts and wests of the globe. In addition to being an important maritime route, the Bosphorus has been indispensable to the social and cultural life in İstanbul since Ottoman times. With historical mansions on the coast and brightly colored fishing boats in the sea, it has been a great source of inspiration for myriad poets, artists, and musicians. Fishing, in particular, has always been a significant feature of the social life around the Bosphorus. In fact, writing about fishing in the Bosphorus is almost a rite of passage for any author who has spent time in İstanbul.

In his column penned in the late nineteenth century, "Vay Lüfer Vay" (Bluefish, Oh My), Ahmet Rasim writes, "Lüfer sözünü duyup da bir parça olsun dönüp bakmayacak İstanbullu farz edemem" (1954: 18; I cannot imagine an Istanbulite not turning his head upon hearing the utterance of the word bluefish). Indeed, *lüfer* (bluefish), also known as the Prince of the Bosphorus, has been the symbol of not only the Bosphorus, but also of İstanbul for centuries. In *İstanbul Balık Kültürü* (2015) (Fishing Culture in İstanbul), Asaf Muammer identifies the late nineteenth century and the early twentieth century as a special period for fishing, calling it *Lüfer Devri* (The Bluefish Period). He states that just as we have an important *Lale Devri* (The Tulip Period) in Ottoman history, we also have a Bluefish Period, a time when *lüfer* was abundant in the Bosphorus and fishing was a ritual celebrated with music and poetry (30).

An example of this ritual can be found in the Turkish modernist Ahmet Hamdi Tanpınar's novel, *Huzur* (1949) (*A Mind at Peace* 2008), where one of the leading characters recalls the infamous bluefish outings on the Bosphorus:

> Toward the end of September, the bluefish runs offered another excuse to savor the Bosphorus. ... An illuminated diversion stretching out along both shores beginning from Beylerbeyi and Kabataş in the south, extending north to Telli Tabya and the Kavaklar near the Black Sea, and gathering around the confluence of currents, the bluefish catches gave rise, here and there, to waterborne fetes, especially on darkened nights of the new moon. In contrast to other excursions

that developed as part of a venture demanding long outings, this carnival dance developed then and there, with everyone. (226)

As observed by Tanpınar, in contrast to most fishing outings that took place offshore, bluefish runs happened at the center of the city, gathering fishermen and observers together in a collective ritual. During these rituals, the famous bluefish entered human language through an extended vocabulary, assuming different names according to its size: *defne yaprağı*, *çinekop*, *kaba çinekop*, *sarıkanat*, *lüfer*, and *kofana*.

Perhaps one of the most humorous texts to articulate the importance of fishing to İstanbul residents is the satirist Aziz Nesin's short story, "Boğaziçi Hastalığı" (1957) (Bosphorus Disease). The narrator, a resident of İstanbul, spends an ordinary day in the city, where the topic of fish is everywhere he turns. In the morning, he randomly picks up a book from his library and it is Sait Faik Abasıyanık's short story, "Sinağrit Baba" (1950) (Sinagrite Father).[4] He then picks up another book and it is Ruşen Eşref Ünaydın's book, *Boğaziçi Yakından* (1938) (The Bosphorus Close-Up). He puts them both down and picks up a newspaper that has the following headline: "'Boğaz'a balık akını' … Balıkçıların bir ilanı: Vatandaş Balık Ye!" (Nesin 1957: 36; "Influx of fish to the Bosphorus" … An ad from fishermen: Citizen, eat fish!). Just as the narrator prepares to leave the house, his wife asks him to buy turbot fish for dinner. He finally goes out on the street to distract himself from all the fish talk, but to no avail. He encounters fishermen who shout loudly to sell their catch of the day. He hops on the ferry and is overwhelmed by the incessant talk of a stranger who tells him about the fish seasons in the Bosphorus, the impact of sea salinity levels on fish, methods for cooking fish, and the best places to fish. At last, the narrator asks the man if he works at the Fisheries Institute to which the other simply replies, "İstanbulluyum" (41; I am from İstanbul). In a witty tone, Nesin portrays the overwhelming interest in fish as the symptom of an Istanbulite's disease.[5]

Given the strong emphasis on the culture of fishing in Turkey, it is not surprising that early literary portrayals of the sea almost exclusively focused on the livelihoods of fishermen. Produced between the 1950s and 1980s, fishing narratives were among the first to elucidate life on the water and marine life as seen from the boat. They importantly called attention to the materiality of water rather than using the sea merely as a literary symbol. These narratives occupy a significant place in literary history as they have, to a great extent, shaped how the sea is culturally imagined in Turkey. However, their portrayals of the marine environment is mostly limited to the experiences of fishermen who see the sea as a source of sustenance, to the conditions above the water, and to the fish that have some kind of economic significance. Other aspects of marine life, unfamiliar marine species, and the impact of human activity on marine ecosystems remain either secondary or overlooked.

For example, in fishing narratives that take place in the Black Sea, infamous for its severe storms, the emphasis is often on the difficulty of navigating the open waters. Strong winds and high waves that whip up the sea take center stage in such novels as Rıfat Ilgaz's *Yıldız Karayel* (1981) (Pole Star Mistral),[6] which takes place in a town in the Kastamonu province on the Black Sea coast. The novel is filled with references to *karayel* (mistral; literally "dark wind"),[7] a destructive wind that blows from the northwest and gives a pitch black color to the sea; "sarı yel" (116; yellow wind) that blows from the south; "poyraz dalgaları" (249; *poyraz* waves) created by the wind blowing from the northeast; and "soluğan" (256; ground swells and currents). Various other waves and currents, to borrow Predrag Matvejević's words, "play an important role in the dramaturgy of the sea, its scenes and peripeteias" (1999: 23). They determine how fishermen navigate this tempestuous body of water and whether they make it home.

Another similar example is Yaşar Miraç's poetry book, *Karadeniz Hırçın Kız* (1988) (Black Sea, Petulant Girl). Miraç writes playful and melodic poems that address the open water conditions awaiting Laz[8] fishermen. One poem, which shares the book's title, addresses the sea: "al bizi kollarına / çalkala dalga dalga / köpük köpük / ... / kemençeler çalarken / ... / bi horon / tutuşalım" (83; take us into your arms / shake us in waves / in foam / ...] / while they play the kemenches / ... / let us play / *horon*). Myriad sounds and motions of the sea enter the poem in the form of musical rhythms and dance moves. The storms, the fortuitous waves, and the accumulating sea-foam are all elements of a festive moment that resembles *horon*, a fast-paced traditional folk dance unique to the Black Sea Region. The poem—much like Ilgaz's novel—places emphasis on the "lively materiality" of seawater (Coole 2010: 92), recalling new materialists' engagement with the dynamism and agency of matter (Barad 2007: 170). Rather than presenting the seascape as a passive background setting, they portray water as an agent capable of affecting the movement of fishermen who depend on the sea to make a living. However, there is not much emphasis on the underwater environment. At the center of the narrative is a predominantly male culture challenged by natural forces.

If we shift the focus to the fishing narratives in the Sea of Marmara, we can see that they share several common motifs with the literatures of the Black Sea: men navigating the sea, families waiting back home, fishing techniques, and displays of strength. However, perhaps because Marmara has relatively milder climate and sea conditions, writers engage more closely with the underwater environment and often depict human-animal encounters. For example, Yaman Koray's epic novel, *Deniz Ağacı* (1962)[9] (Sea Tree), recounts the adventures of Marmara Island fishermen in the 1960s by focusing on the story of Ahmet, who is an expert in harpoon fishing. At the heart of the novel lies Ahmet's encounters with the great swordfish, the fastest swimmer of the sea and a source of both awe and terror for the fishermen trying to catch it. Koray gives a detailed account of life on the sea and touches upon very important issues including Ahmet's struggles to compete with other fishermen who own large vessels and industrial fishing tools. The emphasis, however, is still primarily on the lives of fishermen and the swordfish catches.

What may strike the contemporary reader is that although *Deniz Ağacı* was written only six decades ago, the number of species mentioned in the novel—such as bluefin tuna, mackerel, and swordfish—has dramatically declined. As early as the 1970s, Yaşar Kemal began to point out to this decrease in marine biodiversity by addressing unsustainable fishing practices. In fact, he was one of the first writers to highlight the ecosystemic changes in the marine environment. In his essay, "Denizler Kurudu" (The Seas Dried Up), penned in 1972, Kemal narrates the lives of Menekşe fishermen in the Bakırköy District of İstanbul. They recall the 1950s with nostalgia, when there used to be such an influx of fish into the Sea of Marmara that their boats were filled with the bounty and the entire city of İstanbul was blanketed with an intoxicating fish smell (Kemal 1985a: 141). The fishermen then complain about the impact of the latest industrial fishing techniques such as trawling, dynamite fishing, and the use of lamps and radars, all of which dry out the seabed and eradicate marine species. Kemal also meets a fisheries scientist who informs him that industrial fishing during the breeding season leads to the extinction of certain species (203). Since the Sea of Marmara is a breeding bed for fish arriving from the Black Sea and the Aegean Sea, catching undersized fish—before they can grow and migrate elsewhere—disrupts the cycle of marine life.

In both "Denizler Kurudu" and his İstanbul novel, *Deniz Küstü* (1978) (*The Sea-Crossed Fisherman* 1985b),[10] Kemal also alerts readers to the illegal hunting of dolphins for their oil. He notes that in addition to posing a threat to the dolphin species, overhunting also impacts the migration routes of fish. Dolphins not only keep predatory fish at bay, but they also intercept fish migrating from the Black Sea toward the Aegean Sea, locking them in the Sea of Marmara. If dolphins are killed, Kemal writes, Marmara would ultimately become devoid of fish and be overtaken by invasive species (163, 169). Kemal's writings are unique in that they merge fishing narrative with environmental report to call attention to marine biodiversity and species extinction. However, even in his work, the narrative revolves primarily around cultures that base their existence on the sea.

According to marine biologist Mert Gökalp, until recently, most publications about marine life in Turkey have focused on edible or marketable fish (2011b). The diversity of marine creatures outside the economic cycle has remained largely invisible. The emergence of underwater photography and videography in the 1980s, however, made it possible for the public audience to see and grow curious about the richness of marine life. Diving had already had a long history in Turkey prior to the 1980s, but it was not until the late twentieth century that it was perceived as a method for exploring and preserving marine habitats.[11] Underwater videography in Turkey was spearheaded by Haluk Cecan, who made the first underwater documentary titled *Seyir Günlüğü* (Diary of a Journey) for the Turkish Radio and Television Cooperation in 1988. After that, he produced numerous documentaries that reveal the rich biodiversity and underwater heritage of the seas in and around Turkey.

Cecan once noted that despite living intimately with the sea, most people in Turkey have limited knowledge about marine life (2007). He thus found it important to submerse his camera into previously unexplored depths to make marine environments visually accessible to everyone. Approaching marine life with utmost care, he exposed such issues as the impact of industrial fishing and irresponsible tourism on marine ecosystems. To give a few examples, *Sessiz Dünyada Gezintiler* (1991) (Excursions in the Silent World) follows the loggerhead turtles (*Caretta caretta*) and the Mediterranean monk seals on the verge of extinction, while *Anadolu Mavisi* (1999) (Anatolian Blue) calls attention to marine pollution. For Cecan, underwater environments are spaces of interspecies encounters that can foster a sense of connection between humans and marine animals. Infamously noting, "Bir ıstakozla arkadaşlık kurdum ama onu anlamakta zorlandım" (Cecan 2007; I made friends with a lobster, but I had a hard time understanding him), Cecan elicited curiosity toward marine creatures, calling attention to their unique abilities as well as to the limitations of human knowledge and perception.

A brief glimpse into the history of underwater videography and photography in Turkey is important for reflecting on their contribution to environmental awareness. Diving and underwater imaging appear ever more increasingly in blue humanities discussions about submarine immersion and embodied observation. Stacy Alaimo states: "To begin to glimpse the seas, one must descend, not transcend" (2016: 161). Similarly, Elizabeth DeLoughrey and Tatiana Flores argue "for a kind of submergence under the sea as an ethical engagement with our nonhuman others" and as a method for "theorizing the ocean, not as blank space or *aqua nullius* for human agents to cross but rather as a viscous, ontological, and deeply material place, a dynamic force" (2020: 133). In debates about underwater submergence, there are two crucial points foregrounded by blue humanities critics that are relevant to this chapter. First, submarine immersion allows for novel encounters with unfamiliar marine creatures. As Alaimo asserts, underwater photography and videography use astonishing visual images to elicit "recognition and response" from the viewer who cannot otherwise access the "vast, unthinkable, pelagic expanses" (2013: 151, 159). Alaimo refers to Rancière's definition of politics as "an intervention in the visible" (Rancière 2010: 37), as a basis for conclusion that "aesthetic presentations of fluid life forms of life can be understood as manifestations of care, wonder, and concern" (Alaimo 2013: 141). Alaimo makes the important move of connecting visibility with recognition, and perception with care. Sharing knowledge about submarine environments through visual media is one way, among others, to create empathy toward marine life and to strengthen preservation efforts.

Second, an increased understanding of aquatic life forms demands a critical revision of the limitations of human embodiment and perception. As Melody Jue observes, diving suspends the conditions in which humans navigate the terrestrial realm, such as clear vision and gravity-dependent movement (2020). In such distinct milieus as the subaqueous realm, many of the senses and epistemes we take for granted prove to be contingent. In their discussion of underwater photography, DeLoughrey and Flores thus draw attention to the importance of "nonrepresentationalist methods" that "consider the world from within" (2020: 139). Building on the Caribbean poet-historian Kamau Brathwaite's theory of "tidalectics" and repurposing Karen Barad's use of "diffraction," they propose "a diffracted ethics of the visual logics of oceanic representation," which foregrounds "the bending of a line of sight, the way an object in the water, when viewed from above or below, is distorted" (138). Taking the nontransparent nature of seawater as a basis, they point to the limits of optic transparency and challenge the viewer to think about the role of milieu in determining what and how we see. In contrast to Alaimo, who foregrounds the positive implications of aesthetic oceanic representation for raising environmental awareness, DeLoughrey and Flores propose that we shift our focus from representing watery bodies to how water, as a medium, destabilizes our understanding of embodiment, embeddedness, and visual perception. This, they argue, may alter how we perceive the marine ecosystem and engage with more-than-human others.

As methods of submarine immersion and embodied observation, diving and underwater photography are becoming increasingly important in Turkey. Like Alaimo, several underwater documentarists maintain that giving visibility to marine life may inspire people to care more genuinely about it. One example is the underwater photographer Kerim Sabuncuoğlu, whose work illuminates both the diversity of marine species and the impact of human activity on marine habitats. Sabuncuoğlu's photograph titled *Sessiz Çığlık* (Silent Scream), taken in Bodrum, captures the image of a moray eel feeding on an octopus arm impaled by a concealed fishing hook that goes straight through the moray's jaw (Sabuncuoğlu 2021). Unable to escape the hook and tangled in the fishing line, the moray eel dies as a result of ghost fishing, a term describing what happens when abandoned fishing gear in the sea "continues to fish." Another important documentarist is Mert Gökalp, a marine biologist and underwater photographer and videographer. Gökalp points to marine creatures' lack of visibility in Turkey, noting that nothing has been published about marine life since the Turkish-Armenian zoologist Karekin Deveciyan's 1915 book, *Türkiye'de Balık ve Balıkçılık* (Fish and Fishing in Turkey) (Gökalp 2011b). Asserting that learning about marine environments is a necessary step in advocating for their well-being, Gökalp published *Türkiye Deniz Canlıları Rehberi* (2011a) (The Guidebook of Turkey's Marine Creatures), the first book of its kind to offer a detailed study of approximately four hundred marine species. In a more recent publication, *İstanbul'un Deniz Canlıları* (2022) (Marine Creatures of İstanbul), Gökalp introduces a variety of marine creatures through both photographs and scientific descriptions of species, and calls attention to leading environmental problems such as overfishing and industrial pollution. He also directed two documentaries: *Lüfer-Boğaz'ın Prensi/Bluefish-Prince of Bosphorus* (2017) and *Orfoz "Resifin Efesi"* (2021) (Dusky Grouper "The Lord of the Reef"). The first documentary traces the annual migration of bluefish from the Black Sea to the Mediterranean Sea, showing the decrease in their numbers due to human impact on coastal areas and lack of regulations in industrial fishing. The second documentary explores the biodiversity of the Mediterranean Sea and the conservation efforts for endangered groupers in Kaş-Kekova and the Gulf of Gökova in Southern Turkey.

A final example is the work of Alptekin Baloğlu,[12] who raises questions about what we see when we gaze at the sea, echoing DeLoughrey and Flores's concern with the limitations of human vision. Baloğlu's book of photographs, *Bosphorus by the Sea/Denizden Boğaziçi* (2010), focuses exclusively on the Bosphorus, which has always held an important place in visual and literary culture. The sea, however, has often been praised, narrated, and photographed from the surface. Baloğlu presents a unique perspective by positioning half of his camera's fisheye lens underwater and the other half on the immediate surface of the sea, literally in the permeable limit between terrestrial and aquatic landscapes. The result is a series of images that capture both the cultural and ecological riches of the Bosphorus: the historic landmarks along the coast and the biodiversity of marine life underwater. Baloğlu shows that these two spheres are intimately related and deeply entangled, as opposed to how we might typically think of them as isolated from one another. Similarly, in his book, *İstanbul'un Sualtı Yaşamı* (2006) (Underwater Life in İstanbul), Baloğlu captures images under the waters of İstanbul, particularly in the densely populated and polluted areas like Haliç (the Golden Horn), to show how marine creatures, such as endangered seahorses, navigate these areas. Bringing the marine life under the city to our attention, he both expands our limited perspective on the sea and raises environmental awareness about the lesser-known inhabitants of İstanbul.

Paying attention to both the literary narratives of fishing and visual narratives of the underwater world provides us with a more comprehensive view of the marine environment. The writers I brought into this discussion were among the first to depict life on the sea and to call attention to the dynamic agency of seawater rather than presenting it merely as a symbol or as an inert matter. Some of them also called attention to marine species and to the impact of industrial fishing on underwater ecosystems, playing an instrumental role in raising environmental awareness. The underwater documentarists examined here were among the first to use submergence as a method for elucidating the dynamic materiality of water and the increasing depletion of marine life. They evoked a profound sense of connection to marine species. When considered together, these two different types of narratives, which pertain to life above *and* below the water's surface, help us conceptualize land-sea connectivity in a way that more thoroughly acknowledges the accountability of humans toward more-than-human nature.

Marine Pollution: Urbanization, Industry, Infrastructure

An inner sea that hosts one of Turkey's largest ports and a significant portion of industry and trade centers along its coast, the Sea of Marmara has suffered from heavy pollution since the 1950s. İstanbul, the largest city to have a coast on this sea, has been an important industrial center since the mid-1800s due to its location. In the early 1900s, however, industrial growth accelerated with such speed that İstanbul became home to 55 percent of Turkish industries by the mid-twentieth century (Doğan 2013: 520). Since this time, the city has continued to expand radically as a result of increasing industrial activity, rapid population growth, and urban sprawl.[13] Consequently, the Sea of Marmara, particularly the Bosphorus and the Golden Horn, became immensely polluted. The Black Sea, which meets the Sea of Marmara in Northern İstanbul, is also affected by this pollution to a varying extent. This section continues the discussion started in the previous one and examines the impact of land-based activities on the Sea of Marmara and the Black Sea, shedding light on undesired material transits between terrestrial and marine environments.

In addition to İstanbul, the industrial port city of Kocaeli, located to the northwest of the Sea of Marmara, is also one of the most polluted areas to date. Dilovası, a district in Kocaeli, contains about 15 percent of Turkey's total manufacturing industry, including chemical and basic metal industries. The Dilovası Organized Industrial Zone (DOIZ) is home to approximately one hundred and seventy-four companies, and 13 percent of these operate within the metal products industry sector, which emits a particularly large amount of pollutants (Hamzaoğlu et al. 2011: 370). Researchers have shown that heavy metal pollution from industrial wastewater affects both surface and ground waters and permeates the streams that pour into the Sea of Marmara, the Black Sea, and the İzmit Bay, posing a serious threat to the marine ecosystem as well as to public health. Professor Onur Hamzaoğlu, public health and epidemiology expert, has spearheaded important investigations into the effects of chemical pollutants on environmental and public health in Dilovası and the surrounding region. Hamzaoğlu et al. have called attention to high concentrations of air and water pollution (2014: 81) and to the high rates of cancer and other maladies among local residents (2011: 372).

The industrial activity in İstanbul and Kocaeli continues to adversely affect both the Sea of Marmara and the communities living around it. Authors such as Yaşar Kemal and Latife Tekin have persistently addressed these issues in their novels, revealing the impact of industrial pollution and ineffective waste management on the environment. Published in 1984, Tekin's *Berci Kristin Çöp Masalları* (*Berji Kristin: Tales from the Garbage Hills* 1993) recounts the story of a community that lives near the landfills and lives off picking waste. Modeled after the shantytowns and informal settlements constructed on the outskirts of İstanbul following internal migrations, the neighborhood of "Garbage Hill" is inhabited by individuals marginalized by the society due to their poverty and diverse ethnic backgrounds. Several factories are established in their neighborhood, which are later ironically named "Flower Hill Industries," and the area turns into an industrial zone. The locals endure a series of tragic events while living amid dumping grounds and factories. They grow so accustomed to health problems that their level of exposure to toxic matter determines their social and marital status:

> Their proverb for marriage between equals was "A bride with dust in her lungs to the brave lad with lead in his blood." The saying gained ground when, one after another, the young car battery workers married girls from the linen factory. Young men who had worked in the car battery factories for two or three years could contract lead-poisoning and become impotent and the only match they could find on Rubbish Road was with the pale wan linen workers. (Tekin 1993: 56)

Tekin details the deteriorating health conditions of the laborers working at different factories. Those working at Mr. Izak's refrigerator factory turn "as white as the yogurt; the refrigerator fumes got into their wide-open eyes, their throats were hoarse and torn from coughing" (88). Metal workers attending underground machines wash themselves before coming up aboveground, "desperate to clear their stifled lungs and blow out the metal dust lodged in their throats as soon as they could" (98). After a while, they name the factories "after their effects; some made the lungs collapse, some shriveled the eye, some caused deafness" (55–6). Industrial pollution transfigures both the land and the (non)human bodies living on the land. Cases of poisoning increase as a strange epidemic in the drinking water causes ulcers and red beak-like sores on people's skins. People not only drink toxic water but also wash in "the hot bluish water in which the factory serum and medicine bottles were washed" (28), growing bright, blue spots on their bodies. As ground and surface water sources become more and more contaminated, both humans and animals fall ill: the hens "curled up with drooping necks and died" (27) and the gulls "had their legs bandaged" (113).

Berji Kristin casts light on the material power of waste, treating garbage and industrial by-products as matter capable of transforming the environment and the bodies embedded in it.[14] Although the exact location of the novel is not stated, this marginal community could symbolically be placed in the outskirts of any big city in the Marmara Region, where the immense growth of industrial activity exposes residents to severe environmental health issues. A similar critique is also present in Yaşar Kemal's novel, *The Sea-Crossed*

Fisherman. Kemal describes the gradual transformation of İstanbul and the Sea of Marmara, focusing on waste discharge from various industries in the area surrounding the Golden Horn:

> And all around was the huge miry swamp, the Golden Horn, nothing but a cesspit now, a garbage dump, full of carrion, dogs, cats, huge rats, gulls, horses, a stagnant sea with never a wave, its flow forgotten, bleakly reflecting the neon lamps, car lights, and the dull hazy sunlight, strewn with deadwood and the sweepings of hundreds of kilos of vegetables, tomatoes, eggplants, oranges, leeks, melons and water-melons from the Vegetable Market, torpid, its surface skimmed with years and years of acid-stinking burnt oils from the surrounding factories, reeking with a noisome nauseating odor like no odor in the world. (1985b: 181)

An inlet of the Bosphorus that separates the European side of İstanbul into two shores, the Golden Horn was heavily polluted in the 1950s due to the domestic and industrial discharges from densely populated neighborhoods. Kemal describes this area as "a world of iron rust, forming a raddled slimy layer over the water," whose "all-pervading rotten stench" is mixed with the smell of tobacco from the cigarette factory and the odor from the lumber depot (181, 165). Drowning in garbage, "dense factory smoke," and "viscid, poisonous" air (182), the Golden Horn stands as the symbol of urban decay. Since Kemal first wrote this novel in 1978, various initiatives have been introduced to improve the area's water quality, including waste removal and the import of fresh sea water from the Bosphorus' Black Sea shore (Sofuoğlu 2019). The Golden Horn is in a relatively better state today, but industrial pollution is still an issue of grave importance around the Sea of Marmara.

One recent major impact of industrial pollution is the problem of mucilage. Since 2021, the Sea of Marmara has been covered by a thick layer of mucilage, a gelatinous substance produced by all plants and microorganisms. Mucilage is naturally found in the marine ecosystem, but it has exploded in growth in Marmara to the extent that it threatens the integrity of the ecosystem and is suffocating marine life. The leading causes of this mucilage outbreak—the worst in history—are excessive marine pollution, dumping of untreated industrial and domestic waste into the sea, increased levels of development along the coasts, and rising temperatures. According to Levent Artüz, hydrobiologist from the Marmara Environmental Monitoring Project, a critical moment contributing to the mucilage outbreak occurred as a result of the deep sea discharge system introduced in 1989. The decision was made to discharge one of Turkey's most severely polluted rivers, the Ergene River, into the Sea of Marmara (Çolak 2021).

Another major factor causing marine pollution is urban transformation and infrastructure projects. The Sea of Marmara is under constant threat by development-induced pollution from densely populated coastal cities like İstanbul. Since Adalet ve Kalkınma Partisi (Justice and Development Party) (AKP) came to power in 2002, they have been criticized for initiating a number of controversial urban development projects. Recent examples include the third bridge Yavuz Sultan Selim (2016) and the İstanbul Airport (2018) constructed in the northern part of İstanbul, which previously consisted of large forests. Causing mass deforestation in Kuzey Ormanları (Northern Forests), known as the city's lung, these projects destroyed the habitat of distinct flora and fauna, placed significant drinking water reservoirs at risk, and opened previously unpopulated areas to urban sprawl.

Currently, an even more contested megaproject is planned to be carried out in İstanbul. Proposed by the AKP in 2011 and described by President Recep Tayyip Erdoğan as his "crazy project," Canal İstanbul is a 45-kilometer-long artificial waterway planned to run from the Black Sea into the Sea of Marmara. If completed, the canal would cut through İstanbul, radically transforming the city's topography, and would run parallel to the Bosphorus, which is currently the only water channel connecting the Black Sea and the Sea of Marmara. It would create an island out of Western İstanbul, connecting it to Thrace only with bridges (Saydam 2014: 84). The government claims that Canal İstanbul would route the busy sea traffic in the narrow water passages of the Bosphorus thirty kilometers to the west, thus relieving the volume of maritime traffic on the strait and improving safety by preventing tanker accidents.

The opposition, however, argues that Canal İstanbul would have several negative effects on the different bodies of water in the vicinity. First, it would run through the Terkos Lake, Sazlıdere Stream, and Küçükçekmece Lagoon, putting the city's drinking water reservoirs at risk. Second, the construction process would pollute the seas as well as the forests and farms in the vicinity. Third, the canal would upset the delicate ecological balance of both the Sea of Marmara and the Black Sea. As oceanographer Cemal Saydam explains, the Black Sea receives water flow from several rivers running through Turkey (e.g., Sakarya, Yeşilırmak, and Kızılırmak) and Europe (e.g., Danube, Dnieper, Southern Bug, Dniester, and Don), which carry large amounts of industrial waste and fertilizer runoff. If completed, the canal would lead to an increased flow of polluted water from the Black Sea to the Sea of Marmara, hence placing too much pressure on this inland sea already embattled with pollution. For Saydam, this could lead to a radical decline in the oxygen level of the Sea of Marmara, resulting in the deterioration of marine life and possibly in a heavy stench throughout İstanbul due to the increase in hydrogen sulfide (2014: 47-8). Furthermore, because the Sea of Marmara carries oxygen to the naturally oxygen-devoid Black Sea through undercurrents, the change in Marmara's water quality would also affect the flow of oxygen to the Black Sea.[15]

These environmental issues all speak to the negative implications of the interplay between different seas. As Yaşar Kemal writes in "Denizler Kurudu," "Marmara'nın düzenini bozarsan, Karadeniz'in de düzeni bozulur, Ege'nin de … Dünya bir beden gibidir. Bir denizin düzenini bozarsan öbür denizleri de etkiler" (1985a: 193; Disturbing the ecosystem of the Sea of Marmara is bound to disturb that of the Black Sea and the Aegean Sea … The world is like a body. Intervening into the ecosystem of one sea impacts the other seas as well). Preventing the problems occurring in one sea from traveling into another is an enormous challenge. Such is the dynamic materiality of water, whose motions overwhelm cartographic boundaries, at times to our detriment.

Another potential issue concerning Canal İstanbul is in regard to the geopolitical position of the Black Sea, which connects the various nations that surround it—Russia, Ukraine, Bulgaria, Romania, Turkey, and Georgia. A significant ecological and geopolitical corridor between the east and the west, the north and the south, the Black Sea is a crossroad of "commerce, energy, and culture where the interests of four major international actors overlap: the European Union (EU), the United States (U.S.), NATO, and Russia" (Tsanov 2007: 1). As a result, maritime governance in the Black Sea often requires regional cooperation.[16] For example, issues such as the passage of commercial or naval ships are sensitive matters regulated by the 1936 Montreux Convention.[17] If, as the Turkish prime minister previously announced, Canal İstanbul sidesteps the Montreux Convention, concerns exist regarding how the world would respond to the existence of two water passages in Northern İstanbul (the canal and the Bosphorus), each with a different status (Öymen 2014: 70–2). If the canal alters the international dynamics and leads global actors to increase their military presence,[18] how would these changes affect marine life? Furthermore, the Black Sea is a high-energy region and a significant oil transit route from Russia and the Caspian region countries to the EU. In *Black Sea Files* (2005),[19] Ursula Biemann thus refers to the Bosphorus as the "bottleneck of global oil circulation."[20] How would the canal, a potential second bottleneck, affect global oil circulation and marine pollution deriving from tanker discharge? Admittedly, at this stage, Canal İstanbul looks more like a big question mark than anything else. What is clear, however, is that every decision made on the Turkish shores impacts and is impacted by a web of environmental-political factors playing out on many other shores.

Although the canal is a newly proposed project, it can be seen as an extension of the urban transformation projects that gained speed in the early 2000s. The Sea of Marmara and the Black Sea, two connected seas in Northern Turkey, sit close to highly populated cities with dense industrial activity and infrastructure development. They are increasingly growing more polluted due to land-based activities that contaminate water with debris, sewage, fertilizer runoff, pollutants produced by manufacturing and construction industries, and oil discharge from tankers. Depleting aquatic ecosystems and harming public health, pollution is increasingly becoming an issue that requires urgent measures. Writers like Tekin ve Kemal have addressed the environmental by-products of industrial activity and urban development, paying close attention to the toxic substances that infiltrate the sea and other water bodies. Yet, there is still room for new literary production that can shed light on the damage inflicted on marine ecologies. If, as Kemal notes, the earth is a body comprising interconnected ecosystems, then we must carefully consider the detrimental repercussions of land and sea entanglements and strive to preserve marine life before it dries up completely.

Blue Anatolian Mediterraneanism

Whether referred to as *hē thálassa* ("The Sea" in ancient Greek), *Mare Nostrum* ("Our Sea" in Latin), *Mittelmeer* ("Middle Sea" in German), or *Akdeniz* ("White Sea" in Turkish), the Mediterranean Sea has always triggered the imagination of writers and has been the setting of numerous literary and mythical narratives. Despite the diverse civilizations that inhabited the region throughout its long history, there has often been a tendency to view the Mediterranean region as a harmonious whole. As Sotera Fornaro points out, "The Mediterranean seemed a homogeneous sea to travelers of the eighteenth century; a crossing from North to South, a bridge to the 'Greek resorts' that represented the roots of European culture … a space of poetry and imagination, inhabited by the heroes and gods of Greek mythology" (2018: 109–10). Erasing all evidence of difference during these idealistic crossings, travelers located an originary Mediterranean identity in ancient Greece and in its strong cultural lineage, which forms the backbone of Western European modernity.

Such homogeneous representations of the Mediterranean, however, are no longer accepted among scholars. As Peregrine Horden and Nicholas Purcell note in *The Corrupting Sea: A Study of Mediterranean History*, "We should not take its unity as an uncontroversial geographical datum. Before the development of satellites, the Mediterranean as a whole was invisible" (2000: 10). Then how can one conceptualize this expansive aquatic space without turning to satellites and cartographic practices that give politically tangible form to the perpetual motion of water? In his poetic breviary, *Mediterranean: A Cultural Landscape*, Predrag Matvejević highlights the difficulty of piecing "the Mediterranean mosaic together," noting that "nations and races have conjoined and disjoined here over the centuries; more peoples have lived with one another and clashed with one another here than perhaps anywhere on the planet. Overplaying their similarities and interchanges and underplaying their differences and conflicts is so much bravado" (1999: 10). Matvejević defines the Mediterranean by way of negation, asserting that its boundaries are "neither ethnic nor historical, state nor national; they are like a chalk circle that is constantly traced and erased, that the winds and waves, that obligations and inspirations expand or reduce" (10).

Building on Matvejević's work, Serenella Iovino similarly calls for the need "to de-essentialize the Mediterranean" and "to cognize this sea as an *impure* crossroad for happenstances, relocations, and socio-environmental emergences" (2013: 6). Iovino describes the Mediterranean Sea in terms of the material and discursive forces that participate in its making:

> On a geo-physical level the Mediterranean is a coalition of water and land, of mountains and abysses, of lush vegetation and arid deserts. On a geo-political level, it is the field of encounters (and clashes) between trans-Atlantic *Realpolitik* and the Global South, the East and the West of the world, and very often a theater of political and religious conflicts and of massive internal migrations. (2)

Rather than perpetuating the ideal of a singular Mediterranean identity through a myth of origin, Iovino pays attention to the "unremitting state of transformation" of the Mediterranean "context" (4).

This section contributes to the ongoing debates on Mediterranean culture and identity by focusing on Turkish Mediterraneanism, which "developed not from historians who were following [Fernand] Braudel's approach, but from writers who identified themselves at least in part with the humanities and literature"

(Özveren 2015: 214). The first generation of Turkish Mediterraneanists were writers, scholars, and philologists who came together in the 1960s and started the literary-intellectual movement called Blue Anatolianism. Spearheaded by Cevat Şakir Kabaağaçlı, also known as Halikarnas Balıkçısı (The Fisherman of Halicarnassus),[21] Blue Anatolianists developed a strong interest in the ecological and historical riches of the Anatolian Mediterranean. They highlighted the natural-cultural heritage of the region and used this heritage as a basis for constructing a national identity.

Matvejević notes that given the heterogeneity of the Mediterranean mosaic, one must always begin her "tour of the Mediterranean by choosing a point of departure: coast or scene, port or event, cruise or narrative" (7). My point of departure is the Bodrum Peninsula in Southwestern Turkey, located at the junction of the Aegean and the Mediterranean seas. My scene is that of an exile in the 1920s. This is where and when the story of Cevat Şakir Kabaağaçlı began. Born in Crete in 1890 and raised in Greece and Turkey, Kabaağaçlı spent his adult years in İstanbul, where he worked as a writer, translator, and caricaturist for weekly magazines. His life took an unexpected turn when he published an article titled "Hapishanede İdama Mahkum Olanlar Bile Bile Asılmaya Nasıl Giderler" (How Do Prisoners Sentenced to Death Go Knowingly to Be Hung?) in *Resimli Hafta Dergisi*. Published under the penname Hüseyin Kenan in 1925, the article critiqued the practice of executing war deserters without first trying them in court (Kudret 1976). Because of this article Kabaağaçlı was sentenced to be a *kalebend* (prisoner) in the Bodrum Castle[22] for three years. At the time, the Bodrum Peninsula was not yet the tourist attraction that it is today. It was a small village where the primary means of sustenance was fishing and sponge diving. Kabaağaçlı thus knew very little about this remote place when he was first ordered to go there.

In his memoir, *Mavi Sürgün* (2017) (Blue Exile), first published in the 1960s, Kabaağaçlı offers a detailed account of his exile to Bodrum. Following the protocols of conventional autobiography, *Mavi Sürgün* comprises a series of adventures culminating in a life-altering conversion. Kabaağaçlı departs from İstanbul to embark upon a long journey using trains, buses, and horses. Toward the end of his travels, he asks the two gendarmerie that escort him whether he can walk the remaining distance to Bodrum. The long walk along the changing Aegean landscape turns into an epiphany. When he first reaches the Aegean Sea and hears its powerful roars, Kabaağaçlı feels liberated and says, "Al sana Cevat, işte Arşipel! … Ver mavini serinleyeyim biraz" (2017: 142; "Here, Cevat, is the Archipel![23] … Give me your blue so I can cool off a little"). His awe peaks when he arrives at Bodrum and enters a house whose courtyard door opens out onto the beach. At this moment, we witness a metamorphosis from Cevat Şakir Kabaağaçlı to the Fisherman of Halicarnassus.

> Çocukluktan beri ilk defa çocuk gibi hıçkıra hıçkıra ağlayarak kapıya diz üstü düştüm. ... Diz üstü düşmek, bir çeşit fırlamak, havalanmaktır. Babıali yokuşunun boyunduruğuna vurulmuş olan Cevat, boş bir kalıp olarak yerde yığıla dururken, onun ortasında—içinde sanki bir milyar kuş, sevinçle cıvıldaşarak—**Halikarnas Balıkçısı** irkilip, dikilmeye koyuluyordu. (156–7; original emphasis)

> For the first time since childhood, I fell on my knees weeping. ... Falling on the knees is a kind of release, a letting go that also allows a rising up. As Cevat, accustomed to the yoke of the Babıali ascent, lay on the floor like an empty mold, the **Fisherman of Halicarnassus** was preparing to stand up—with a billion birds joyously chirping inside him.

The moment of transformation into the Fisherman of Halicarnassus is described as a return to a long-forgotten point of origin: "Tanıdım, tanıdım! İşte o! ... Üç buçuk yaşımdayken babam Atina'da büyükelçiydi, 'Faleron'da', hafızamın dünyaya ilk göz açtığı çağda, o denizi görmüştüm ... Kaç yıldır, bir vakitler şimşek gibi gördüğüm bu dünyanın özlemini çekip duruyormuşum da farkında değilmişim" (157; "I recognized! I recognized! That's it! ... When I was three-and-a-half, my father was an ambassador in Athens. I had seen that same sea in 'Phaleron' at a time when my memory was first awakened to the world ... I had not realized that for many years I had been longing for this world that I once saw in a flash). The child, who long ago encountered the Aegean Sea in Greece for the first time, emerges anew to inhabit the adult body and psyche as "the Fisherman of Halicarnassus." Returning to his origins to recuperate a dormant Mediterranean identity, Kabaağaçlı defines his innermost self as a being deeply connected to the sea. His second encounter with the "Archipel" determines his fate as an author-ecologist, a fate that he describes as his destiny since childhood. In this autobiographical work, Kabaağaçlı crafts a Mediterranean identity for himself before taking the next step of theorizing about Mediterranean history in subsequent works.

The remaining part of *Mavi Sürgün* is largely an account of how Kabaağaçlı spends his time in Bodrum. Once he arrives there, he realizes that the Bodrum Castle is no longer used as a prison. He is thus condemned to stay within the premises of this remote village, where he freely moves around, meeting fishermen and sponge divers and listening to their stories about the Mediterranean Sea.

Since he is banned from sailing, it is through his conversations with these men, whose lives are dedicated to the sea, that he becomes acquainted with marine life. He also puts a lot of time in reading and writing about Mediterranean history, archeology, and mythology. A historian by training, he approaches Bodrum as an ancient text to be read through references to Homer, Herodotus, and Heraclitus of Ephesus. Ancient names of places (e.g., the Archipel) recurringly appear in his writings so as to create a continuum between antiquity and modernity. He lists numerous archeological treasures to allude to the classical civilizations that inhabited the region. References to mythical and historical figures make up an essential component of his narrative. For example, he compares the heroic seafarer Odysseus with historic figures such as Turgut Reis, the sixteenth-century commander of Ottoman naval forces in the Mediterranean, so as to create a continuum between ancient Greek and Ottoman-Turkish histories.

After spending eighteen months in exile in Bodrum, Kabaağaçlı is ordered by the court to complete the remaining time of his sentence in İstanbul. During this time in İstanbul, he restlessly anticipates his return to Bodrum, collecting fishing equipment and seeds of various plants from Turkey, Europe, and South America. Once he completes his sentence, he wastes no time in returning to Bodrum, where he ultimately stays for twenty-five years. In his second time around in Bodrum, Kabağaçlı immerses himself fully in the ecological life of the peninsula. He plants the seeds he previously gathered into the different parts of the peninsula: Bella sombra seeds from Brazil, citrus fruit seeds from Southern Anatolia, yellow cassia seeds from Paris, and passiflora and palm seeds from different parts of the globe (Kabaağaçlı 2017: 224–5). Most importantly, he introduces *bougainvillea*, which has since become the symbolic shrub of Bodrum. No longer a prisoner, he begins to navigate the Mediterranean Sea in his boat *Yatağan*—fishing, exploring inlets, and writing (216). He writes about the abundance of sea life, fishing and sponge diving, floral diversity, and horticulture.

Kabağaçlı approaches the sea both as a historical and mythological text waiting to be read and a rich ecosystem waiting to be explored. In other words, he pays attention to both the cultural meanings attributed to the sea—"the sea's discursive constructions"—and "its irrefutable materiality" (Oppermann 2019: 445). At times, as in his short story "Ege'nin Öfkesi" (1947) (The Rage of the Aegean Sea), the sea is represented as a mythic figure imbued with the power to bless and to curse. At other times, as in his novel *Aganta Burina Burinata* (1946)[24] (*Aganta! Burina! Burinata!* 2018), the materiality of water comes to the foreground when Kabaağaçlı portrays the physical challenges of navigating open waters.

Kabaağaçlı's fascination by the Mediterranean Sea results in a novel mode of sea travel named "Mavi Yolculuk" ("Blue Voyage" or "Blue Cruise"). A phrase still used in the tourism industry today, the concept originates with Kabaağaçlı and fellow intellectuals, such as Azra Erhat and Sabahattin Eyüboğlu,[25] who go on long sailing trips along the Aegean and Mediterranean coasts in local sponge divers' boats. During these voyages, they immerse themselves in the natural and cultural heritage of the Mediterranean. While swimming in a sea filled with dolphins, groupers, parrotfish, and red mullets, they also turn to mythical narratives such as Arion and the dolphin to add a mythic, poetic quality to their marine excursions. In her book *Mavi Yolculuk* (Blue Voyage), Erhat shares a detailed account of their excursions, describing how they make temporary homes from the boats, where they fish, cook, write, and read together (2018: 58, 16).

It is during these journeys that a unique vision of Turkish Mediterraneanism called *Mavi Anadoluculuk* (Blue Anatolianism) first emerges. Developed by Kabaağaçlı in conversation with Erhat, Eyüboğlu, Melih Cevdet Anday, and Vedat Günyol,[26] "Blue Anatolianism," also known as "Anatolian Humanism," is built on the premise that "the contribution of Anatolia in general, and Ionia in particular, to Mediterranean and world civilization had been greatly obscured by the philhellenic, Eurocentric, and Orientalist biases, if not the outright ignorance of the historians of civilization" (Özveren 2015: 212). Since many ancient civilizations sprang from Anatolia, they argue, Anatolia should take back its well-deserved place in Mediterranean genealogy. Blue Anatolianists thus demand a reconsideration of ancient Anatolian civilizations that gave birth to the Mediterranean culture, whose roots are typically attributed to Greece. They not only call attention to such civilizations as Lydians, Phrygians, and Carians, which inhabited Asia Minor, but also revisit the works of poets like Homer to reveal their connections to Ionia, hence ancient Anatolia.

For example, in her introduction to *Hesiodos: Eseri ve Kaynakları* (1977) (Hesiod: Work and Sources), which she translated with Sabahattin Eyüboğlu, Erhat remarks that in the earlier stages of their translation, they always compared Hesiod with Homer. They concluded that Homer was superior to Hesiod, just as Ionia was artistically superior to Boeotia, and Anatolia to Greece (1). However, upon more research, their view of Hesiod changed as they identified his Anatolian roots. Erhat notes that since Hesiod's father had migrated from Anatolia to Greece, his work carried traces of Anatolian traditions (15, 92). She even states that Hesiod's work could, in some ways, be considered more Ionian and Anatolian than Homer's epics (3). In other words, despite their altered perception of Hesiod, Erhat and Eyüboğlu continue to maintain their initial emphasis on the historical importance of Anatolia.

Privileging the Ionian culture and identifying Anatolia as the territory of the Ionian civilization, Blue Anatolianists contend that they must cease to search for the roots of Western civilization in Europe—and, by extension, in Greece—and instead focus on the cultural heritage buried in Anatolia. Europe, Erhat argues in *Mavi Anadolu* (Blue Anatolia), has taken away this heritage and estranged Turks from their history (2020: 6). For her, "Türkiye'de kökleşebilecek bir hümanizma" (6; a humanism that could take root in Turkey) requires that they shed light on the diverse civilizations that inhabited Asia Minor through the ages. Erhat remarks that most of the ancient pioneers of contemporary civilization, from literature to medicine, once lived in Anatolia: "Epos, yani destan türü Homeros'un *İlyada* ve *Odysseia*'sıyla İonya'dan, ... lirizm, Paroslu Arkhilokhos'la, Lesboslu Alkaios ve kadın şair Sappho ile Adalardan ... çıkmıştır. ... ilk filozoflar Thales, Anaksimandros, Anaksimenes Miletli" (2018: 75–6; Epos, the epic form, emerged in Ionia from Homer's *The Iliad* and *The Odyssey*, ... lyricism in the Islands from Archilocus of Paros, Alcaeus and Sappho of Lesbos. ... the first philosophers Thales, Anaximander, Anaximenes were from Miletus). Erhat thus concludes that the actual source of many Greek miracles is Anatolia (77).

To promote a historical consciousness of Anatolian civilizations, Erhat and Kabaağaçlı then initiate a number of projects. An expert of classical texts, Erhat translates the works of Homer and writes *Sappho Üzerine Konuşmalar ve Şiir Çevirileri* (1978) (Conversations on Sappho and Poetry Translations) with Cengiz Bektaş. Erhat's translations play an important role in blue voyages as they explore the natural-archeological sites they visit via renowned epics. Natural landscape becomes a living, breathing text inscribed with historical and mythological significance, and the visitation of significant sites allows for "canlı öğrenim" (Erhat 2018: 101–2; live education).

Looking back at the premises of Blue Anatolianism today, there is much to say about its legacy. Blue Anatolianists made an invaluable contribution to the literary and environmental culture in Turkey. Kabağaçlı penned several novels, short stories, and essays that shed light on marine life and sea cultures in the Aegean and Mediterranean regions. Erhat paved the path for the translation of important works and encouraged the teaching of classical languages at a time when the Turkish education system was undergoing major reforms. Furthermore, they provided the necessary momentum for the development of archeological excavations (Erhat 2020: 3–4). In *Anadolu'nun Sesi* (The Voice of Anatolia), Kabaağaçlı asserts that as recently as the early 1900s, no one knew about the Hittite civilization in Anatolia, buried under the earth for thousands of years: "O zamanki tarihler, Finikelilerden Yunanlılara geçiyordu dosdoğru" (1971: 13; According to the chronicles back then, history jumped directly from the Phoenicians to the Greeks). Blue Anatolianists helped uncover the historical importance of ancient Anatolian and Mediterranean civilizations. Furthermore, at a time when tourism was largely restricted to major cities like İstanbul and İzmir, and comprehensive guide books about Turkey were predominantly published by the French press, Erhat and her colleagues placed the forgotten parts of the Mediterranean coast back on the map (Erhat 2018: 161).

However, there is also an inherent contradiction in the ideology of Blue Anatolianism, particularly in their promotion of both humanism and nationalism. While they embraced the legacies of various civilizations that thrived in the Anatolian Mediterranean, they did it according to a nationalist agenda. On the one hand, they reacted against the predominant nationalist discourse of their time, arguing against a racial basis for national identity. Rooting Turkish identity in the cultural melting pot of Anatolia, they advocated for a new conception of Turkishness based on place (rather than race), which they called "Türkiyelilik" ("being from Turkey"). As Kabaağaçlı remarks, "Türkiye'nin … tarihi Türkiye'de gelmiş geçmiş koşullarca etkilenmiş ve o koşulları etkilemiş bütün etnik ve kültürel varlıkların tarihidir. … Türkiye tarihini Selçuk, ya da Osmanlı İmparatorluğundan, şu sultan, bu sultandan başlatmak, onu göbek bağından değil, belinden sepetlemesine kesmektir" (1971: 9; Turkey's … history is the history of all the ethnically and culturally diverse communities that have shaped and have been shaped by Turkey's past. … To start Turkish history from the Seljuk or Ottoman Empires, from this or that sultan, is to cut it not from its umbilical cord, but from its waist).

On the other hand, Blue Anatolianists perceived the Mediterranean Sea as a symbolic limit separating Turks from Greeks. Despite appropriating the works of classical figures like Homer on the basis of their connections to Anatolia, Kabaağaçlı marginalized the Greeks as well as the Rum community, the Greek Orthodox Christians of Turkey. As critic Herkül Millas states, although Kabaağaçlı spent his childhood in Athens and in Büyükada, an island in the Sea of Marmara with a predominantly Rum population, he often marked the Rum community as an "other." Millas observes that, in *Aganta Burina Burinata*, there are only two Rum characters, one of whom is a woman working at a brothel and the other is a man accepted by Turks only on the basis of being like "one of them" (2005: 158-9). Nermin Yazıcı identifies a similar problem in Kabaağaçlı's novel *Deniz Gurbetçileri* (1969) (Exiles of the Sea), which recounts a ban on sponge diving that prohibits divers from using the conventional techniques employed by Turks and only allows diving with diving suits, a method used by the Greeks. Yazıcı notes that the ban fuels the existing competition between Turkish and Greek/Rum divers (2011), leading Kabaağaçlı to make the following remark: "Rum dalgıç armatörleri ise motorları ile Türk kıyıları süngerlerini diledikleri gibi yağmalıyorlardı. Amerika sünger piyasası 'Greek silk sponges' diye Türk süngerleriyle dolup taşıyordu (1969: 255; Rum divers were plundering the Turkish coasts in their motor boats. The American sponge market was overflowing with Turkish sponges sold as 'Greek silk sponges'). Depicting Rums as plunderers, the passage reflects Kabaağaçlı's anxiety about losing to Greeks what essentially "belongs" to Turks, especially under the watchful eyes of the West. Despite the humanistic claims of Blue Anatolianism, a fairly monolithic and nationalist "we" thus leaks into Kabaağaçlı's writing (Belge 2006).[27]

Blue Anatolianists' efforts to reclaim Turkey's Mediterranean heritage was primarily a reaction to the genealogy of Western history, which, they argued, highlighted the Greek origins of Mediterranean civilizations, overlooking Anatolian history. Yet it can also be seen as a response to the rivalry between Turkey and Greece throughout the early twentieth century. As political scholar Leonidas Karakatsanis writes, "It was the war against the Greek troops occupying Anatolia that consolidated the nation-building process during the Turkish War of Independence in 1919-22" (2014: 13). Indeed, Turkish narratives about the War of Independence often portray the Aegean Sea as a sea of victory, where the new Turkish nation was "purged" of its enemy, the Greek, who got defeated and retreated westward to the Aegean coast. Following this war, there were several political tensions between the two nations.[28] In 1923, Turkey and Greece signed the Treaty of Lausanne, agreeing to a forced population exchange, based on religious identity, between the Turkish nationals of the Greek Orthodox religion (living in Turkey) and the Greek nationals of Muslim religion (living in Greece). The exchange reflected both countries' attempts to homogenize their populations and was grounded on an ideology at odds with the notion of the Mediterranean as a melting pot.[29] Although the Greek Orthodox communities from İstanbul were excluded from the exchange, they were subjected to violent attacks, as manifested in the September Events of 1955 and the displacement of the Rum population post-1964.[30]

While this historical background puts Blue Anatolianists' internalization of the dominant national discourse in context, it does not explain the readily apparent contradictions in their endorsement of both humanism and nationalism. Kabaağaçlı's attempt to highlight the importance of Anatolia to Mediterranean history within a humanist framework while placing Muslim Turks at the center of his discourse, overlooking the interwoven histories of Turks and Rums in Anatolia, is a significant inconsistency that must be acknowledged. As Kenan B. Sharpe observes, "One cannot claim participation in the Mediterranean world, and attempt to appropriate its texts and cultural artifacts, without at the same time opening oneself up to the possibility of 'contamination' by other peoples" (2018: 176). At this point, I thus find it productive to turn to other authors such as Sait Faik Abasıyanık, Sevgi Soysal, and Yani Vlastos, whose more inclusive portrayals of sea cultures present an alternative to the vision of the Blue Anatolianists.

A contemporary of Kabaağaçlı, Sait Faik authored numerous stories about life on the sea and on the islands, elucidating the tangled lives of Muslim Turkish and Greek Orthodox communities. Although he is not a writer of the Mediterranean per se, he spent several years on the Burgaz Island, an island in the Sea of Marmara, writing about the people he encountered during his daily excursions: "fishermen, youngsters, loiterers, the owners and patrons of coffeehouses" (Halman 1995: 3). Rather than using characters to present grand ideologies, Sait Faik focuses on the subjective experience to portray "human frailty, foibles and follies" (9). His characters hop from one island to the next, at times talking to seagulls, as in "The Armenian Fisherman and the Lame Seagull" (2004b), and other times, discovering the complexities of friendship and erotic desire, as in "Coming of Age on Kaşıkadası" (1995a). When Sait Faik writes about the multicultural texture of the islands, he does not resort to genealogy or political commentary. Instead he shares stories of Rum and Armenian islanders, fishermen, and artisans by blending "the vernacular with lyrical touches, a tender humanistic empathy, and ironic twists in the story line" (Halman 2004: vii). For example, "Bir Kaya Parçası Gibi" (1952) (Like a Piece of Rock) recounts a fishing excursion led by an experienced Rum fisherman named Barba Vasil,[31] who teaches his companion how to navigate the sea under foggy conditions without surrendering to anxiety. Another story, "*The Stelyanos Hrisopulos*" (1995c), revolves around the Rum fisherman Stelyanos who takes care of his ill grandson Trifon, supporting the child's dream of building a ship—named after his grandfather—to "go to the edge of the sea" (139).

In a 1936 letter addressed to Yaşar Nabi Nayır, the founder and editor of the literary journal *Varlık*, Sait Faik remarks that the owners of *Yücel* magazine, where he first intended to publish "*The Stelyanos Hrisopulos*," found his story too "cosmopolitan" (Abasıyanık 1972: 89). Disappointed by the magazine's response, Sait Faik pulled his piece and decided to publish it in *Varlık*. In his letter, Sait Faik asserts that his story is a "humain bir yazı" (humanist piece of writing) and that one should not be considered non-Turkish for being Rum or perceived as a lesser human for being named Hrisopulos (89). Portraying the island culture as a complex and beautiful tapestry, he remarks: "The world is teeming with people: many of them, who look alike, bathe at beaches … Your eyes are nearer to me than my eyes, your hands are as nervous as mine … Whatever your color … I can understand your language, smell your smell. … It is clear to me that I love people more than flags" (1995b: 155). Prioritizing the stars in the sky over the stars on national flags, Sait Faik pays attention to the abiding interactions between people that wash in the same sea and whose lives touch one another, hence maintaining a "sense of optimism about the human capability of building a better society" (Halman 1995: 8).

The intertwined lives of Muslim Turkish and Greek Orthodox communities have also been the subject of other works, such as Sevgi Soysal's *Yürümek* (Walking), a 1970 novel critiquing societal taboos against the backdrop of a politically tumultuous time in Turkey. The narrator, Ela, visits the İmroz Island (Gökçeada) in the Aegean Sea, where she spends time with a group of Turkish and Rum locals who dine and dance together in Stavro Stavropulos' tavern (150). This festive atmosphere ends abruptly when someone denounces the Greek Orthodox Church to the authorities for sending secret signals to the Greek island opposite İmroz. All of a sudden, the tavern is shut down and people retreat to their homes. The next morning, the military arrives on the island and surrounds the beach with barbed wire. Although locals have no reason to fear each other, they grow estranged from one another given the alarming atmosphere. Soysal portrays the typically peaceful coexistence of the two communities that is shattered by political tensions. Like Sait Faik, Soysal does not resort to identity politics, but she lets her characters speak for themselves through the daily interactions that occur among diverse ethnic and religious communities who call the Mediterranean their home.[32]

Similar motifs can also be found in Rum literature.[33] One example is Yani Vlastos's autobiography, *Baba Konuşabilir Miyim?* (2013) (Father, May I Speak?), which recounts his childhood in Çengelköy, İstanbul, in the 1950s when Turkish, Rum, Kurdish, and Albanian residents lived together harmoniously. The Turkish-Greek dispute over Cyprus and the September Events, however, led to serious conflicts between Muslim and Rum communities, ultimately spiraling into uncontrollable violence across the city. In the book, Vlastos recalls the time when Rum houses, shops, and churches were looted and Vlastos's family had to hide in the neighbor's house in fear. As he writes, they followed the news from both the Turkish and Greek media: "Atina Radyosu'nu İstanbul Radyosu'nun hemen yanında, orta dalgadan dinleyebiliyorduk" (73; We could listen to the Radio of Athens and the Radio of İstanbul side by side, via midwave broadcasting). While it appears that Vlastos is making a simple observation, I find this a poetic and telling moment in the story. Not proper Greek according to the residents of Greece and not proper Turkish according to Muslim Turks in Turkey (138), the Rum community had to keep one ear on Turkish politics and the other on Greek politics. They situated themselves in the middle of the two countries, which are so close to one another that they remain within the physical range of midwave broadcasting, despite the mutual enmity keeping them far apart.

After 1955, Vlastos's life is never quite the same, but the critical moment occurs in 1964, when the Greek nationals of İstanbul are deported from Turkey. Although Vlastos's family is not expelled, upon witnessing the radical change in the sociopolitical landscape and the increasing exclusion of the Rum community, they too decide to move to Greece. In Turkey, the Rum were even discouraged from speaking their own language in public,[34] a fact reflected in the book's title. Vlastos's small daughter asks, upon their move to Athens, whether she can finally speak *Rumca*[35] (307). During their move, Vlastos and his family ride a ship from Turkey to Greece. As he writes, "Seyahatimizi yaptığımız *Akdeniz* vapuru bu yolculuğu sık sık yapıyor[du] … İstanbul'u, Boğazı, Adaları, ve sevdiğim her şeyi geride bırakarak … belirsiz bir istikbale doğru yol alıyordum" (306–7; The ship named *Mediterranean*, which we took [to Greece], often made this journey … I was heading toward an indefinite future leaving behind İstanbul, the Bosphorus, the islands, and everything else that I loved). The aquatic distance between Turkey and Greece, close enough to cross by boat, distant enough to foster political animosity, is navigated by a boat named *Akdeniz* (Mediterranean). Ironically, Vlastos's move is a result of the political divide between Turkey and Greece, but the name of the ship that takes them to Greece alludes to the Mediterranean region as a whole, emphasizing the shared geography over national divisions.

A glimpse at various works written between the 1950s and 1970s reveals that the Mediterranean Sea has, throughout history, embodied various culturally and politically charged meanings. For Blue Anatolianists, it was an ancient body of water, which bore witness to the history of Anatolian civilizations in the Mediterranean. For Sait Faik Abasıyanık and Sevgi Soysal, it was a fertile ground where the coexistence of ethnically and religiously diverse populations countered nationalist ideologies. For Yani Vlastos, it was a geography of exile between Turkey and Greece. Considered in their entirety, these texts demonstrate that the Mediterranean Sea is a "vast archive" (Matvejević 1999: 23), which contains the histories of the countless communities that crossed its waters. This means, as Franco Cassano observes, that we can no longer turn to the Mediterranean to "reassign ownership of that sea to someone. ... We do not go to the Mediterranean to seek the fullness of our origins but to experience our contingency" (2012: xlvii). Despite the various political meanings attributed to it, the Mediterranean Sea resists the solidity of fixed borders and the myth of a pure "we," and acts as a palimpsest, where different cultures wash into one another, culminating in an ever-changing landscape.

Mare Plasticum: The Mediterranean Plastisphere

The postcards depicting the enchanting Mediterranean coasts conceal a secret: The azure waters of the Aegean and Mediterranean seas are home not only to endangered marine species, but also to the material residues of various land- and marine-based human activities. Sewage, urban and industrial wastewater, agricultural run-off, solid wastes, radioactive substances, discharged oil, and chemicals are only a few agents of this secret underwater life. The primary actor, however, is plastic. The Mediterranean Sea, once praised by Blue Anatolianists, is currently awash in plastic waste generated primarily by nearby coastal countries: Turkey, Spain, Italy, Egypt, and France (Alessi and Di Carlo 2018: 10). Mediterranean marine pollution is truly a transnational problem. If the proprietary sense of *mare nostrum* still resonates today, it should serve to highlight the complicity of neighboring countries in the changing ecological system of *mare plasticum*.[36]

Turkey is one of the major plastic pollution sources in the Mediterranean and is struggling with waste management. In addition to its own industrial and domestic waste, Turkey is currently the largest destination for waste exported from the EU, with a volume of around eleven million tons in 2019. This amount has tripled since 2004 due to China's decision to ban the import of foreign waste in 2017, which led to a change in the direction of the global flow of waste and an increase in Turkey's role in the global waste economy ("Turkey" 2020). Since Turkey does not have a well-established circular economy that enables the elimination of waste through the efficient production, use, and recycling of raw materials, how it handles imported plastic is a matter of great concern. Nihan Temiz Ataş, Biodiversity Projects Lead at Greenpeace Mediterranean, asserts that it is not clear "what percentage of imported waste is actually being recycled, incinerated or stored in landfills" (Uğurtaş 2020). As a result, it is not easy to monitor or to cut off the flow of plastic into the sea.

Plastic flow in marine environments does not follow a stable temporality.[37] It increases dramatically during tourist seasons, when marine litter in the Mediterranean increases by 40 percent. Found between the French island of Corsica and the Italian island of Elba, the Mediterranean Garbage Patch—a floating island of plastic waste—measures several dozen miles long and is the sixth largest accumulation zone in the world for marine litter. Despite holding only 1 percent of the world's waters, the Mediterranean concentrates 7 percent of all global microplastics (Alessi and Di Carlo 2018: 10). While such macroplastics as bags, bottles, and straws harm marine animals, it is the record level of microplastics—fragments less than 5 millimeters—that are the most hazardous to the sea's ecosystem. Microscopic zooplankton accidentally consume plastic fragments that they then transmit up the marine food chain. Animals such as sea turtles and seabirds fall into "olfactory traps," eating the plastic they mistake for food because of the odor emitted by the algae and bacteria that colonize it (15, 17). Plastic contaminants cause deformities and interfere with important biological processes, setting up a tragic example to what Alaimo calls "transcorporeal transits" (2010: 13), the material flows through the environment that transform human and more-than-human bodies.

Plastic plays other clever tricks. It accumulates organisms, building unique communities that are distinct from the ones living underwater: "Different types of plastics accommodate different inhabitants: there are about 1,000 types of microorganisms that inhabit the *plastisphere*, including those that cause diseases in humans and animals, such as vibrios" (Alessi and Di Carlo 2018: 20; my emphasis). Transforming bodies and ecosystems as well as manipulating the boundary between organic and inorganic, animate and inanimate, plastic is the new cyborg of the underwater world. It forms its own colonies by acting "as a chemical sponge, soaking up and concentrating other pollutants" in the oceans (Weyler 2017). It becomes a vehicle for transportation, as it travels thousands of kilometers with ocean currents, carrying invasive alien species across oceans. It could be said that the life of plastic in the terrestrial realm is monotonous, with a prescribed function and limited temporality due to its disposability. Its real life, however, begins after disposal and once it reaches the sea—where it gradually achieves a vibrant agency. Moving in different directions and speeds, constantly mutating and being mutated, it acquires a "vitality intrinsic to materiality" (Bennett 2010: 3) that brings it "alive with movement and with a certain power of expression" (Bennett 2005: 447).

Contemporary artists from Turkey increasingly explore the impact of plastic pollution on marine ecosystems. One example is the US-based Turkish artist Pınar Yoldaş, who creates infradisciplinary art projects that address the Anthropocene and engage with posthuman critique. Of particular relevance to this discussion is her synthetic biology project titled *An Ecosystem of Excess*.[38] First exhibited in Berlin in 2014, the project poses an intriguing question: "If life evolved from our current, plastic-debris-filled oceans, what would emerge?" (Yoldaş 2015: 359). Inspired by real-life bacteria that metabolize plastics, Yoldaş imagines a futuristic evolutionary story about "pelagic insects, marine reptiles, fish, and birds endowed with organs to sense and metabolize plastics as a new Linnaean order of post-human life forms" (359). Using speculative biology as a point of departure, Yoldaş combines various methods available to science, fiction, and visual arts to construct a taxonomy of marine creatures. She imagines "life forms that can turn the toxic surplus of our capitalistic desire into eggs, vibrations, and joy" (359).

In this alternative ecosystem, plastic is no longer considered a toxic material whose existence is a cause for distress. The damage is done, the grief is over. Plastic has already become a naturalized part of nonhuman bodies and organs. One example of the exhibited specimens is "STOMAXIMUS: Plastivore Digestive Organ," described as a maximized stomach:

> The evolutionary success of a plastivore is dependent on the ability to sense and metabolize plastics. ... This poly-chambered digestive organ is capable of metabolizing a variety of plastics, including high- and low-density polyethylene, polypropylene, polyvinyl chloride, polystyrene, polyurethane, polyethylene terephthalate, acrylonitrile butadiene styrene, phenolics, nylon, polycarbonate, and acrylic. (360)

Other exhibited organs include "E-PLASTOCEPTOR: Plastosensory Organ" and "PETRONEPHROS: Kidney For The Plastivore" (362–3). In Yoldaş's own words, "Starting from excessive anthropocentrism, *An Ecosystem of Excess* reaches anthropo-de-centrism by offering life without humankind" (359). She imagines how the world would look like in a hypothetical future where humans go extinct after acting as agents that alter the earth's hydrologic and geologic processes. In this post-Anthropocene world, the focus becomes the irreversible plastification of nonhuman creatures and their constant mutation to metabolize synthetic material.

The exhibition method of *An Ecosystem* mimics the scientific method of displaying organisms. Yoldaş uses glass lab containers that showcase different life forms floating in water. These organisms are accompanied by supplementary sketches and brief textual explanations that combine scientific discourse with environmental criticism. Yoldaş uses irony to detail the extent to which synthetic materials have shaped the biological processes of organisms and highlights some of the advantageous qualities they acquire over time. For example, in order to critique balloon pollution in the Pacific Ocean, she introduces a species called the "Pacific Balloon Turtle." As a result of digesting colored latex, "in a Lamarckian twist, the shell of the Pacific Balloon Turtle demonstrates pneumatic qualities. The elastomer lining on top gives this nimble animal an edge by allowing it to float when it is exhausted" (365). Another example is the "Pantone Birds," whose "beautiful colors" (368) are a result of the bottle caps they digest. Yoldaş provides a detailed description of the process of pigmentation in the avian population, using Pantone's color system and referring to color codes such as "Coca Cola Red" and "Dasani Blue."

Playfully obscuring the boundaries between fact and fiction, and art and science, Yoldaş invites the audience to experience the transformation of resilient marine species. While she holds humans culpable for these changes, she does not agonize over what lies ahead. As Burcu Baykan observes, "far from invoking dystopian scenarios of death, collapse, and catastrophe, [Yoldaş] is concerned with imagining a possible future in which a novel ecosystem transpires from the residues and enduring traces of the human species on Earth" (2021: 261–2). Yoldaş foregrounds the ability of more-than-humans to survive via mutation. We may not outlast the Anthropocene, but other creatures of the earth will, in one form or another. The joke, it seems, is on us.

In recent years, other artists have also explored the issue of marine pollution from different perspectives. Based in Ordu, a city in the Black Sea Region, Alper Aydın explores the tensions between human and natural systems by engaging with the unique geographical features of his milieu. His sculpture titled *Unwanted Guest* is a massive wave-shaped fishnet "threatening to swallow everyone" (Aydın 2019). Aydın takes a scene commonly encountered underwater and reproduces it on land to call attention to ghost nets in the sea, which cause grave harm to coral reefs. Another artist from the Black Sea Region, Mehmet Türkçelik, works with waste matter and found beach objects. Based in Filyos, Zonguldak, Türkçelik works exclusively with material washed ashore by the storms over the Black Sea: *çatuk* (driftwood), pieces of glass and metal, pebbles, seashells, fishnets, bones, and roots. He notes that waste materials and pieces of wood from the surrounding regions ultimately find their way into his "sea-smelling atelier" (Göçmen 2019). These materials are, for him, filled with narrative potential. Rather than distorting—by cutting and carving—the material already transformed by the sea, he works with the found form. The sculptures and masks that Türkçelik makes reveal the constant material flow—organic and inorganic—between marine and terrestrial environments.

Alican Abacı's short film, *Only One World Left* (2019), similarly reflects on the mobility of matter and recounts the toxic journey of human by-products and their subsequent entry into the food chain via the marine environment. Shot in Kaş, a seaside town on the Mediterranean coast renowned for its rich marine life, the film begins by taking viewers on a tranquil journey as they follow free diver Melike Selçuk's seamless movement underwater. The serenity of the deep blue sea is suddenly interrupted by a plastic globe thrown into the water. Abacı's camera then ascends to the surface and begins to show various isolated instances of human acts that contribute to marine pollution: a hand squeezing a plastic bottle, a hand throwing away a cigarette butt, an abandoned plastic bag flying in the air. After these various forms of litter find their way into the sea, Abacı once again submerses his camera underwater. The narrative pace and music slowly accelerate to reflect the mood shift. This time, we witness the diver navigating a sea of plastic bottles and bags, military tanks and sunken fishboats, until both she and the plastic globe are trapped in a huge sheet of plastic wrap. Abacı's film captures the flow of toxins across terrestrial and marine habitats and confronts the viewers with the excess of capitalist consumption buried in the depths of the sea.

These artists practice what new materialists like Stacy Alaimo and Jane Bennett express in theoretical terms. Tracing the multidirectional flow of matter across the environment, their creations not only shed critical light on land-sea entanglements but also counter the "persistent (and convenient) conception of the ocean as so vast and powerful that anything dumped into it will be dispersed into oblivion" (Alaimo 2016: 113). Yoldaş, Aydın, and Türkçelik map the trans-corporeal transits between land and sea, and human and nonhuman bodies, via different forms of artistic expression. They imagine new species, give visibility to underwater life, and work with found material to show the anthropogenic impact on marine environments. Countering the notion of a stable marine ecosystem independent of human intervention, they encourage the audience to reflect on their "corporeal intimacy with 'the seas'" and on the various consequences of this intimacy (Alaimo 2016: 126).

Shifting our focus from a perception of the world as comprising distinct entities to one that emphasizes flows and circulations, the seas call into question several boundaries we presume to be intact. Large bodies of water encourage us to experience the contingency of terrestrial demarcations by losing, even if momentarily, the feel of *terra firma* beneath our feet. Variously (dis)connecting ecosystems, cultures, and species, water evokes a complex interplay across porous frontiers. At times, this interplay is precisely what allows us to question the rigidity of political boundaries by reminding us of cultural exchanges that make the Mediterranean into a vibrant civilizational mosaic. Other times, the dynamic materiality of water is what allows pollutants to spread far and wide, creating an ever-growing Mediterranean plastisphere.

Moving from the north to the south, from the Black Sea to the Mediterranean, this chapter presents a glimpse into the dynamic aquatic geography of Turkey. It demonstrates that the sea is an important feature of both the physical landscape and cultural identity, and that how we perceive the different bodies of water is not independent of the available narratives about them. A thorough understanding of the marine environment thus requires that we listen closely to stories, which reveal both the cultural significance and the material reality of the four seas, approaching them variously as precarious ecosystems, geopolitical crossroads, dumping grounds for toxic waste, sites of mytho-historical identification, passages of exile, and spheres of plastic. This may precisely be the task that confronts us as we strive to better apprehend and protect the aquatic realm, one of the primary life-support systems for this planet we call home.

Notes

1 See Murathan Mungan's poem, "Kadırga" (1992) (Galley), which recounts a tale of love between two modern-day "pirates" who find one another on the shores of the Aegean Sea.
2 See Orhan Veli Kanık's poem "Ayrılış" (2005) (Separation), which uses the symbolic motif of a departing ship over the vast sea to articulate the pain of separation.
3 See Nazım Hikmet's poem "Hasret" (2002) (Longing), where the speaker longs to "return to the sea" in order to live and to die as a free man. Hikmet was forced to leave Turkey because of his political views and lived in Moscow for several years until his death. Since this poem was first composed in 1927, during his early years

in Moscow, the sea also alludes to a space of exile and to the possibility of returning to one's homeland.

4   The protagonist of this short story is a wise, loner common sea bream fish, who searches for the right fisherman to end his life, knowing precisely what awaits him in the afterlife: to be presented on the dinner table (Abasıyanık 2002).

5   In their book on İstanbul's cultural life, Pekin and Dinç make a similar observation: "İstanbullu balık zamanlarının ustası olmuştur. Uskumru, lüfer, palamut, istavrit ocak ayında lezzetlidir. … Şubatta kalkan mevsimi başlar. … Martta kefal, levrek ve kalkanın en lezzetli zamanıdır" (2004: 35; Istanbulites are masters of the seasons of fish. Mackerel, bluefish, bonito, horse mackerel are delicious in January. … In February, the season of turbot begins. … March is the month of gray mullet, sea bass, and turbot). The list continues until the year's end.

6   The novel is named after two cold winds that blow from the north and the northwest.

7   As one character remarks, "Sen bilmezsin bu deli rüzgarı! … Rengi olur mu rüzgarın? Karadeniz'de her gördüğün şeyin, her işittiğin, kokladığın şeyin bir rengi vardır" (Ilgaz 1981: 116; You don't know this mad wind! … Can you imagine a wind having a color? Everything you see, hear, smell in the Black Sea has a color).

8   The Laz people whom Miraç writes about are an ethnic group of Caucasian origin living in the Black Sea Region and speaking Laz language. A close engagement with the sea can be found in the works of several Laz artists. See Helimişi Xasani's poem "Deniz ve Laz" (The Sea and the Laz): "Laz balıkçıklar çok tez unutur / Dalgalar onlara neler eder / Sabah yine denize kendi gider" (Laz fishermen quickly forget / What the waves do to them / Come morning, they return to the sea, unhesitantly) (2006). See also Laz musician and environmental activist, Kazım Koyuncu (1971–2005), who recorded several songs in Laz, Homshetsi, and Turkish with his band "Zuğaşi Berepe" (The Children of the Sea) in addition to putting out solo albums. The Black Sea is the mental geography of most of Koyuncu's songs, including "Hey Gidi Karadeniz" (Oh, the Black Sea) and "Atın Beni Denizlere" (Throw Me into the Sea) (Koyuncu 2020).

9   The novel is titled after a peculiar marine plant that fishermen consider a lucky charm.

10 See Özdağ (2008) for a detailed ecocritical analysis of Kemal's *The Sea-Crossed Fisherman*.

11 The interest in underwater life in Turkey dates back to sponge diving. After the Cretan immigrants settled in the Bodrum peninsula in the early 1920s, sponge diving became a common practice. The period 1946–65 was known as the golden era of Bodrum sponge diving, but the sponge disease of the 1980s and the beginning of artificial sponge production put an end to this activity (Binder 2023). In the 1950s, the growing interest in underwater archeology made Turkey a desired

diving spot for German and American archeologists, who contributed to important excavations along the Aegean and Mediterranean coasts. In the 1980s, diving gained increasing popularity as an independent sport, leading to the establishment of Türkiye Sualtı Sporları Federasyonu (The Turkish Underwater Sports Federation) in 1980.

12 Baloğlu published the first underwater photography book in Turkish, *Sualtından Yansımalar* (Reflections from Underwater), in 1999.

13 Urban sprawl was followed by a booming construction industry, which made liberal use of asbestos-containing material until 2010, when asbestos use was banned. However, due to a 2012 law that allows for urban renewal in seismic risk areas, asbestos-containing materials are being removed during demolitions. This has strongly impacted the health of construction workers and the communities living in the vicinity, resulting in a high number of mesothelioma cases (Odman 2019).

14 See Ergin (2017) for a detailed ecocritical analysis of *Berji Kristin: Tales from the Garbage Hills*.

15 In addition to these ecological concerns, how the government would manage the evacuation of Western İstanbul "islanders" in case of emergencies like earthquakes is an additional issue that needs to be addressed (Gürdeniz 2014: 85, 91).

16 By the 1990s, for example, the water quality in the Black Sea had declined so radically due to agricultural, industrial, and energy-intensive activities that Turkey, Bulgaria, Georgia, Romania, the Russian Federation, and Ukraine signed the Convention on the Protection of the Black Sea Against Pollution (1992), making a regionally shared commitment to improving water quality.

17 Signed by Turkey, Bulgaria, France, UK, Japan, Greece, Romania, Yugoslavia, and the Soviet Union, the Montreux Convention Regarding the Regime of the Straits regulates maritime traffic through the Turkish Straits.

18 Military activity in the Black Sea has a substantial impact on marine life, in addition to contributing to a breakdown in the enforcement of environmental regulations. As Marian Paiu from the Romanian NGO Mare Nostrum states, pods of dolphins are killed during live fire training, and many suffer from the uptake in the use of sonar and military hardware (Schwartzstein 2016).

19 Biemann documents the Baku-Tblissi-Ceyhan (BTC) oil pipeline in its construction phase. BTC carries oil across Azerbaijan, Georgia, and Turkey. It is one of Turkey's several investments in South Caucasian and Middle Eastern energy reserves to decrease the country's dependence on Russian gas.

20 Not only do oil tankers cross the Black Sea and the Bosphorus to reach the global market, but several pipelines also run through Turkey, including "Blue Stream" (2005) and "TurkStream" (2020), two major trans-Black Sea pipelines.

21 Kabaağaçlı adopted the pseudonym Halikarnas Balıkçısı (The Fisherman of Halicarnassus) in reference to Bodrum's ancient name and historian Herodotus of Halicarnassus.
22 Built in the fifteenth century, the Bodrum Castle served as a military garrison and a fortress prison under the reign of the Ottoman sultan Abdulhamid II.
23 "Archipel" (from "archipelago") is the ancient name used in reference to the Aegean Sea.
24 The title is an expression in lingua franca used by seafarers until the nineteenth century. It is a word of command asking that the sail ropes be held tight to gain speed and exhilaration when moving toward open waters.
25 Erhat was a classical philologist and Eyüboğlu was a professor of French literature. They both worked at the Translation Office set up in 1940 by the Minister of Education, Hasan Ali Yücel, and paved the path for the translation of classical works. In the aftermath of the 1946 elections, which radically changed the political atmosphere in Turkey, both Erhat and Eyüboğlu lost their academic positions.
26 Vedat Günyol was a renowned translator and critic. Melih Cevdet Anday was a poet and initiated the *Garip* (Strange) Movement with Orhan Veli and Oktay Rıfat in 1941.
27 According to critic Murat Belge, Kabaağaçlı's historical novels, such as *Uluç Reis* (1962) and *Turgut Reis* (1966), rely on strong hierarchical oppositions between Muslims and Christians, Turks and Westerners, which stand in contrast to Kabaağaçlı's humanistic theories. Focusing on sea warfare and the Ottoman naval commanders' conquests, Belge argues, these novels celebrate the courage of Ottoman leaders, while ridiculing Christian men and vulgarizing Christian women (2006).
28 See, for example, the disputes over the fate of the Republic of Cyprus and the Aegean islands' territorial waters.
29 Ironically, the exchange, which changed the lives of more than one and a half million people, did not lead to the kind of homogenization desired by politicians. The deported communities on each side shared the predominant religion of their new countries, but their national origins still marked them as "other:" Rums deported to Greece were labeled as "the Turkish seed" (*Turkos sporoi*) and the Muslims deported to Turkey were stigmatized as "the Greek seed" (*Yunan dölü*) (Iğsız 2018: 3).
30 Also known as İstanbul Pogrom, or İstanbul Riots, the September Events of 1955 comprised a series of mob attacks targeting İstanbul's Greek Orthodox minorities. The attacks began after the radio broadcasted the false news that someone had bombed the house in Thessaloniki, where Mustafa Kemal—the founder and the first president of the Turkish Republic—was born. Following public demonstrations in the Taksim Square, clusters of people gathered to destroy Rum-owned houses,

churches, and shops in İstanbul. The September Events resulted in the mass emigration of the Rum population (Güven 2011). In 1964, the government reneged on the 1930 Greco-Turkish Convention that established the right of the Greek nationals of İstanbul to live and work in Turkey.

31 The character is presumably inspired after a real person named "Pendik'li Barba Vasil," a Rum priest who left his church to lead a life on the sea and became a fisherman in Pavli Island near Pendik (Muammer 2015: 78).

32 For a contemporary discussion of the subject, see Deniz Gezgin's novel *Ahraz* (2012) (Deaf), which takes place in a Turkish village by the Aegean Sea and elucidates the tensions between Turkey and Greece, among other things.

33 Rum publications were once a central component of the Ottoman intellectual life. As Foti Benlisoy remarks, in the early twentieth century, there were many multilingual publications put forward by the Rum population who variously spoke Kurdish, Armenian, Turkish, and Albanian. They also published Turkish books and newspapers written in the Greek alphabet. These publications came to a halt in Turkey in the 1960s due to the hostile political climate (Benlisoy 2013). Recently revived by Istos Publishing, cofounded by Benlisoy, the forgotten literature of Turkey's minorities is gaining visibility again.

34 Vlastos refers to the revival of the 1920s campaign that had the slogan "Vatandaş Türkçe Konuş" (Citizen, speak Turkish!) (2013: 136).

35 The language spoken by the Rum community.

36 The expression "mare plasticum" is borrowed from the book titled *Mare Plasticum – The Plastic Sea: Combatting Plastic Pollution Through Science and Art* (2020), edited by M. Streit-Bianchi, M. Cimadevila, and W. Trettnak.

37 Alican Abacı's film, *Antalya'da Denizden Çıkanlar* (2020) (What Comes Out of the Sea in Antalya), shows that pollution has increased dramatically following the Covid-19 pandemic. In addition to typical pollutants like plastic bottles, tires, and fishing nets, Abacı finds a large number of disposable masks and gloves on the seabed off the coast of Antalya, a Mediterranean city.

38 See Yoldaş (2015) to view the photographs of the exhibition.

2

Climate

Anthropogenic Change, Accountability, and Belatedness

Contemporary debates on climate change increasingly revolve around time. The sense of urgency instilled by extreme weather events engenders a distinct fear of belatedness, namely the anxiety of running out of time to curb global warming. The tension between taking timely versus belated climate action is central not only to climate mobility but also to the increasing corpus of climate fiction. This chapter tackles climate change following a fourfold analysis centered on the notions of temporality, belatedness, and intergenerational accountability. I examine literary works produced from the 1950s to this day to discuss both the evolving state of climate change in Turkey and the shifting perceptions of this vast phenomenon.

Prior to delving into a discussion of climate change, a brief detour is necessary to explain that the term "belatedness" has historical baggage in Turkish culture. It concerns Turkey's complex relationship to Western modernity. Renowned modernist Ahmet Hamdi Tanpınar's novel, *Saatleri Ayarlama Enstitüsü* (1961) (*The Time Regulation Institute* 2013), captures the significance of this term in relation to Turkish history. The novel is a satirical take on the failure to adjust to modernizing reforms carried out during the period that spans from the fall of the Ottoman Empire to the foundation of the Turkish Republic. Tanpınar portrays the loss of historical and cultural continuity through the allegory of unregulated timepieces. Central to the story is the eccentric "Time Regulation Institute," whose goal is to synchronize all the timepieces of a nation trying to catch up with Western modernity. As Özen Nergis Dolcerocca writes, "The Institute is a parody of accelerating modernization in a nation plagued by its belatedness: it regulates the citizens' timepieces, synchronizing all cultural clocks with the world historical time" (2017: 179). The Institute ensures synchronization via a system of fines, demanding "the collection of five *kuruş* for every clock or watch not synchronized with any other clock in view" (Tanpınar 2013: 11). Citizens whose timepieces run slow are required to pay an additional fee. As the narrator remarks, "there is undeniably a difference between fast and slow timepieces, and this difference is an extremely important one" (15).

This chapter demonstrates that many concepts once tackled by Tanpınar—from "belatedness" to "temporal irregularity" to "lack of adjustment to change"—still hold great relevance today, but they have acquired entirely new connotations in the age of climate change. As massive ecological phenomena shake up the pillars of modernity[1] and global warming threatens to melt the "Homogeneous, empty time" (Benjamin 2003: 395) of Western historicism, we no longer merely fear falling behind in the race for progress. In the face of climate-induced planetary transformations, which bring about an entirely new sense of temporal disorientation, we now fear lagging behind on climate action. In the context of the climate crisis, the "difference between fast and slow timepieces" is indeed critical, for the belatedness of action costs more than just a few *kuruş*.

Bearing this difference in mind, I begin my discussion in the first section by focusing on a cohort of authors, such as Fakir Baykurt, Necati Cumalı, and Yaşar Kemal, who wrote extensively about climate-related environmental issues in Anatolia in the 1950s and 1960s. Although they did not have access to the information on anthropogenic climate change that we have today and did not use terms like the "climate crisis" per se, they showed that Anatolia was suffering from such challenges like extreme temperatures and water scarcity. These challenges still exist today and have only become more alarming over time as climate change has accelerated. These authors have not received sufficient attention in current ecocritical debates about climate change, and I argue that an examination of the geographical and historical context captured in these texts contributes to a better understanding of the climate issues in Turkey today.

In the second section, I call attention to the immense transformation that Anatolia, the land portrayed in the literary texts of the previous section, has undergone over the past decades due to the climate crisis. I combine scientific and political analysis as a framework for understanding the background and the current state of climate politics in Turkey, including the major contributors and key environmental vulnerabilities. I briefly address the culpability of energy and mining industries, the history of climate mobilization, and the increasing cases of environmental migration. This section provides the reader with a brief survey of climate issues in contemporary Turkey prior to shifting the focus to the emerging genre of climate fiction in the following sections.

Sections three and four focus on two examples of climate fiction that take readers on myriad journeys across time: Buket Uzuner's *Uyumsuz Defne Kaman'ın Maceraları: Toprak* (2015) (*The Adventures of Misfit Defne Kaman: Earth* 2018a) and Oya Baydar's *Köpekli Çocuklar Gecesi* (2019) (The Night of the Children with Dogs). Each novel investigates the many challenges posed by a warming and commodified earth and envisions alternative societies, although the authors accomplish this in different ways. Uzuner composes an ode to the earth radically altered by climate change and proposes an ecocentric politics in light of ancient and modern texts on ecology, Central Asian and Siberian myths, and shamanic practices dating back to pre-Islamic Turks. In reaction to the ever-growing neoliberal pressures on the natural environment, Uzuner evokes ancestral wisdom and mythopoesis to cultivate a land ethic.

In contrast to Uzuner's evocation of the past, Oya Baydar's novel presents a dystopian, near-futuristic version of contemporary society, issuing a warning about the possible scenarios that await us should we keep up with the current pace of political and environmental degradation. Both authors respond to climate change via intergenerational dialogue, but whereas Uzuner resorts to ancestral teachings, Baydar turns to the younger generation for an answer. While dwelling on the temporal uncertainty of climate change and the varying social perceptions of climate temporality, Baydar foregrounds the importance of youth activism as an antidote to belated climate awareness.

Because climate fiction is an emerging genre in Turkey, there is both a limited body of literature and a fairly limited critical scholarship on the genre. Few critical studies of Uzuner's novel have foregrounded the shamanistic elements in her work more than the climate issue, and Baydar's novel has not yet been read with an eye on the central issue of time. This chapter not only reads these novels in a fresh light but also expands the horizon of climate criticism by seeking a continuum between modern literatures and contemporary examples of climate fiction. While paying close attention to the issues that emerge in response to Turkey's unique geographical, cultural, and political milieu, it also sustains a dialogue with ongoing climate debates without Turkey.

Vulnerable Lands: Anatolia before the Climate Debate

A broad peninsula lying between the Black Sea and the Mediterranean Sea, Anatolia is the Asian part of modern-day Turkey. The birthplace of many civilizations, Anatolia hosted various empires—including the Hittite,

Roman-Byzantine, and Ottoman—throughout its long history. With an interior landscape of high arid plateau and rugged mountain ranges, Central Anatolia has also been an important agricultural center since ancient times, where the first harvest appeared in mid-ninth millennium cal BC (Baird et al. 2018). Due to its rich cultural, archeological, and agricultural significance, Anatolia holds a very unique place in the Turkish imagination. The frequently used phrase *Anadolu toprakları* (Anatolian lands) carries multiple connotations; it refers to both the Anatolian "soil/earth," a rich source of life and nourishment, and the Anatolian "land," a historically important territory.

Anatolia has been a source of inspiration for numerous writers, musicians, and filmmakers who have captured its ecological, cultural, and historical textures. For example, botanist and nature writer Hikmet Birand's *Anadolu Manzaraları* (1957) (Anatolian Landscapes) is a book of essays dedicated to the biodiversity of Anatolian forests and steppes.[2] Folk poet and *saz*[3] virtuoso Âşık Veysel Şatıroğlu recited many songs about Anatolia including the infamous "Kara Toprak" (1971) (Black Earth), which articulates the significance of soil as both a source of life and an ultimate resting place. Nuri Bilge Ceylan's films, such as *Bir Zamanlar Anadolu'da* (2011) (Once Upon a Time in Anatolia), revisit myriad existential and political questions by exposing life in the Anatolian villages.

Some of the most interesting literary works about Anatolia were written by those who attended *köy enstitüleri* (village institutes), which were established in the early 1940s with the purpose of educating the rural populace.[4] Of the approximately forty thousand villages in Turkey in 1935, nearly ten million citizens had never received education, meaning that 80 percent of the village population was illiterate (Altunya 2012: 83–5). The state decided to establish the village institutes to bring about a "conscious resurgence of the village from within" (Tonguç 1939: 88; Altunya 2012: 84). The goal was to train the rural youth in their own milieu so that they could become teachers and educate the younger generations in the villages in the future. Built in areas with arable land, the institutes offered training in several areas of expertise, including agricultural practice and a strong arts education. In addition to cultivating the land, students read the classics of world literature, published literary journals, and studied with renowned musicians and writers such as Âşık Veysel and Yaşar Kemal (Dündar 2000: 40, 74). By the mid-1940s, however, rising right-wing politics and the increasing Islamization of Turkey caused the institutes to fall under suspicion as communist sympathizers. In 1954, four years after the right-wing Democratic Party came to power, they were shut down.

Ultimately, an entire generation of prominent Anatolian writers came out of the institutes, such as Talip Apaydın, Fakir Baykurt, Mahmut Makal, Hatun Birsen Başaran, and Mehmet Başaran. Knowledgeable about both the land they lived on and cultivated and about diverse literary traditions, these writers produced a unique constellation of literary works dedicated to the vast Anatolian landscape.[5] They wrote against the backdrop of the 1950s, when the feudal system was gaining strength; the landowners became richer while villagers became poorer and were often obliged to migrate where they could find employment. In a rapidly modernizing nation deeply divided along cultural and economic lines, Anatolian writers held a mirror up to the lives of the villagers in the less visible rural areas. Often written in the style of social realism, their works were, for the most part, classified as *köy edebiyatı* (village literature).[6] While Mahmut Makal's *Bizim Köy* (1950) (Our Village) is seen as a precursor, the genre has been redefined through diverse novelistic, poetic, and essayistic works such as Talip Apaydın's book of observations *Bozkırda Günler: Köy Notları* (1952) (Days in the Steppe: Village Notes) and Mehmet Başaran's poetry book, *Ahlat Ağacı* (1953) (The Wild Pear Tree).[7]

During this period, there were other Anatolian writers, such as Yaşar Kemal and Necati Cumalı, who wrote about similar issues in rural areas, but did not attend the institutes. Their works were also often classified under the genre of village literature. Today there is a substantial body of critical scholarship on this genre, but the focus of this scholarship is on the value of the political criticism and social realism found in these works. The environmental elements in these literary texts have been largely overlooked, because environmental issues typically held a secondary place in the political debates post-1950s. The period between 1950 and 1980 was a tumultuous time in Turkey marked by several military coups, tensions between left- and right-wing politics, and various economic disruptions. Literary and political debates thus concentrated primarily on this turbulent history. As contemporary author Latife Tekin observes, her generation of writers were so preoccupied with political activism in the 1970s and 1980s that they paid little, if any, attention to nature (2014). Since the 2000s, due to the increasing interest in ecocriticism in Turkish academia, there has been a renewed interest in village novelists, but their works are still not examined with an eye to climate issues.

The purpose of this section is to revisit the works of three writers associated with village literature—Fakir Baykurt, Yaşar Kemal, and Necati Cumalı—to show that they were among the first to address climatic and environmental challenges in Anatolia. Although they had no knowledge of anthropogenic climate change and did not use terms like the "climate crisis" per se, they showed that Anatolia was suffering from such challenges as extreme heat, dryness, and water scarcity. These authors called attention to Anatolia's proneness to desertification prior to contemporary claims that the earth is rapidly deteriorating due to climate change. I thus propose that we read contemporary works of climate fiction in a continuum with this literary heritage.

I first focus on Fakir Baykurt, a notable Anatolian author, teacher, and a graduate of the village institute.[8] Baykurt's 1967 novel, *Kaplumbağalar* (Tortoises), is a particularly important work in terms of its in-depth focus on Anatolian ecology and climate in the 1960s. The novel takes place in an Alevite[9] village named Tozak and recounts the hard work of villagers who construct a vineyard and an orchard on a crooked stretch of barren land resembling "yamalı bir yoksul yorganı" (1967: 7; the poor's patch quilt). The novel opens with an emphasis on the scorching heat: "Tozak kırı yanıyor. Güneş Tozak kırına kocaman bir ateş topu gibi çöktü. … Otlar kavrulmuştu. Serin yeller de acaba neden esmiyor? Eserse arada 'çanak kurutan' esiyor. O da hangi cehennemden esiyorsa, Tozak kırına daha beter yangınlar getiriyor" (7; Tozak prairie is burning. The sun has settled on the prairie like a giant ball of fire. … The weeds are scorched. Why do cool winds not blow? If anything, *çanak kurutan*[10] occasionally blows. From whichever hell it emerges, it brings worse fires to the Tozak prairie). Following the leadership of the old villager, Kır Abbas, and the village teacher, Rıza, locals labor endlessly under conditions of extreme heat to turn an unproductive piece of land into fertile ground.

When the land finally begins to bear fruit, the cadastre committee arrives and informs the locals that the land has been claimed by the state. The statesmen that come to the village make a mockery out of Mustafa Kemal's maxim, "The peasant is the master of the nation," which they repeat *ad nauseam* while effectively stealing from the peasants. Despite many appeals and petitions, the villagers receive no legal support and decide to settle matters in their own way. One evening, upon Kır Abbas's call, everyone meets in the vineyard, gathers the grape harvest, and quickly turns it into molasses and wine. Kır Abbas then asks the shepherds to bring their cattle to destroy all evidence of agricultural production. When the bureaucrats arrive, they find nothing but a destroyed area and they decide to leave. Once again abandoned by the state, the locals return to being residents of a village without water and without an orchard.

Kaplumbağalar focuses extensively on extreme weather conditions and water scarcity. While Abbas checks out every well to satisfy his thirst when working on land, his wife and daughter-in-law save every drop of water they can during their house chores. The drought, which is at the center of the narrative, impacts every single aspect of the characters' lives. The heat affects not only the crops but also the humans and animals whose emaciated bodies become an extension of the blazing landscape. Younger people like Abbas's son, Yusuf, and newborn animals in the farm are often described as frail and underfed. Neither Yusuf's mother nor the newly calved cow receives enough nutrition to breastfeed their offspring. By contrast, when grape plantations temporarily bear fruit, Baykurt's writing turns luscious—filled with juicy descriptions of multicolored grapes, molasses, and wine.

As evident in the title, tortoises are an important motif in the novel. From beginning to end, we encounter hundreds of tortoises who inhabit Tozak and who share resemblances with their human counterparts. At times, Baykurt draws on human and animal analogies[11] to describe the characters' looks, as in "Kır Abbas'ın küçük kaplumbağa gözleri" (46; Kır Abbas's small tortoise eyes) and "adamın kaplumbağa elleri" (305; the man's tortoise hands). Other times, Baykurt touches upon the shared vulnerability of both humans and animals in the face of extreme heat. Although the tortoises are habituated to living in arid conditions, they have a hard time coping with the temperatures in Tozak; many of them die due to dehydration (19, 56). Both animals and villagers struggle to survive in a difficult landscape, searching for water and shade. In the initial pages, for example, we read about both an old tortoise and old Abbas walking strenuously under the sizzling heat, looking for "bir parça kölge" (14; a piece of shade), before all the liquid in their bodies—"su, kan, ilik" (14; water, blood, marrow)—evaporates. When the vineyards bear fruit, the tortoises take shelter there, hiding their babies in the shade of the grapevines. After the vineyard is destroyed, the animals abandon the village and head toward other destinations as if they realize there is no other way of surviving. *Kaplumbağalar* conveys the extent to which the climate impacts all the living beings—human and animal—in this region.

A similar emphasis on extreme temperatures and water scarcity can also be found in Necati Cumalı's short story, "Susuz Yaz" (1962) (Dry Summer), and Yaşar Kemal's short story, "Ekin" (2004b) (Crop). Cumalı's story revolves around two brothers, Osman and Hasan, who live together, along with Osman's wife Bahar. One day, Hasan builds a dam across a spring running through his land to irrigate his property, and he deliberately blocks the water from reaching his neighbors' farmland. When their plots begin to dry out, villagers cut down Hasan's trees for revenge, which results in a slowly unfolding chaos that leads to intrafamilial and sexual violence. The story, whose title is literally translated as "summer without water," alludes to "thirst" in reference to both water scarcity and Hasan's greed in considering everything—from land to water to women—as property. Set in a difficult landscape with a difficult fate, Cumalı's "Susuz Yaz" focuses on violent conflicts over water. Yaşar Kemal's "Ekin" (Crop), first published in the 1950s, is similarly about a social conflict triggered by water shortage. The main character runs away from his village after wounding someone during a violent dispute over "bir damla su" (Kemal 2004b: 161; a drop of water) to irrigate his farmland. The story ends with him hiding among the crops in Çukurova's "sarı sıcak" (59; yellow heat),[12] listening in fear for the approaching footsteps of an angry mob.

Writers like Baykurt, Cumalı, and Kemal portrayed the strenuous struggles over water in semi-desertified Anatolia, a region already riddled with socioeconomic disparity. They wrote about what they observed and showed how climatic and economic challenges can culminate in disastrous rural living conditions, where even the most basic agricultural activity becomes a challenge. Today, we know that most of the issues they raised in the 1950s and 1960s have worsened due to climate change. As I discuss in the next section, starting in the 1970s, severe climate-induced droughts have been observed in Anatolia (Şahin 2016). At the time they wrote, authors like Baykurt did not have access to this information. Therefore, they did not dwell upon whether the aridity they portrayed was due to Anatolia's usual continental climate or something new and exceptional was happening, causing permanent degradation of land. Yet they depicted Anatolian land and climate with such meticulous detail that they still help us immensely in understanding why this region has become particularly vulnerable to climate-induced desertification.

Yaşar Kemal was deeply attuned to these problems and repeatedly wrote about Central and Eastern Anatolia. In his writings about his native Çukurova region, he remarks how the "fertile Anatolian soil" has, over the years, evolved into an "agricultural desert" (2009: 274). Such issues as desertification, deforestation, erosion, and decreasing biodiversity hold a central place in Kemal's work. In particular, he focuses on forests, because in such arid lands as Central Anatolia, forests play a central role in storing underground water and in resisting desertification.[13] In "Yanan Ormanlarda Elli Gün" (Fifty Days in Burning Forests), first published in 1955, Kemal dwells on forest destruction in great detail and contemplates future risk scenarios. Originally published as a series of articles commissioned by the newspaper *Cumhuriyet*, this work consists of Kemal's interviews with villagers, rangers, and environmental lawyers in the western and southern coasts of Turkey. Kemal first identifies the leading factors that contribute to deforestation. As he notes, one of the primary causes of forest fires is the villagers' use of burning to clear trees and create agrarian land. Additionally, sometimes the villagers destroy forests one tree at a time. They harvest *yalabuk*—the thin white pellicle between a tree's bark and bole—to eat the sweet parts, which causes the trees to dry up. They then turn "boğulmuş ağaç" (Kemal 1971: 363; choked trees) into wood for sale and turn the choked forest into agrarian land. Contractors are among the other leading agents of forest destruction. Kemal interviews *tahtacılar* (woodworkers), a nomadic group that makes a living by cutting down trees in the Taurus Mountains. They report that before 1937, contractors were able to buy entire forests from the state. They then hired *tahtacılar* to cut down the woods and sold the timber to other countries (404). In 1937, when the first set of forest policies were introduced to legally define forests,[14] contractors were no longer allowed to buy forests. However, they still bought land registers from villagers and cut down forests a few acres at a time with no legal consequences.

Kemal then cautions the reader that deforestation can lead to desertification, because trees play a crucial role in absorbing and storing rainwater:

> Orta Anadolu'dan geçerken o kıraçlık, o kuraklık, o zalim tabiatın verimsizliği, kısırlığı karşısında adamın yüreği ağzına geliyor. Orta Anadolu'nun o Allahın belası tabiatında insan yaşayabiliyorsa, o kurağa, kızgın saca benzeyen bozkıra yılda hiç olmazsa bir kere olsun yağmur düşüyorsa o da kıyılardaki orman şeritlerinin yüzü suyu hürmetinedir. (1971: 422)

> When passing through Central Anatolia, one almost jumps out of his skin at the sight of the barrenness, dryness, and infertility of that cruel nature. If anyone can survive in that damned nature of Central Anatolia, if rain falls on that dry steppe resembling a hot sheet of metal at least once a year, it is for the sake of the coastal forest strips.

Kemal playfully notes that the occasional rainfall on the dry Anatolian land occurs merely out of respect for the forests. If there were no forests, the rainfall would wash away the treeless soil, leaving only sharp rocks behind, and the soil would take hundreds of years to regenerate. An environmental lawyer informs Kemal that erosion on drylands may aggravate desertification and presents forest protection as a serious ecological, political, and existential issue (406).

Kemal travels across Turkey, gathering observations and eyewitness accounts, to show that given the myriad challenges in an already semi-desertified Anatolia, it is a major risk to continue forest destruction. He concludes "Yanan Ormanlarda Elli Gün" by referencing Franz Heske, forestry professor and guest scholar at İstanbul University in the early 1950s, who claims that forests have an immense impact on the country's water sources and climate, and that major droughts should be expected in Turkey if forests continue to be decimated (Kemal 1971: 419).[15] The first exposé to highlight the connection between deforestation and climate,[16] Kemal's work from seven decades ago is a critical warning against the future risk of radical desertification.

The issues raised by such authors as Baykurt, Cumalı, and Kemal have only become more alarming in the past few decades due to increased climate impact. What they set out to critique post-1950s—climatic conditions and agrarian challenges, water scarcity and food insecurity, desertification, and regional and economic disparities—have taken center stage in contemporary climate debates. It is thus no coincidence that when tracing a genealogy of climate fiction in Turkey, contemporary writers like Tekin and Uzuner mention past writers such as Kemal and Baykurt (Akkuş 2018; Tekin 2014). It is crucial to read these earlier works alongside contemporary works of climate fiction. If taken more seriously, these early warnings could perhaps have elicited a more effective response to environmental devastation, and even prevented the anxiety of belated climate action, which is a central concern in Uzuner's and Baydar's novels discussed later in this chapter.

Warming Climate: Contributing Factors and Impacts

The Anatolian land, once portrayed by village writers, has undergone rapid transformation over the past decades due to climate change. A brief overview of the current state of the climate crisis in Turkey is thus necessary prior to turning to the genre of climate fiction. In the profiles prepared by Carbon Brief, Turkey is currently listed as the world's twentieth largest emitter of greenhouse gasses (GHGs), and Turkish emissions are reported as having risen faster than for any other Annex I[17] country—more than doubling between 1990 and 2013 (Timperley 2018). On the one hand, as climate policy scholar Ümit Şahin states, the government has initiated a number of "action plans, as well as projects, awareness-raising, and capacity-building activities" (2020: 184) in reaction to Turkey's increasing climate footprint. Turkey became a party to the United Nations Framework Convention on Climate Change in 2004, signed the Kyoto Protocol in 2009, and ratified the Paris Agreement in 2021. In 2015, it submitted a climate pledge stating a goal of 21 percent reduction in GHG emissions by 2030. The Ministry of Environment and Urbanization was renamed as the Ministry of Environment, Urbanization and Climate Change in 2021 as a symbolic change to reflect these initiatives. On the other hand, as Şahin adds, there is an inconsistency between the government's action plans and ongoing actions: "Turkey's emissions-reduction pledge is far from operational because it plans to double its emissions, and energy and other sectoral policies are not consistent with an emissions-reduction commitment" (184).

This inconsistency is evident in the fact that energy- and pollution-intensive sectors played a larger role in Turkish economic growth during the 2003–9 period than they did in the previous period (Aşıcı 2015: 1738). The economic growth path taken under the AKP led to massive urban transformation projects and infrastructure investments—such as the third airport, the third bridge, and the planned Canal İstanbul discussed in the previous chapter—making it nearly impossible for Turkey to reach the stated goal (1735). Furthermore, Turkey still relies on domestic coal reserves to meet its energy demand (*Seventh* 2018: 7). Although Turkey updated its climate target at COP27[18] in 2022 and promised to bring GHG emissions 41 percent below business-as-usual levels by 2030, it also set 2038 as a peak emissions year. This means that Turkey's emissions will actually increase 33 percent by 2030, hence confirming Turkey's unwillingness to reduce emissions in absolute terms (Şahin 2022). Climate Action Tracker thus rates Turkey's Nationally Determined Contribution (NDC) target as "Critically Insufficient" ("Türkiye" 2023).

Since the early 2000s, nongovernmental organizations have highlighted these inconsistencies and played a vital role in making climate issues publicly visible. The 2005 Greenpeace protest of the coal-fired power plant in Çanakkale was the first to call attention to global warming and the need to divest from fossil fuel. On the Global Climate Action Day in 2005, the first civil protest against climate change took place with the efforts of Açık Radyo (Open Radio), a regional, not-for-profit radio station, and Küresel Barış ve Adalet Koalisyonu (Global Peace and Justice Coalition) (Ünal 2019). In the following years, climate movement gained further strength as a result of the İstanbul rally organized by 350.org and Küresel Eylem Grubu (Global Action Group) in 2010, the demonstrations during the Gezi Park Protests and the Global Power Shift campaign organized by 350.org in 2013, and Halkların İklim Yürüyüşü (People's Climate March) organized by Küresel Eylem Grubu in 2014. Although environmental activism slowed down after 2015 due to the Turkish political climate, Greta Thunberg's call to action in 2018 provided renewed momentum for youth action in Turkey. The global climate strikes in 2019 were, in part, initiated by young students, such as Atlas Sarrafoğlu and Ege Adman (Ünal 2019). Climate activism continues today with the support of several organizations, including Kuzey Ormanları Savunması (Northern Forests Defense), 350.org, Fridays for Future,

Genç Yeşiller (Young Greens), Yokoluş İsyanı (Extinction Rebellion), and Yeşil Düşünce Derneği (Green Thought Association). Independent media outlets, such as *Yeşil Gazete*[19] (Green Newspaper), *İklim Haber* (Climate News), and Açık Radyo, and cultural center Müze Gazhane[20] (Gazhane Museum)—which hosts the first climate museum—also play important roles in raising awareness about the climate crisis.

Climate activism can be seen as the extension of a strong environmental opposition that has existed in Turkey since the 1980s. In 1984, the protests against a coal-fired power plant project in the Gökova Bay, a famous tourist attraction, marked the beginning of a nation-wide environmental debate. In 1988, the first Yeşiller Partisi (Green Party) was established. In 1990, the biggest environmental action in Turkish history took place against the Aliağa coal power plant in İzmir, when thousands of people created a human chain along the sixty kilometer road between İzmir and Aliağa, and successfully prevented the project (Şahin 2020: 178–9). In the early 1990s, rural people were at the center of the protests against the Bergama gold mine. As Şahin observes, "While the Bergama case and the anti-nuclear movement characterized the 1990s, the new period of environmental activism in the 2000s was dominated by campaigns against small hydropower plants, urban transformation, and megaprojects" (179). During Büyük Anadolu Yürüyüşü (The Great Anatolian March) in 2011, ten marching caravans from different parts of Turkey arrived at the capital city Ankara in protest of the exploitation of natural resources. Yaşar Kemal supported the march with a letter mourning the radical changes around the Taurus Mountains, noting that "Doğaya düşman bir ülke olduk" (Kemal 2011; Our country has become an enemy of nature).

The primary target of environmental mobilization today is the energy industry. As documented in a 2018 report, of all the GHG emissions, the energy sector has the largest portion at 72.8 percent. The breakdown of energy production in 2018 includes 37.3 percent from coal, 29.8 percent from natural gas (largely imported), 19.8 percent from hydroelectric energy, 6.6 percent from wind, 2.6 percent from the sun, 2.5 percent from geothermal energy, and 1.4 percent from other resources (*Seventh* 2018: 19). The primary contributing source of GHG emissions in the energy sector is coal-fired power plants, with the largest one located in Zonguldak, a city on the western coast of the Black Sea (*İklim Meselesi* 2017).

Over the past few decades, the critical scholarship on coal has primarily focused on a leftist critique of the mining industry, prioritizing labor struggles, wage injustice, and unsafe working conditions. For example, Yavuz Özkan's film *Maden* (1978) (Mine) and Metin Köse's fiction trilogy—*Mükellefiyet* (2010)

(Liability), *Göl Dağı* (2012) (The Lake Mountain), and *Büyük Yürüyüş* (2014) (The Great March)—all portray the dangerous and unjust working conditions of coal miners. Similarly, Yaşar Miraç's bilingual Turkish and German poetry book titled *Kömürkirchen* (2015) (Coal*kirchen*) sheds light on the lives of coal miners, underground work sites, and mining-induced health problems. In one poem titled "Soma'da," the writer mourns Soma Faciası (Soma Disaster), the worst mining fatality in Turkish history, when 300 miners lost their lives in the Eynez coal mine fire in 2014.

In addition to focusing on labor exploitation, writers and filmmakers have recently begun to pay attention to the environmental impact of coal mining and the fossil fuel industry. Umut Vedat's *Kara Atlas* (2015) (Dark Atlas) and the National Geographic documentary titled *İklim Meselesi* (2017) (The Climate Issue) are two such examples that reveal the contradiction between Turkey's pledge to reduce GHG emissions while still relying heavily on carbon-intensive infrastructure projects. To resolve this conflict, the Turkish government lists hydroelectric and nuclear power plants among leading renewable green energy sources for the future (*Seventh* 2018: 21). Yet to what extent are these truly green or clean? As Mine Islar writes, hydropower became a state-regulated market after a 2001 amendment made to the Turkish Electricity Market Act, which allowed private companies to lease the rights to rivers for forty-nine years for hydroelectricity production (2012: 377). Water grabbing has a deeply negative impact on water quality. According to water rights contracts, companies are only responsible for leaving "10% of the flow considered necessary for sustaining fish populations, biodiversity and water quality," but the experts assert that 40–60 percent of water is necessary to sustain river ecosystems (387). The impact of hydroelectric power plants (HPPs) is worse if several plants are built along a single river basin, as in the İkizdere Valley in the Black Sea Region, where twenty-one hydropower projects are licensed on one river (386).[21] Additionally, the fact that HPPs depend on rainfall, a source predicted to become increasingly depleted, means that they are an unreliable energy source.

The second alternative to fossil fuel, according to the government, is nuclear power. Following the establishment of the Bureau of Nuclear Energy in 1972, Akkuyu (Mersin) was chosen as the first site to develop a nuclear power plant (Akbulut, Adaman, and Arsel 2017: 176–7). This plan was delayed for decades due to financial reasons and the Chernobyl disaster of 1986.[22] After the AKP came to power in 2002, there was a renewed interest in nuclear power and the government signed bilateral agreements for two nuclear plants: Akkuyu with Russia in 2011 and İnceburun (Sinop) with Japan in 2013. The Akkuyu nuclear power plant is currently under development, but it continues to be a controversial project. The opposition[23] points to many risks including the likelihood of earthquakes in Turkey, the lack of safety measures involved in the planning and construction phases, and the problems with safeguarding nuclear waste. Climate change scholar Levent Kurnaz notes that carefully constructed nuclear plants can cause less damage than coal-fired plants, but Sinop's proximity to an active fault is deeply disconcerting (2011). Turkey is a seismically active country and has suffered massive earthquakes in the past, including the earthquake of August 1999 in Kocaeli and the catastrophic earthquakes of February 2023 in Maraş.[24] Subsequent seismic action across the country has continued to remind us of Turkey's vulnerable position regarding the hazardous risk of nuclear accidents.

In the face of the climate crisis, we are simultaneously faced with colossal energy demands and the need to decarbonize quickly. We are asked to choose either coal-fired or nuclear power plants when Turkey is, according to Kurnaz, in an advantageous position for attaining 100 percent renewable energy (2019). While the investment in solar and wind power has increased notably over the past few years, there is still a potential for much greater use of alternative energies. Whether the government will improve its energy politics by utilizing these sources more productively in the future remains to be seen. What is certain at this moment is that many of the predicted climate impacts are already visible in Turkey.

A report prepared by the Intergovernmental Panel on Climate Change identifies Turkey as highly vulnerable to climate-induced drought, land degradation, and desertification (Mirzabaev et al. 2019). The *Seventh National Communication of Turkey*[25] also states that in the period between 1960 and 2010, the annual total precipitation has increased considerably in the northern parts of Turkey and decreased in the Aegean, Mediterranean, and Southeastern Anatolian regions (2018: 126). A significant part of inner Anatolia and Southeastern Anatolia are considered arid lands prone to desertification, while a large part of the Mediterranean and Aegean regions are designated as sub-humid areas that may be affected by desertification processes (148). Şahin observes that "subsequent periods of drought are already visible in Turkey ... The most severe and widespread drought periods in the last 40 years were in 1971–1974, 1983–1984, 1989–1990, 1996, 2001, 2007–2008, and 2013–2014" (2016). Along with climate fluctuations and droughts, several issues come to the fore such as depletion of water resources and food security. According to climate scientist Ömer Lütfi Şen, Turkey is already qualified as a "water stress" country

(2013: 22), and climate change, along with population growth, is only expected to increase the stress.

Adverse climate events often trigger one another, creating an avalanche of problems. The deterioration of agrarian land makes mass migration necessary. The agricultural sector has historically played a fundamental role in the Turkish economy as the largest single employer, accounting for about a quarter of the workforce in the entire country. In the past two decades, however, approximately two and a half million small-scale farmers have been forced to migrate to urban centers for employment because of extreme weather events downplaying agricultural efficiency[26] (Holt 2019). There has been considerable migration in the country due to both climate- and development-induced environmental degradation. In addition to an increase in droughts since the 1990s, the Konya Plain, home to the earliest known farming communities, now suffers from the use of illegal water wells that lead to a drop in the underground water table and to the formation of large sinkholes (*obruk*) (Erdi Lelandais 2016: 93). Similarly in Suruç, a district of the city of Urfa near the Atatürk Dam,[27] decreasing rainfall and falling groundwater levels since the 1970s have caused farmers to emigrate from the area (Kadirbeyoğlu 2010).

In addition to drought and migration, climate change has fueled massive forest fires, caused floods, and impacted water resources and food production in Turkey. In the summer of 2021, wildfires burnt 178,000 hectares of forest area in the Mediterranean Region, becoming the worst fire recorded in Turkish history (Akgül 2021). The same summer, the Black Sea Region experienced excessive rainfall, floods, and landslides that destroyed numerous buildings and took many lives. While the lack of emergency preparedness contributed to the vastness of the disasters, climate change was undeniably the primary factor. At this point, one cannot but ask why we continue to be unprepared for climate change. Can we, today, still afford to think of climate impact as unpredictable?

Perhaps the continuing perplexity about the climate crisis is caused, in part, by our belatedness in paying attention to the timely warnings issued by earlier authors like Baykurt and Kemal. The creation of an informed response to temporally vast phenomena such as climate change requires a bridging of the past, present, and future. Just as the environmental mobilization of the 1980s provided the foundation for contemporary climate activism, village literature of the 1950s prepared the literary grounds on which contemporary climate fiction rests. With these continuums in mind, I next examine two works of climate fiction that expose how radically the Anatolian lands—described in the earlier works—have been altered in the past few decades. I focus on two writers in particular, Uzuner and Baydar, who embark upon various journeys across time to call attention to the importance of intergenerational dialogue in envisioning alternative climate futures.

Land Degradation, Shamanism, and Mythopoesis

Although climate fiction is an emerging genre in Turkey, contemporary novelists have been addressing anthropogenic climate change since the early 2000s. One of the first literary responses to climate change came from Latife Tekin. Her novel *Unutma Bahçesi* (2004) (Garden of Forgetting) portrays a small group of people building a utopian garden, which, they predict, will become an island once climate change causes the sea level to rise. Her poetic manifesto, *Rüyalar ve Uyanışlar Defteri* (2009) (Notebook of Dreams and Awakenings), by contrast, recounts the narrator's nightmares about a dystopian Turkey riddled with droughts, scorching winds, and water scarcity. *Rüyalar* mimics the nonlinear language of dreams and oscillates between different temporal frameworks—the past, present, and future—to offer a multidimensional critique of the environmental decay brought about by neoliberal politics. Tekin urges the reader to awaken from this nightmare and to give a timely response: "kalk doğrul, uyunacak gece değil" (79; get up, it is no night to sleep).

The first comprehensive response to climate change, following Tekin, came from contemporary author Buket Uzuner. Her nature tetralogy, *Uyumsuz Defne Kaman'ın Maceraları* (*The Adventures of Misfit Defne Kaman*), is both a warning about the climate crisis and an ode to the four elements discussed in each book: *Su* (2012) (*Water* 2014); *Toprak* (2015) (*Earth* 2018a); *Hava* (2018b) (*Air* 2020); and, *Ateş* (2023) (Fire). Like Tekin, Uzuner takes readers on various journeys between the past and the present in order to generate hope for the future. The protagonist of all four novels is Defne, a young environmental journalist and activist whose grandmother teaches her everything she knows about ecology. Defne and her grandmother frequently return to the long Anatolian past to argue for an ecocentric politics based on their knowledge of Central Asian myths and shamanic practices.

Defne lives in İstanbul and travels across Turkey to write environmental and political news articles that often get her into trouble. Uzuner uses Defne's investigative journalism as a pretext to set each novel in a different city. In *Water*, which takes place largely in İstanbul, Defne investigates the protests against the hydroelectric power plants in the Black Sea Region, issues related to water pollution, and the hunting of marine animals.[28] In *Earth*, she travels to Çorum to write an article about the smuggling of historical-archeological artifacts and investigates the impact of climate change on the Anatolian land. In *Air*, Defne gets into trouble with the fictional Ministry of Climate Change Denial for writing an article on the risks of nuclear power plants. Taking place largely in Kapadokya, Nevşehir, the novel is filled with references to increasing droughts, air pollution, and the energy industry. In *Ateş* (Fire), she travels to Mardin, a historic city in Southeastern Anatolia and close to the Turkish-Syrian border, where climate-induced fires spin out of control. In addition to forest fires, Uzuner touches upon war and migration as Defne volunteers in a preschool for Syrian children and adopts a child saved from Aleppo. Saluting Mardin's ethnically and religiously eclectic demography, Uzuner alludes to various Kurdish, Assyrian, and Armenian mythologies, among others.

Despite the distinct milieu chosen for each work, the general structure of all four novels is similar. They all comprise multiple narrative layers: the larger narrative about Defne's adventures is interrupted by her journalistic exposés, excerpts from *The Book of Water/Earth/Air/Fire*, intertextual references to contemporary and ancient texts, and occasional postmodern commentaries by the narrator. In terms of genre, they read somewhat like detective novels and somewhat like modern mythologies. Defne always disappears at one point while investigating a case and reappears later in the story. Each time she disappears, an animal appears in her place and evokes mysterious connections between the shamanic past and the present-day reality. Although the novels are written in response to climate change, they are different from the more conventional examples of climate fiction in that the climate crisis is not front and center. While a series of events such as environmental protests, police investigations, travels, and wars transpire in the foreground, climate change always lurks in the background like a specter that haunts the Anatolian land. In each novel, there is a climate-induced catastrophe such as a forest fire, flood, or drought occurring in the backdrop. Most of the climate criticism takes place on the levels of dialogue between characters, who address these issues and highlight the urgency of slowing down climate impact.

I focus on the second book from the tetralogy, *The Adventures of Misfit Defne Kaman: Earth* (2018a), which begins with the story of Kemal Yörüklü, a tour guide from Çorum who has recently lost his wife. Kemal and his son Karaca visit Defne's grandmother, Umay Bayülgen, upon hearing about Umay's healing powers as a pharmacist and herbalist. Over time, Karaca develops a strong bond with Defne, who becomes like an older sister to him. The story then jumps to a few years later when Defne visits Çorum to investigate the smuggling of historical-archeological artifacts. Defne learns that Karaca has become an eco-hacktivist and has hacked the digital system of the Çorum Archeological Museum. At this point, both Defne and Karaca disappear and the remaining part of the book reads like a mystery novel with family and friends searching for them.

Beyond this main plotline, *Earth* pays close attention to the vulnerability of the Anatolian land, which was also a central concern for earlier writers like Baykurt and Kemal. Originally titled *Toprak* (which can be translated as "soil," "land," or "earth"), the novel is an ode to Anatolia's "ancient, fertile soil" (Uzuner 2018a: 298) degraded by climate impact and neoliberal politics. Uzuner critiques human-induced climate impact on the land by building historical, ecological, and textual bridges between the past and the present. First, she uses archeology to elaborate on ancient civilizations' interactions with the land. The story takes place in Çorum, the Northern Anatolian city, which was once the center of the Hittite Empire. Defne and archeologist Güneş Aytan often converse about the importance of healthy soil and agriculture in ancient civilizations to critique the unsustainable agrarian practices in contemporary society. Second, Defne and Nine Umay (Grandma Umay) often evoke the shamanic past to unearth ancestral wisdom and to develop an ethical relationship to the land. Uzuner contends that shamanic cultures had strong ties with the natural environment and that remembering this heritage may allow us to envision a better future for the planet. Third, Uzuner gives intertextual references to ancient epics and Turkic myths to provide mythopoeic solutions for ongoing environmental crises.

The story revolves primarily around Defne and her grandmother Nine Umay, a botanist and a modern shaman who owns a "healing greenhouse" (91) with plants gathered from all over the world. Nine Umay is portrayed as a wise woman deeply respected in her community. Her name derives from ancient Turkic-Mongolian mythology and Tengriism,[29] where "Mother Umay" (Umai or Mai) is the earth-mother and goddess of fertility. In Mongolian, the word "'Umai' means womb or uterus. The earth was considered a 'mother' symbolically" (İnan 2012: 97). In Tengriism, Mother Umay is also the wife of Bay (Bai) Ülgen, the deity who created the "earth, sky and all beings, claiming water, food, bountifulness and the richness of the earth" (Batur and Özdağ 2019: 331). Embodying the symbolic powers of both Mother Umay and Bay Ülgen, Defne's grandmother Umay Bayülgen has several shamanic traits: she is a socially recognized healer, an interpreter of dreams, a transmitter of local lore, an herbalist decocting potions and medicine, a soul-traveler to the upper- and netherworlds to negotiate with ancestor spirits, and a mentor for future shamans (Öğüt Yazıcıoğlu 2022: 17). When asked to describe her grandmother's skills as a kaman[30] in contemporary terms, Defne answers by telling people to imagine "a radical environmental activist … an agricultural engineer … an insatiably curious organic chemist" (Uzuner 2014: 76).

As Nine Umay's granddaughter, Defne is also an heiress to the Mother-Goddess Umay. Like most of the symbolic names in the Bayülgen family, Defne's name reflects a strong mythical tie and comes from a dream that Nine Umay has prior to Defne's birth: Nine Umay reconfigures the Greek myth about Daphne and Apollo, and imagines Daphne turning Apollo into a tree and continuing her life in peace. Believing in the revelatory powers of dreams, Nine Umay names her newborn granddaughter "Defne," convinced that she would one day embody the strong feminine spirit revealed in the dream.[31] Defne indeed grows up to become a strong female figure and has a close bond to her grandmother. She often alludes to Nine Umay's teachings about the natural world. For example, as she walks with Güneş on the archeological site of Yazılıkaya, Defne grabs a handful of soil and says, "Nine Umay used to fill my hands with earth and tell me what was in it" (Uzuner 2018a: 300). Defne is trained to read the soil like a text comprising manifold layers of historical, ecological, and mythical wisdom and captures this wisdom in a special notebook called *The Book of EARTH*.[32] She inherits *The Book* from her grandmother, who notes that it has been safeguarded by Defne's family for centuries. Passed on from generation to generation, *The Book* is an "Encyclopedia of Nature, full of healing botanical knowledge with lists of endemic plants and seeds that no longer exist in Anatolia. And it contains mythological stories about the underworld from our ancient traditions. It's a treasure trove of knowledge" (80). *The Book* is updated by each new family member who temporarily serves as its guardian and it imparts ecological wisdom to the younger generations about how to appreciate, preserve, and restore the earth degraded by human-induced climate impact.

Occasionally, fragments from *The Book* are incorporated into the main narrative of the novel. For example, the chapter titled "Mother Earth" is an excerpt from *The Book* and praises the earth through descriptions such as "Our source, our destination," "Terra Firma. The foundation," "seed, nourishment, meal and food," "the Other World, the Under World," and "Continuity, Future, Hope" (127–8). Diversely portrayed as an essential source of life, a mythical place of underground gods and goddesses, and a being "whose body, soul and rights we've violated" (129), the earth assumes myriad material and symbolic meanings. In another fragment titled "Thinking Like a Mountain,"[33] writers cultivate an "earth ethic" (321) built on the shared recognition that the "arid, sick, embittered earth can be healed" (322). Emphasizing the importance and the vulnerability of the Anatolian land vis-à-vis environmental decay, *The Book* serves both as an archive of ancestral knowledge and as a contract among generations to protect the earth, one of the most important sources of life.

In addition to the fragments from *The Book*, the novel is also enriched with references to Turkic epic poems and Central Asian mythologies. Uzuner's novel mimics the earth it praises, by comprising several layers of eco-poetic wisdom that pile on top of one another just like archeological strata. The Turkic epics Uzuner refers to remain in conversation with the overarching themes of the novel. She places emphasis on three epics in particular. The first one is the Kyrgyz epic trilogy of *Manas* from the eighteenth century, which conveys the importance of intergenerational transmission of knowledge and skills, by telling the story of three generations of heroes (Öğüt Yazıcıoğlu 2022: 133). This is a central concern in *Earth*, where Defne inherits the knowledge of her ancestors, as well as that of Nine Umay. The second epic Uzuner refers to is *Kitab-i Dede Korkut* (*The Book of Dede Korkut*),[34] an epic of the nomadic Oghuz Turks who migrated from Central Asia to the Caucasus and the Middle East, transitioning from animism to Islam, and from nomadic existence to permanent settlement (Walker 1992: 23). The epic has, at its center, the alleged author Dede Korkut (Grandfather Korkut),[35] who "combines the roles of wise old man, religious leader, and bard—strongly suggestive of the Central Asian shaman" and who recounts "[Oghuz Turks'] victories, their defeats, their trials and tribulations" (Eleonora 2007: 137, 140). Uzuner alludes primarily to the shamanic and ecological wisdom captured in this book. The third epic she references is *Kutadgu Bilig* (*Wisdom of Royal Glory: A Turko-Islamic Mirror for Princes*), authored by Yusuf Khass Hajib in the eleventh century. The poem is built on the interaction among four leading characters, "the king, the vizier, the sage and the mystic … While focusing on 'real politic,' the narrative also describes a Manichaean alternative in the mystical cosmos … where the king and vizier represent the sun and the moon, and justice extends from the harmony of the world" (Batur and Özdağ 2019: 326). Uzuner reinterprets *Kutadgu Bilig*[36] to inspire the vision of an alternative society consisting of an "eco-civilization" and governed with "ecowisdom" (327).

Although Uzuner does not dwell on the content of these epics in detail, she does reference them as fundamental sources that have taught Nine Umay and Defne about the importance of earth preservation, especially in the age of the climate crisis. As noted in *The Book of EARTH*, "This is what we learned from ... the Epic of Manas and Kutadgu Bilig, from Dede Korkut ... 'MOTHER EARTH' is eternalized in our legends and flows through our hearts" (Uzuner 2018a: 129–30). What is eternalized in the suggested legends and epics is a mythopoeic relationship to nature. In both *Kitab-i Dede Korkut* and *Kutadgu Bilig*, it is via myths that humans attribute agency to natural elements and construct a bridge between human and nonhuman realms. As Patsy Callaghan observes, "Myths as a genre often invite us to read the spaces around the protagonist by giving the natural world itself agency and identity and complexity; in this way, our most ancient stories, read ecocritically, can provide an antidote to the anthropocentrism that might be said to motivate, perpetuate, and aggravate the ecological crises of our time" (2015: 80). Following in the tradition of these old epics, Uzuner produces a modern work of mythology that provides an antidote to the anthropocentric fueling of ecological crises.

In *Earth*, myths become particularly important after Defne's disappearance. Nine Umay spends several nights in Yazılıkaya waiting for her return, praying to the rulers of the three worlds: Erlik Khan, ruler of the "Underworld," nine layers under the earth; Mother Umay, earth-mother and goddess of the "Middle Earth," where mortals dwell; and Tengri Bay Ülgen, the god of the "Upper World," seventeen floors above the skies (Uzuner 2018a: 97, 334). Nine Umay conducts a shaman ritual, coming into contact with the forces of the natural world and praying in a trance-like state for Defne's well-being. As she notes, "In our ancient Shaman traditions ... Every creature in 'middle earth' came to life in order to help another" (225), and that "ecological balance" (226) can only be sustained if the connection between the human and the nonhuman realm is not severed. In the following days, Nine Umay experiences a magical incident: a wild deer appears in Yazılıkaya and forms a mystic bond with her. Enchanted by one another, they wait side by side for days on this historical site. Since the deer has symbolic significance in Anatolian and Turkic cultures, where it is perceived as a sacred animal, Nine Umay considers the animal to be a messenger and a bearer of good news (273).

In fact, in each novel, Defne's disappearance is followed by the mysterious appearance of an animal: In *Water*, a dolphin; in *Air*, an eagle; in *Ateş* (Fire), a horse.[37] Uzuner implies that not only are the two shaman women closely connected to the earth and the natural world, but also that Defne has a shape-shifting, trickster-like quality. As Nine Umay says, "Defne is always moving about, altering her appearance, wandering this way or that, but she always comes back" (Uzuner 2014: 21). Even her nickname, *Ayçöreği* (Crescent Roll), is inspired after the princess in the epic of *Manas* who turns into a swan once she realizes she is in danger (Uzuner 2012: 129). The reference to the crossing of species boundaries both reveals an ethics of coexistence between human and more-than-human beings and refers to a symbolic, mythic retreat. Defne "is traveling away from the mundane and ordinary, to another, exceptional world, where she talks with animals, to be with nature and the ancestors" and "to bring [back] the divine gifts of wisdom" (Batur and Özdağ 2019: 336, 328).

It may perhaps be argued that Uzuner's inclusion of shamanism and Turkic mythology runs the risk of trivializing the gravity of climate issues. Yet her return to the rich Anatolian cultural heritage is motivated by an anthropological curiosity for reviving an ecocentric worldview. As archeologist Güneş remarks in the novel, "anthropology helps us see the order and logic in traditions we used to belittle as primitive and illiterate" (Uzuner 2018a: 234). Uzuner laments the "negative image of the kamans today" and the fact that their legacy is not even upheld as "part of our folklore" (2014: 74–5). With one eye on the past and one eye on the present, Uzuner taps the ancient traditions to ask whether it is possible to live without damaging the natural habitat. She makes the following remark via a news article written by Defne: "*Now you might say that these tales and legends are old and have nothing to do with our world today. But ... now our ancient cultural heritage has reemerged to ask us: How have these ancient people changed? Why do people in Turkey today take craftiness for cleverness, a wallet for a conscience, greed for pride?*" (38–9). Instead of viewing shamans as primitive religious practitioners, Uzuner argues that their perception of the natural world is superior to that of contemporary society. As she notes in an essay on climate fiction,

> Humanity, which called those eras [the pre-monotheistic era of shamanic ancestors] when the economy was not dependent on carbon, primitive, now considers itself modern and civilized while cutting, mowing, burning, drilling, digging, burying, and torturing every non-human living thing like 'inanimate goods'. Today, one of the most vital issues that climate-fiction literature should remind us again is what civilization actually is. (Uzuner 2021)

In a way, then, Uzuner writes *Earth* and the entire nature tetralogy to remind the reader that civilization should be redefined in terms of an ecocentric ethics, whose roots are to be found in shamanic praxes. Defne's dual role as a modern-day shaman and an environmental journalist serves precisely to build this connection between the past and the present. As suggested in *The Book of EARTH*, "Nowadays, they [shamans] are called environmental volunteers" (Uzuner 2018a: 322).

Uzuner is not alone in her endeavor to connect shamanism with contemporary environmentalism. In *Shamanism in the Contemporary Novel*, Özlem Öğüt Yazıcıoğlu studies a constellation of novels, including Uzuner's, that call attention to "the significance of the notion of animated nature ... for the development of an environmental-ethical consciousness" (2022: 5–6). Building on previous scholarship by Juha Pentikäinen and Marjorie Mandelstam Balzer, Öğüt Yazıcıoğlu argues that instead of treating shamanism as an archaic religion, one should examine "indigenous onto-epistemologies in their historical confrontations with Western metaphysics" to investigate the "affective and ethical relations between human and more-than-human characters or entities with agentic force" (6, 13). Uzuner's writing, which turns toward shamanic praxes to resist the anthropocentric view prevalent in modern-day society, can be included within this literature framework.

Uzuner occasionally alludes to the resemblances she observes between shamanic and other Indigenous traditions. In *Water*, for example, she shares a Cree Native American prophecy when critiquing capitalist ecocide and notes that Nine Umay resembles Native American women in both her looks and in her roles as an elder, teacher, and spiritual guide (2014: 34, 71). In *Earth*, Güneş, whose ex-wife is a Native American woman of Cheyenne descent, suggests that Nine Umay's belief in animism is similar to Native American beliefs about more-than-human agentiality (2018a: 276, 234). Several commonalities between shamanic and other Indigenous myths can indeed be found in their respective earth ethics, attribution of agency to nature, and ceremonial prayers for sustaining the connection between humans and the more-than-human nature. For example, in *Earth*, Defne's grandmother prays to the rulers of the three worlds—Erlik Khan, Mother Umay, and Tengri Bay Ülgen—to acknowledge the interdependency of all the different elements and creatures of the earth. Similarly, as Salma Monani and Joni Adamson note, from "the Navajo conception of Father Sky and Mother Earth, to the Mayan conception of Sea and Sky, recorded in the *Popol Vuh* (a corpus of mytho-historical-astronomical narratives), Indigenous groups around the world see themselves as intimately related to the sun, moon, stars, earth, and water" (2017: 3). While these similarities are significant, it is also crucial to acknowledge the differences. Most importantly, shamanism is no longer a living tradition in Turkey, whereas the Indigenous communities across the globe still struggle to protect their traditional lifestyles and territories from neoliberal pressures and are often at the forefront of climate mobilization.

Since shamanism is no longer practiced in Turkey, Uzuner makes it relevant to climate activism by creating contemporary versions of old shaman leaders in strong female figures like Defne, Nine Umay, and the women farmers of Anatolia to whom the book is dedicated. In the dedication, Uzuner writes that farmers have "passionately protected heirloom, organic seeds in their personal treasure chests for generations despite legal measures preventing the trade of local seeds. I am deeply thankful to those WOMEN FARMERS who try to protect the land, the trees, the water and the air of Anatolia … the great granddaughters of Umay—the Mother Nature Goddess of ancient Turkish Shamans" (2018a: vii). Near the end of the novel, after she is found,[38] Defne gives a public speech in Çorum with a similar motif and remarks that *"whoever manages the seeds and the soil will manage the world of the future!"* (462).

The emphasis on seeds, as potential bearers of fertility and futurity, is found everywhere in the novel: in Nine Umay's greenhouse of healing plants; in the archive of botanical wisdom in *The Book of EARTH*; in Defne's personal memories of giving a peach seed as a precious gift to her childhood friend; and in her conversations with Güneş about desertification, soilless agriculture, and local seeds. Uzuner's emphasis on seeds is yet another means of praising the ancient, fertile soil of Anatolia, which holds a central place in the history of agriculture. As portrayed in Sevinç Baloğlu's documentary *Tohum/Seeds* (2018), the first seed (wheat) planted by humanity was domesticated in Anatolia before spreading to Europe. Archeologists today recover ancient seeds in Anatolia that reveal significant information about humanity's transition from nomadic lifestyle to sedentary farming. Uzuner, for example, refers to Boyalı Höyük in Çorum, where they recovered charred pulses and grass pea seeds in a provisions jar (Uzuner 2018a: 121). She notes that seeds were considered quasi-sacred in old Anatolian traditions, passed on as dowry to brides, and carried by yoruk women in their necklaces. These traditions continue today as women's collectives across the country preserve and exchange local seeds to maintain a diverse gene pool and to cope with future climate conditions. Uzuner deliberately calls attention to the struggles of the rural communities who are the first to feel the impact of climate change and stand at the forefront of the resistance against it.

As previously noted, Uzuner does not respond to the climate crisis by placing it front and center in the novel. Instead, she pays close attention to the archeological, shamanic, and agricultural history of Anatolia to gather the ecological wisdom of premodern societies. She revisits the faultlines of contemporary society in light of this heritage and foregrounds such issues as food security and biodiversity via the emphasis placed on soil. In locating the story in Anatolia and in calling attention to the importance of protecting the earth, Uzuner builds on the work of earlier authors such as Yaşar Kemal, who notes that "Vatan önce sağlıklı bir topraktır" (Kemal 2009: 266; Homeland is, above all, a healthy soil). Like Kemal, who elaborates on various factors that have turned Anatolia into an "agricultural desert" (274), Uzuner warns the reader about climate impact, noting that "if EARTH goes, our homes, our land, agriculture, food—all will be gone" (Uzuner 2018a: 130).

Earth begins and ends with an emphasis on healing the Anatolian land that is adversely affected by neoliberal growth and anthropogenic climate change. For Uzuner, if there is such a thing as an earth ethic, it derives from the acknowledgment that "the only living store of memory in this world … is earth" (323). Defne believes that only women farmers can keep this memory alive and thus they hold the key to a sustainable future. After revisiting the past to critique the present, the novel moves to the future: Uzuner concludes the story by commenting on the crucial role of farmers and activists like Defne, who advocate for a new "'Earth Culture' of the 21st century" that will run on "renewable energy" (462) to mitigate climate change and will prioritize the restoration of degraded land. While speculating about possible future trajectories to highlight the immediate need for climate action, *Earth* also ends with a warning about the risk of belated awareness. Following Defne's public speech, the governor remarks, "The climate's been giving us warning signals for years! … Maybe it'll wake up those climate skeptics[39] who think the whole thing is science fiction?" (473).

Climate, Temporality, and Ecodystopia

The tension between taking timely versus belated climate action is the central motif in Oya Baydar's novel *Köpekli Çocuklar Gecesi* (2019) (The Night of the Children with Dogs). Baydar's novel presents a dystopian version of contemporary society and serves as a cautionary tale about future scenarios that may arise should we continue the current pace of political and environmental degradation. The story is narrated by an unnamed woman, who is saved—by youth activists—from a climate-induced global flood that wipes out most of humanity. She recounts, in retrospect, the environmental and political catastrophes that led up to the flood. While the novel focuses largely on the time prior to the flood, the first and the last chapters briefly reveal that only members of the younger generation survive the catastrophe and prepare to start a new life.

I argue that time is of utmost importance to this novel, which simultaneously discusses the temporal uncertainty of climate change, social perceptions of climate temporality, generational time, and narrative temporality. I examine the relationship between climate and temporality in Baydar's novel by offering a twofold analysis. In the first part, I focus on the novel's content and show how Baydar sheds light on multiple, incompatible temporalities manifest in the social perceptions of climate change to address such issues as youth activism, political inaction, and failure to adapt to climate fluctuations. In particular, she emphasizes intergenerational conflict to capture the difference between taking timely versus belated climate action: she contrasts the disastrous results of the older generations' delayed response to climate change with the hopeful elements reflected in the timely activism of the youth. In the second part, I focus on the novel's form to show how Baydar experiments with narrative temporality to capture the temporal uncertainty of climate change. Oscillating between the real and the fictive, Baydar archives some existing catastrophes but also plays with chronology, probability, and timescale to create a temporally fractured narrative. She uses the ability of fiction to bend time—to accelerate it, slow it down, poke holes in it—in order to portray the complex temporality and urgency of climate change.

Baydar explores the question of temporality by utilizing the narrative conventions available to both climate fiction and ecological dystopia. Like climate fiction, ecodystopia is a relatively new genre in Turkish literature, although political dystopia has existed since the 1960s (Atasoy 2016: 561). Ecodystopian tropes can be found in contemporary works such as Latife Tekin's *Rüyalar ve Uyanışlar Defteri* (2009) (Notebook of Dreams and Awakenings) and Zülfü Livaneli's *Son Ada* (2008) (*The Last Island* 2022).[40] However, Baydar's novel is the first ecodystopian narrative in Turkish to focus primarily on climate change.[41] *Köpekli Çocuklar Gecesi* focuses on both the irreversible damage brought about by anthropogenic climate change and retains a glimmer of hope through the activism of the surviving youth. As such, the novel can be considered an example of "critical dystopia," which is defined by Lyman Tower Sargent as "a non-existent society ... located in time and space that the author intended a contemporaneous reader to view as worse than contemporary society but that normally includes at least one eutopian enclave or holds out hope that the dystopia can be overcome" (2001: 222). As Raffaella Baccolini and Tom Moylan note, "critical dystopias allow both readers and protagonists to hope by resisting closure" (2003: 7). Baydar's open-ended novel likewise resists closure and hints at the possibility of overcoming the dystopia: The youth, whose timepieces run ahead of everyone else's, emerge from a ruinous world as the only protagonists of the future.

A brief summary of the novel is necessary to make my later discussion and analysis more clear. The unnamed narrator of *Köpekli Çocuklar Gecesi* is a botany scholar who reflects on planetary ecological and political crises, which lead up to the global flood: Presidents of various countries blaming one another for climate disasters; severe earthquakes and tsunamis occurring around the world; the ten-year global drought pushing millions of people to starvation; and interstate conflicts arising over water issues. While framing climate change as a planetary issue, Baydar also pays close attention to regional politics and places Turkey and the Middle East at the center of her dystopian tale. The narrator recounts a number of environmental and political problems in Turkey: economic and climate crises, increasing droughts, water and food scarcity, agricultural inefficiency, and politicians accusing "imperialist agents" of sabotaging the country's water sources (2019: 191–3). The existing turmoil is made worse by political authoritarianism, the oppression of free speech, public misinformation, and media censorship. Language, too, has become toxic: speaking of peace has become a crime, and of war, a virtue (45).

While focusing on this turbulent time before the flood, the novel also sheds light on the life of the narrator prior to the catastrophe. We find out that she came out of an unhappy marriage and feels guilty for remaining in the safety of her academic life. For example, the narrator often recalls the night she and her son Umut Doğa (Hope Nature) see a thirteen-year-old boy sleeping with a dog on the sidewalk. Umut Doğa wants to take them both home, but the narrator refuses to do so. Retrospectively, she feels like a hypocrite for raising a son with a strong conscience, while at the same time she remains in her comfort zone. As she later learns, her son chooses to secretly help that child and others, and he eventually joins a youth group assisting people in regions under blockade. While the exact location is not stated, the reference to the region over the border possibly implies war-torn Syria. The narrator then loses all contact with her son.

The narrator admires the youth, including her son, who are engaged in various forms of activism. Inspired by her son and by her lover, Adam, an environmental and peace activist, the narrator grows increasingly more interested in the Middle East. Adam is raised by a Norwegian environmental lawyer and activist, who saves him from a genocide targeting an Aramaic-speaking Christian community. A multilingual speaker of Kurdish, Arabic, and several European languages, Adam does not fully reveal his origins. With a symbolic name that stands for the first man or for every man, he notes that, like all children who lose their mother tongue at a young age, he, too, is multilingual and has multiple identities (173). When the narrator tells Adam about her intention to change the course of her life, Adam proposes that she help refugees through work for a United Nations coordination bureau. The narrator then decides to leave behind her academic career and travels to vulnerable regions torn apart by climate disasters and armed conflict.

The regions that the narrator visits remain mostly unidentified in the text. However, Baydar makes implicit references to Syria on a number of occasions when she incorporates actual events into the story. For example, while the narrator describes communities whose lives are destroyed by war and severe droughts, Adam speaks of refugees' dangerous sea voyage from the Mediterranean coast to Europe (175), and mentions the death of Alan Kurdi (162).[42] The reason Baydar pays attention to Syria may be twofold. First, Turkey has been an important country of transit and permanent settlement for Syrian refugees fleeing the war. Second, Syria suffered a massive drought between 2006 and 2010, which was, according to climate scientist Colin P. Kelley et al., primarily a consequence of the human impact on climate systems. The Syrian drought is linked to the long-term warming trend in the Eastern Mediterranean, which also affects Turkey (Kelley et al. 2015).[43] Baydar's novel elucidates the intertwined fates of the two neighboring countries in the face of political turmoil and their shared vulnerability in the face of climate change.

Of primary concern to this chapter is the novel's emphasis on the discrepancy between different "social temporalities of climate change" (Baker et al. 2018: 420). Baydar includes a spectrum of climate crisis responses from different actors to call attention to the critical difference between timely versus belated climate action. On the one hand is the government, which perpetually defers climate action to an indeterminate future so as to advance neoliberal growth. On the other hand are different forms of climate action that emphasize the belatedness of our response to a long-standing problem. Seen in this light, the novel elucidates the ongoing tension between state politics and climate activism, which revolves around two distinct projections of climate temporality.

Baydar's novel also contains characters that join neither side but remain spectators of what Rob Nixon terms "slow violence … a violence that is neither spectacular nor instantaneous, but rather incremental and accretive, its calamitous repercussions playing out across a range of temporal scales" (2013: 2). The narrator acknowledges that she also failed to give a timely response to the gradual environmental and political degradation: "Her şey mantar gibi bir gecede yerden bitmedi. Öyle sanmak bizim aymazlığımızdı. Çevre felaketi gibi siyasi felaketin geleceği de belliydi aslında. İki felaketin kaynağı aynı" (Baydar 2019: 44; Things did not just spring forth from the ground overnight, like mushrooms. Our indifference created that illusion. It was certain that just like environmental disaster, political catastrophe would also come about. Both catastrophes derive from the same source).

At the center of Baydar's novel is the youth, whom she describes as the most responsive to environmental and political deterioration. There are two groups, *köpekli çocuklar* (children with dogs) and *iklim çocukları* (climate children), both of which represent resistance and hope in a world torn apart by wars and ecological disasters. *Köpekli çocuklar* are homeless and orphaned children who suffer from poverty, environmental degradation, forced migrations, and war. The narrator learns of their existence when she travels to a conflict zone with Adam, head of the UNESCO aid mission, and with Doctors Without Borders. A French-speaking doctor reacts to the failure of European countries to provide aid and notes that they would all be dying of hunger if it wasn't for the *children* (125). The narrator first encounters *köpekli çocuklar* amid bombed streets and destroyed homes, after being mysteriously summoned by a dog that leads her to their meeting place. She observes them from a distance and can't hear what they discuss, but once they depart, the narrator hears the hoot of a scops owl, bearer of news and a symbol of wisdom. Her second encounter with the children takes place right before the big flood. Again summoned by a dog, she is brought to the meeting of hundreds of children, who warn her about the impending disaster and share good news: her son is reportedly alive and has joined forces with *köpekli çocuklar*.

Köpekli çocuklar are at the center of this climate fiction, because, as Amitav Ghosh observes, "The Anthropocene has reversed the temporal order of modernity: those at the margins are now the first to experience the future that awaits all of us" (2016: 62). No longer in a hurry to catch up with the accelerating tick-tocks of Western modernity, those at the peripheries are now the first to feel the dizzying sense of uncertainty evoked by irregular climate clocks. Children are the most vulnerable in these contexts. The narrator depicts *köpekli çocuklar* as the youth whose lives are stolen by climate and political crises: "Yakılmış köyler, yıkılmış evler, çoluk çocuk yollara düşmüş insanlar. ... Aç, susuz, perişan göçmen kafileleri" (Baydar 2019: 89; Burned villages, demolished houses, people who take to the roads with their children. … Hungry, thirsty, wretched cafilas of migrants). The disastrous legacy that *köpekli çocuklar* inherit from the previous generation represents the ultimate failure in world politics.

İklim çocukları appear later in the novel and are also essential to the story. They are the youth raised in wealthier countries and deeply aware of the global climate crisis. This is the generation of Greta Thunberg, whose activism is initially described in the novel as charming and harmless, but it later evolves into a powerful global movement. Despite violent attacks, they organize global marches, run the only media source that resists misinformation, and play a vital role in the activist network. *Köpekli çocuklar* play a vital role in this network by acting as messengers and spreading the news of climate emergency. Once it becomes too late to stop the flood, these children start preparing for damage control.

Admittedly, the flood is a recurring eschatological motif in numerous historical and mythical narratives. Baydar references the Epic of Gılgamesh, the Prose Edda, and the Noachian Flood prior to presenting the global flood in the novel as the ultimate determinant of who survives ecocide and who becomes history. When the flood occurs, the narrator survives it only because *köpekli çocuklar* save her from a city submerged in water, leaving her on a sixty-floor skyscraper called the Glasstower. The narrator describes her experience of that moment as dream-like (251). That her life is saved by children and their animal companions seems improbable at best. Yet, as she wonders, if "yeni normal" (101; the new normal) state of the world was brought about by adults, why should salvation not come from the youth?

After the flood, the narrator recalls the many warnings that had come from *iklim çocukları* and the Extinction Rebellion, which nobody had taken seriously. Even she had never expected a flood of global scale to arrive *this early*. Disappointed by her own belated realization, she locates hope in the younger generation. As she remarks, "Köpekli Çocuklar'la İklim Çocukları belki de bir bütünün birbirini tamamlayan parçaları … ortak bir amaç uğruna sistemi zorlama, bir gelecek umudu yaratma çabaları" (210; Perhaps Children with Dogs and Climate Children are the complementary pieces of a whole … they all struggle to instill hope for the future and push the system to the limit for a common goal). The narrator's admiration for these children as well as her son is, in part, due to her previous lack of commitment to ecopolitical matters. Her sense of guilt resurfaces every time she sees a child, such as the time she buys ice cream for a homeless boy. As the cherry-flavored ice cream melts, her hands—covered in red—become complicit in the violence she has passively witnessed for years, eliciting traumatic memories: "*Elim kanıyor. Kan dirseklerime süzülüyor. Kan akan bir nehir yatağında yürüyorum ... Sahra hastanesinin branda bezinden sedyesindeki kanayan çocuk. Beyaz önlüklü adamın, kanı durduramıyorum, çığlığı:* I can't stop the blood!" (146; *My hand is bleeding. Blood is running down my elbows. I am walking on a blood-running riverbed ... The bleeding child on the tarpaulin stretcher in the desert hospital. The scream of the man in the white gown who can't stop the blood:* I can't stop the blood!). The narrator's sense of complicity for leaving a world of atrocities to future generations soon turns into a discussion about generational time and intergenerational justice.

The narrator makes a significant observation with regard to three generations—her parents', her own, and her son's—and their political priorities. She notes that environmental issues were largely overlooked by her parents' generation and only belatedly became a priority for her own generation (104). She tells her son: "Yıllar geçiyor, kuşaklar değişiyor, dünya değişiyor. ... O kuşaklar; işçi sınıfı, sömürü, devrim dediler ... Bizler çevre, doğa, hayvan hakları ... insan hakları ... dedik. Tümünün birliğini, bütünlüğünü bizler de tam kavrayamadık" (103; Years go by, generations change, the world changes. ... Those [older] generations were vocal about working class issues, labour exploitation, revolution ... We have been vocal about the environment, nature, animal rights ... human rights ... We did not comprehend they were parts of a whole). Adam shares a similar sentiment, noting that neither his parents' nor his own generation could comprehend "kutup ayılarıyla devrimin bütünlüğü" (104; the connection between arctic bears and revolution), a fact that is clear to the youth. Adam and the narrator critique themselves and the older generation for separating the environmental from the political.[44] As Baydar explains in an interview, this is her way of confronting herself and her peers who believed that if the socialist revolution actually happened, then other, more "secondary," issues would also be resolved. Baydar admits her own belated realization that the exploitation of both labor and nature is a result of capitalist modernity and that it calls for outright resistance against the system (Çuhadar 2019).

While this belated realization carries a naive undertone, it also shows how people's priorities may undergo drastic changes in response to climate events. It is perhaps to make up for this belatedness that Baydar's writing occasionally exhibits dramatic tendencies, such as the recurring expressions of middle-class guilt and the excessive lists of global catastrophes. Despite these tendencies, however, the novel candidly explores the issue of intergenerational justice and reads like a letter of apology to future addressees. The apology is politically nuanced, because children from developing countries face disproportionate risks and greater vulnerability. This is why the narrator cannot speak of the climate crisis without touching upon socioeconomic inequalities, wars, droughts, and forced migrations. It is also why she hopes that one day *köpekli çocuklar* and *iklim çocukları* join forces to build a better world out of this one divided along cultural, political, and economic lines.

Intergenerational dialogue is a common motif in both works of climate fiction that I have included in my discussion so far. In Uzuner's novel, Defne relies on the teachings of the older generation, represented by Nine Umay, to find solutions to ongoing environmental crises. In Baydar's novel, it is the opposite. The narrator places all her hope in the children, revealing a paradox common to this genre. Adeline Johns-Putra argues that the figure of the child often embodies a paradoxical role in climate fiction as both the object of parental care and the savior of the planet Earth that was destroyed by the same parents (2019). In Baydar's novel, similarly, the protagonist both expresses her concern for the children who face immense environmental threats and overburdens them with the responsibility of healing a broken world. This incongruity becomes more evident in the novel's closing scene, where we find Adam and the narrator together in a cabin atop a mountain following the flood. Adam, wounded with a bullet, and the narrator, infected with a virus, are both about to die and decide to end their lives by poisoning themselves. Their suicide marks the inevitable self-destruction of human civilization as both the subject and the object of ecocide. Yet the lovers do not feel despair. Rather they see themselves as part of a failed system that needs to end in order to make space for new life. The narrator expects the poison to taste bitter, but the liquid, she says, tastes like the elixir of life (Baydar 2019: 268). The ingestion of a substance that is at once poisonous and curative can be read as a manifestation of *pharmakon*. The self-inflicted poison/cure marks the end of the old world and prophesies the beginning of a new, soon-to-be-healed, planet Earth.

Because the novel follows a nonlinear narrative, we know from the first chapter that *köpekli çocuklar*, including the narrator's son, survive the flood and ultimately arrive at this cabin to find the narrator and Adam lying dead in each other's arms. They also recover the narrator's voice recorder, which captures all that went wrong in the past twenty-six years. The narrator's testimony acts both as an archive of environmental change and as a cautionary tale for future generations, much like *The Book of EARTH* in Uzuner's novel. The voice recorder also plays a similar role as this novel by Baydar that we, the readers, are holding in our hands. Just as the youth inherit the voice recorder, we, the readers, take possession of the novel that reads like a transcription of the narrator's testimony. Ultimately, both the youth and the reader are survivors who must ask, "What comes next?"

Baydar does not reveal what the new world order may look like. The novel's final scene takes place with the children finding the dead lovers in the cabin. As they are leaving, Umut Doğa notices a flower, *Matricaria chamomilla*, blossoming between the rotting wood logs. The flower reminds him of his childhood when his mother taught him all she knew about plant life, and it also suggests that new life can emerge from the ruins. Baydar hints at the potential for a long-term, system-wide change. In lieu of a closure, *Köpekli Çocuklar Gecesi* ends with temporal markers that suggest future transformation: "Dünün sonu, yarının başlangıcı" (269; The end of yesterday, the beginning of tomorrow).

Thus far, I presented a thematic analysis of Baydar's work, which portrays humanity's failure to mitigate the climate crisis to comment on the catastrophic results of belated climate action. In the following pages, I shift my focus to a formal analysis of the novel. I explore Baydar's engagement with narrative temporality and her strategies for capturing the temporal uncertainty of climate change on the level of narrative activity. As previously mentioned, *Köpekli Çocuklar Gecesi* takes readers on countless journeys on a planet facing an unprecedented rise in dictatorships, extreme climate events, nuclear and cyber wars, and viral pandemic. If all this sounds somewhat familiar, that is because the novel includes numerous events that have actually occurred and others that gradually unfold as we speak. Interestingly, although she includes factual events, Baydar does not utilize the conventional narrative tools available to realism. As Ümit Şahin notes, the events depicted in the novel cannot possibly take place in the time frame and sequential order that they are described (2019). Most of them transpire within an accelerated time frame, as if witnessed through a time-lapse camera, until they are taken to a point of utter destruction.

I argue that the author deliberately uses a distorted narrative temporality, because it allows her to portray contemporary society in the style of dystopian realism. As science fiction author Christopher Brown asserts, dystopia "depicts the world as it really is, through the refractive prism of extreme metaphor. It's a realism that uses mirrors, sometimes fun-house mirrors" (2017). In Baydar's novel, the fun-house mirrors create a distorted sense of time and an improbable chronology. As I set out to demonstrate, these temporal alterations enable the author to capture the complex temporality of climate change and the society's failure to adjust to climatic rhythms.

First, the disjointed temporality of the novel allows Baydar to elucidate the irregularities of climate temporality. As the narrator says, "En az elli yıl, yüz yıl sonrası için beklenen kuraklık erkenci, biraz da saygısız bir misafir gibi çat kapı gelivermişti" (Baydar 2019: 135). The drought, which was expected to arrive at least fifty or hundred years later, had dropped by early and unexpectedly, like a disrespectful guest). Baydar brings the predicted future forward by five or ten decades to dismantle the comforting distance between *now* and *later*. In their analysis of deep time in the Anthropocene, Franklin Ginn et al. note that apocalypticism "performs a kind of telescoping action, whereby distant temporal registers are brought close … [and] the 'vastness of time' is made present within the time of human life" (2018: 221).[45] Baydar's novel employs this technique and draws the future closer, including it within the boundaries of our short-sighted vision. She compresses the amount of time that is supposed to elapse from today until an indeterminate tomorrow so as to foreground temporal entanglements. As Adam says, "Gelecek bir süredir başladı, çoktan geleceğin içinde, fütür'de yaşıyoruz gibi geliyor bana. Bugün aslında yarındır" (Baydar 2019: 175; The future has begun a while ago; it seems to me that we are already living in it. Today is actually tomorrow).

Second, highlighting the temporal entanglements provides Baydar with the opportunity to critique our miscalculation of probability and our failure to adapt to climatic rhythms. When faced with a phenomenon of immense spatiotemporal dimensions like climate change, there is considerable room for error in forecasting its effects. Baydar laments this tendency to make mistakes about future predictions via numerous examples, such as when the narrator recalls a terrifying sci-fi film she had seen as a child. Although her father had then convinced her that it was improbable for those terrible things to happen to the world, she now realizes that "yirmi-otuz yıl öncesinin kötümser gelecek tasavvuru, bugünün gerçeğine dönüştü" (102; a pessimistic future prediction from twenty-thirty years ago has become today's reality). Noting that yesterday's improbability can become today's reality, the narrator regrets not listening to activists' warnings: "Çevreci grupların giderek kitleselleşen, yaygınlaşan, sertleşen eylemleri bir yandan iktidarların aldırmazlık duvarlarına, öte yandan … kitlelerin aymazlığına çarpıyordu. *Biraz da kızıyorduk felaket tellallarının kötümser kehanetlerine*" (20–1; Environmentalist groups' mass demonstrations, which grew increasingly more severe, collided with the wall of indifference of the ruling powers on the one hand, and … with the heedlessness of the masses on the other. *We were frustrated with the pessimistic prophecies of doomsayers*). The narrator critiques the imaginative failure of the belated majority, including herself, who did not act because they viewed activists' timely warnings as pessimistic prophecies.

Köpekli Çocuklar Gecesi demonstrates that climate change complicates our frames of temporal reference and our perception of futurity. It thus serves as an example for contemporary discussions on climate temporality. As Timothy Clark argues, climate change disproves the supposition that "future time and the terrestrial space can act as bottomless repositories for waste or for issues that thinking wishes to avoid" (2010: 133). Critiquing the notion of "inexhaustible externality in both space and time" (133), Clark remarks that the future can no longer be perceived as an infinitely distant and abyssal dumping ground for evaded thoughts. Similarly, Timothy Morton asserts that "distance is only a psychic and ideological construct designed to protect me from the nearness of things" (2013: 27). Morton utilizes concepts such as viscosity and intimacy to argue that global warming has already "intruded into ecological, social, and psychic space" and that it "spells doom now, not at some future date" (104). In a similar manner, Baydar's novel shows that climate change unravels the notion of temporal distance. In reaction to those who perceive climate change as a distant threat and delay climate action *ad infinitum*, Baydar presents a dystopian setting where the future is here and now, pressing against the present.

Portraying temporal entanglements is an efficient means of conveying the urgency of climate change. Given the irregularities of ecological clocks and altered climate cycles, the novel cannot narrate the climate crisis by conveniently referring the reader to a remote future. Rather it calls attention to nature's broken timepieces and our lack of adjustment to irregular climatic rhythms, whether the adjustment is temporal, political, economic, or psychological. As Paul Huebener writes, humans are at once "nature's clock breakers and nature's broken clocks" (2020: 501). Baydar's characters also embody this dual role: they are both inflicting irreversible damage on the world and suffering from the devastation caused by their own hands. In the struggle to adjust to rapid, unseasonal changes, only a few succeed.

Baydar utilizes different narratorial tools to convey the characters' difficulty in keeping up with the irregular temporality of climate change. Comprising temporal and spatial leaps, the novel moves nonsequentially between past remembrances and imaginary futures, and between experiential and hypothetical frames of reference. Time is not evenly sliced; temporal boundaries are not clearly demarcated. The narrator erratically navigates the distant past and the recent past, the time prior to and after the flood, and various moments in Turkish history. The novel dismantles temporal coherence, and the fixed, singular notion of time loses its currency in a fractured world. Temporal leaps also call attention to the incommensurability between human and geological timescales. In an uncertain world, where human civilization has a slim chance of surviving the global flood, the narrator records what she witnesses for a future listener, "son insan ya da ilk yeni insan" (Baydar 2019: 191; the last human or the first new human). The anticipation of an unknown future addressee lends a spectral quality to the novel, challenging readers to consider the possibility of a planet Earth where humans do not exist. To borrow Morton's words, with its "mind-bending time- and spatial scales," climate change "forces humans to coexist with a strange future, a future 'without us'" (2013: 139; 94). The narrator and Adam often talk about the geological history and the future of the earth, acknowledging their finite existence on an evolving planet.

As they speculate about the future, they realize that climate change involves "profoundly different temporalities than the human-scale ones" (Morton 2013: 1). Regretting that words like "soon" or "tomorrow" have lost meaning, the narrator notes, "Bir zamanlar; 'bugün'ün yaşandığı, 'yakında'nın bir anlamı olduğu, yarının beklendiği, geleceğin sonsuz göründüğü doğal bir zaman, doğal bir yaşam vardı" (Baydar 2019: 49; Once upon a time, there was a natural flow of time, a natural flow of life in which 'today' was lived, 'soon' had a meaning, 'tomorrow' was waited for, and the future seemed infinite). Post-climate temporality disturbs habitual frames of temporal reference that revolve around the notion of natural flow, which alludes to a succession of discrete moments dashing forward like a river. Similar to Alexis Wright's notion of "collapsed history" (Wright 2001: 239), an "indigenous mode of storytelling … related to the idea of 'all times' existing simultaneously" (Rowland 2019: 544), past, present, and future coexist in a disorienting manner in the novel. The narrator cannot construct a linear narrative where temporal fractures can be mended and rationalized. Unstable climate events and their unpredictable rhythms hinder the possibility of measuring time and of dividing it into logical, sequential units.

The narrator's difficulty in creating a coherent narrative also exemplifies what Timothy Clark calls "unprecedented difficulties of interpretation and imagination" imposed by "scale effects" (2010: 136). Focusing on the scalar derangement between human activity and its impact on climate, Clark points out that a seemingly trivial act at one scale may always turn out to be devastating at another, and vice versa. For example, as she reflects on the past, Baydar's narrator is unable to identify particular acts that may have later triggered the climate catastrophe. She contemplates numerous events, one after another, without being able to formulate an intelligible narrative. This exemplifies the challenge of "keeping pace intellectually with an event [climate change] whose scale, complexity and incalculability is such as to resist representation or being conceptualised" (Clark 2010: 132).

Köpekli Çocuklar Gecesi addresses the difficulty of interpreting the vastness of climate events in myriad other ways. The mysterious viral pandemic that spreads after the flood is perhaps the most striking example. The narrator suffers from an unnamed viral infection that leads to partial amnesia.[46] Because scientists cannot identify the origin of the virus, they cannot produce an antidote to it. Those who contract the virus can no longer recall the past or distinguish the real from the imaginary, which explains why the narrator needs a voice recorder to remember recent history. The anxiety of belatedness already instilled by the climate crisis is further increased by the virus. The narrator races against time to complete her recording before her memory is erased altogether. The virus makes it harder than before to reason about and unravel the complexity of climate change. On a symbolic level, it is a metaphor for the loss of memory in an indifferent society, where people choose to forget the issues they cannot easily resolve. As a doctor says, "unutmak hatırlamaktan daha iyi şu sıralarda" (Baydar 2019: 14; these days, it is better to forget than to remember). Baydar insinuates that the partial collapse of cognitive faculties caused by the virus may be a numbing and coping mechanism to deal with climate change, which is "a peculiarly monstrous cultural/political/economic/philosophical/ethical and scientific hybrid" (Clark 2010: 137). Yet, while some groups are eager to forget, others strive to remember everything that happened and actively work toward change.

Climate change overwhelms habitual modes of thinking, challenging us to pay attention to "forces of unthinkable magnitude that create unbearably intimate connections over vast gaps in time and space" (Ghosh 2016: 63). Ecopolitical dystopias like *Köpekli Çocuklar Gecesi* take up this exact challenge to include the unthinkable within our sight. Akin to the immense proportions of the climate crisis, Baydar's novel provides us with a monstrous vision of what awaits us. Jumping disjointedly through the timeline, the novel evokes a heightened awareness of temporal entanglements to elucidate the immediacy of climate change effects. While echoing the irregular rhythms of broken ecological clocks and of a broken society, the story also conveys hope through the space of resistance claimed by global youth movements.

Placing contemporary climate fiction on a continuum with earlier literary traditions reveals that the climate has long been sending warning signals to humanity. Writers such as Baykurt and Kemal showed that, when combined with socioeconomic disparity, climate vulnerability in Anatolia may potentially produce disastrous challenges, such as food and water insecurity and irreversible desertification. At the time they wrote, most of the climate-related challenges they discussed were projected into the future as possible risk scenarios. Today, however, the climate crisis can no longer be perceived as a future risk, as it began altering the planet long ago. Contemporary authors like Uzuner and Baydar thus write with a greater sense of urgency, placing such issues as climate disasters, intergenerational accountability, and the need for timely action on center stage.

In light of the increasing uncertainty unfolding around us, literature plays an essential role in clarifying the magnitude and the irreversible impacts of climate change. Despite the diverse topics they bring into discussion, ultimately both works of climate fiction that I have examined return to the issue of accountability and reveal that changing climate patterns "are the mysterious work of our own hands returning to haunt us in unthinkable shapes and forms" (Ghosh 2016: 32). Using the potential of literary narrative to evoke a language of complicity and responsiveness, they ask us, before it is too late, to adjust our timepieces to the reality of irregular climatic rhythms and to work for change now, in this very moment.

Notes

1 See Leigh Glover's *Postmodern Climate Change*. Glover argues that climate change is "a problem of modernity" and that only by "recognizing the limits of modernity," and by questioning "the legitimacy of modern systems of knowledge, social organization, and environmental management," can we produce effective responses to it (2006: 3).
2 A botany professor, Hikmet Birand paved the path for the study of plant sociology in Turkey. He is the author of *Türkiye Bitkileri – Plantae Turcicae* (1952), among others, and the cofounder of Herbarium Turcicum (ANK) in Ankara. Due to his notable contributions to botanical studies, several plants were named after Birand, including *Cousinia birandiana* and *Verbascum birandianum* (Baytop 2009–10).
3 A long-necked string instrument used in Ottoman classical music and Turkish folk music.
4 Spearheaded by the Minister of Education Hasan Ali Yücel and the Director of Primary Education İsmail Hakkı Tonguç, village institutes were established as part of the cultural, economic, and educational reforms carried out in Turkey following the foundation of the Turkish Republic in 1923.
5 Previously, Anatolian life was portrayed primarily by outsiders such as Reşat Nuri Güntekin (1889–1956) and Yakup Kadri Karaosmanoğlu (1889–1974).

See Güntekin's travelog *Anadolu Notları* (1936) (Notes on Anatolia) and Karaosmanoğlu's novel *Yaban* (1932) (Savage).

6 Not everyone from the institutes agreed to this classification. For example, Fakir Baykurt did not want to be seen as a writer of village novels, because he wanted to avoid a reductive taxonomy. If classification is a must, he could perhaps best be defined as "Köy Kökenli Emekçilerin Yazarı" (Sezer 1999: 37; the writer of laborers with village roots).

7 To read more about village institutes and village literature, see the roundtable discussion among Mahmut Makal, Talip Apaydın, Orhan Kemal, Kemal Tahir, and Fakir Baykurt in *Beş Romancı Tartışıyor* (1960) (Five Novelists in Debate) and Makal's *Köy Enstitüleri ve Ötesi* (1979) (Village Institutes and Beyond).

8 Baykurt was tried for his role in *Türkiye Öğretmenler Sendikası* (Teachers Union of Turkey) in the aftermath of the 1971 military coup and moved to Germany in 1979. Although he continued to write in Germany, it is the novels he authored in the 1950s and 1960s—such as *Yılanların Öcü* (1954) (Revenge of the Snakes), *Onuncu Köy* (1961) (The Tenth Village), and *Kaplumbağalar* (1967) (Tortoises)—that voice the difficult conditions of village life in Anatolia.

9 The term *Alevi* denotes the Muslim Shi'a community that constitutes the largest religious minority in Turkey, a predominantly Muslim Sunni nation.

10 *Çanak* refers to the soil where crops take root; *kurutan* means "drying." *Çanak kurutan* is the name given to a hot wind that dries crops.

11 At times, the oppressive relationship between the state and the villagers is projected onto the relationship between the villagers and the tortoises. Like the statesmen who rule over the peasants, Kır Abbas presides over the lives of the tortoises that quietly go about their ways. As part of a local tradition, he kills tortoises to make accessories out of their shells for newborn babies' cribs (Baykurt 1967: 140).

12 The expression "sarı sıcak" (yellow heat) refers to the scorching heat in Turkey's southern provinces.

13 Kemal discusses the risks of forest destruction in several works. One example is the collection of essays titled *Zulmün Artsın* (1995) (May Your Oppression Increase), where Kemal mourns both the state indifference toward deforestation and the state censorship of novels composed by Fakir Baykurt and Mahmut Makal. He addresses the equally detrimental oppression of both the ecological and literary landscapes in the period following the 1971 coup.

14 In 1945, forests were nationalized and came under the protection of the newly established *Orman İşletme Müdürlükleri* (Directorates of Forest Management).

15 Heske is the author of *Türkiye'de Orman ve Ormancılık/ Wald und forstwirtschaft in der Turkei* (1952) (Forests and Forestry in Turkey). The work Kemal references here, however, is an article titled "Comment améliorer l'hydrologie de l'Anatolie grâce à la biologie et à l'écologie" (Heske 1953).

16 Although Kemal does not address this point, today we know that forests indeed play an essential role in lessening the impact of climate change by absorbing atmospheric carbon dioxide. When cut or burned, trees release the carbon back into the atmosphere. Deforestation is thus a major contributor to global carbon emissions.
17 The United Nations Framework Convention on Climate Change (UNFCCC) divides countries into three groups according to differing commitments. Annex I Parties include the industrialized countries that were members of the Organization for Economic Co-operation and Development (OECD) in 1992, plus countries with economies in transition (the EIT Parties), including the Russian Federation, the Baltic States, and several Central and Eastern European States. See https://unfccc.int/.
18 Short for "Conference of the Parties," COP is the annual climate change conference held by the United Nations. It includes representatives of all the countries that are signatories to the United Nations Framework Convention on Climate Change.
19 *Yeşil Gazete* emerged from within Türkiye Yeşilleri (Turkey's Greens) in 2008 (Gürçay 2018).
20 Müze Gazhane is located in Hasanpaşa Gazhanesi (Hasanpaşa Gasworks Complex), which was built in 1892 to meet the energy needs of the city. It burned coal to produce gas, which was then used for lighting and heating. The Gasworks Complex operated until 1993, when natural gas came into use. Since it was an important industrial heritage site, the complex was re-functionalized as a cultural center in 2021. Today, ironically, it is home to the first climate museum in Turkey.
21 There has been strong anti-HPP resistance in Turkey, leading to the establishment of collectives such as Türkiye Su Meclisi (Turkish Water Assembly) and Derelerin Kardeşliği Platformu (Kinship of Rivers Platform).
22 Following the Chernobyl accident, winds carried the radioactive clouds toward the Thrace and Black Sea regions, contaminating fields, livestock, and crops of tea, hazelnut, and tobacco.
23 There has been a strong anti-nuclear movement in Turkey since the 1970s. In addition to the publication of anti-nuclear papers such as *Akkuyu Postası* (The Akkuyu Post) and *Ağaçkakan* (Woodpecker), the opposition also established the Anti-Nuclear Platform in 1993.
24 Turkey is situated in the zone of collision between the Eurasian Plate and both the African and Arabian Plates. Much of the country lies on the Anatolian Plate bounded by two major strike-slip fault zones, the North Anatolian and the East Anatolian faults. While the 1999 earthquake was devastating, resulting in the death of over seventeen thousand people, the 2023 earthquake was one of the largest disasters to hit the country in the past century. Striking southern and central Turkey, the 2023 earthquake resulted in more than fifty thousand fatalities,

destroyed numerous cities, and left approximately one and a half million people homeless.
25 The *Seventh National Communication of Turkey* is a comprehensive report on Turkey's vulnerability to climate impact and its adaptation strategies. It is prepared in line with the liabilities of Turkey under United Nations Framework Convention for Climate Change, to which it is a party.
26 As food engineer Bülent Şık states, agricultural production is directly impacted by climate change. Crops now contain lower concentrations of micronutrients due to the high levels of carbon dioxide. Furthermore, increasing temperatures accelerate insects' multiplication, resulting in the use of heavier pesticides (2018).
27 Located on the Euphrates River, the Atatürk Dam became operational in 1992, as part of *Güneydoğu Anadolu Projesi* (GAP) (Southeastern Anatolia Project).
28 In *Water*, Uzuner also touches upon honor killings. Although this is the only novel where Defne explicitly investigates gender violence, each novel from the tetralogy has an implicit ecofeminist tone: Uzuner approaches the oppression of women and nature as inextricably linked and critiques both sexist and speciesist ideologies.
29 Tengriism is an ancient shamanistic religion practiced in Central Asia, whose chief deity is the celestial god Tengri.
30 As Uzuner explains, "ancient Turkic shamanism traditions were known as kamanism in the Proto-Turkish spoken in Asia" (2014: 74) and a shamanist was known as kaman(ist) or kamist.
31 Defne's last name is Kaman, which further adds to the nominal symbolism in the novel.
32 *The Book of EARTH* is one of the four notebooks that appear in each novel from the tetralogy. The others are titled *The Book of WATER*, *The Book of AIR*, and, *The Book of FIRE*. They all comprise lyrical descriptions of the element in question and use a language that has a chant-like rhythm.
33 The title of the fragment refers to Aldo Leopold's notion of "thinking like a mountain" in *A Sand County Almanac* (1949).
34 The first written copy of *The Book of Dede Korkut* is dated roughly to the fifteenth century.
35 Defne's grandfather is named Dede Korkut (Grandpa Korkut) after the alleged author in the epic.
36 *Kutadgu Bilig* also plays a practical role in the novel. After Defne disappears, the police receive anonymous coded messages that correspond to couplets from *Kutadgu Bilig*. The police read the couplets to resolve the mystery and to find Defne.
37 Tulpar, the winged horse in Turkic mythology.

38 At the end of the novel, both Defne and Karaca are found alive. It is revealed that Karaca was pressured by smugglers into hacking the Çorum Museum system and Defne was taken hostage while trying to save him.
39 Climate skeptics are everywhere in Uzuner's tetralogy. In *Air*, there is an ironic "Ministry of Climate Change Denial," whose primary purpose is to prove that climate fluctuations have nothing to do with the fossil fuel industry or neoliberal growth (Uzuner 2020: 20).
40 Over the past few years, there has also been an emerging corpus of science fiction, such as Murat Ukray's *Çöl Gezegen* (2021) (Dune) and Aslı E. Perker's short story "Günübirlikçiler" (2018) (Daytrippers) that imagine catastrophic climate futures.
41 It should also be noted that *Köpekli Çocuklar Gecesi* is Baydar's first ecological novel. Her previous novels focus largely on sociopolitical issues such as history and remembrance, migration, and the collapse of socialism. Although some of her earlier works, such as *Çöplüğün Generali* (2009) (The General of the Garbage Dump), engage with environmental issues, their primary focus is political history.
42 The three-year old Syrian boy who drowned, along with his mother and brother, while trying to cross the Mediterranean Sea.
43 Kelley et al. note that, along with Syria, other countries in the greater Fertile Crescent—a crescent-shaped area in the Middle East including Southeastern Turkey—also experienced the drought between 2006 and 2010. They remark that, despite being impacted by the drought, Turkey suffered less from it due to its geographic diversity and investment in the southeast region's irrigation. The Turkish government launched *Güneydoğu Anadolu Projesi* (GAP) (Southeastern Anatolia Project) in the 1970s as a comprehensive initiative to develop water and land resources, including projects on irrigation and energy production on the Euphrates–Tigris basins ("What's GAP?" 2015).
44 While Baydar's intergenerational comparison is meant to highlight the centrality of climate action for contemporary youth, it would not be fair to interpret her sense of belatedness in terms of environmental issues as symptomatic of an entire generation. After all, there has been a strong environmental mobilization in Turkey since the 1970s. Baydar's self-criticism may be better understood in the context of her latest work, *80 Yaş Zor Zamanlar Günlükleri* (2021) (Aged 80, Diaries of Difficult Times), where she mentions her own belatedness in accurately analyzing Turkish politics.
45 In their introduction to the special issue of *Environmental Humanities*, Franklin Ginn et al. make this observation in response to Richard D. G. Irvine's reading of Mongolian Buddhist prophecies published in the same issue.
46 Baydar uses the motif of viral-induced amnesia in an earlier novel, *Çöplüğün Generali* (2009) (The General of the Garbage Dump), where the public is

deliberately made to forget recent history via a man-made virus named "3 Monkeys Virus." Spread through the city's water supply network, "3 Monkeys Virus" subdues an oblivious society into conformity. The unnamed virus in *Köpekli Çocuklar Gecesi* is not deliberately produced in a lab like the "3 Monkeys Virus," but it could still be seen as a consequence of anthropogenic climate change since it appears in the aftermath of climate-induced catastrophes.

3

Routes

Movement, Environment, and Politics

Contemporary author Ayhan Geçgin's novel, *Uzun Yürüyüş* (2015b) (The Long Walk), recounts the young protagonist's epic walk from İstanbul to the rugged mountains in Eastern Turkey. Driven by the desire to escape the social and political pressures of modern urban life, he seeks a quiet place untouched by human civilization. However, during his long journey, he discovers that he cannot get out of the historical context in which he is involved, no matter how remote the terrain or how far the distance traveled. Although he initially thinks of the social and the natural worlds as a dichotomy, he ultimately realizes that the boundary between them is more permeable than he imagined.

This chapter invites the reader to a similarly long journey across Turkey to trace the entanglement of nature and society, environment and politics, by paying attention to different forms of human mobility in Anatolia. I examine the myriad ways that humans navigate natural environments—mountains, valleys, seas, and deserts—to show that nature is continually reinscribed with political significance. My analysis builds on existing ecocritical scholarship, which problematizes the distance between nature and society, claiming that "Historical conditions have abolished an extra-social nature" (Morton 2007: 17). However, I also introduce a new angle to this discussion by focusing specifically on human mobility. The emphasis on movement adds a temporal dimension to ahistorical conceptions of place and historicizes natural environments by shedding light on different communities that have variously passed through, settled in, or avoided certain terrains.

I utilize "route" as a key concept, because it evokes both a geography and the movement within that geography. I follow the routes of various people—nomads, rural walkers, itinerant poet-singers, outlaws, exiled populations, and migrants—who navigate the diverse topography of Anatolia for various reasons. As I examine the changing trajectories of human mobility, I include voluntary and forced movement in my discussion, and analyze fictional and autobiographical narratives from different periods.

Currently, there is no ecocritical study about movement and its various implications for revisiting the continuum between environment and politics in Turkey. The existing literary scholarship on human mobility predominantly focuses on internal migration from villages to urban centers. There is also only a limited body of criticism on the culture of walking, which primarily gives attention to narratives of urban *flânerie* in renowned modern novels. Other forms and agents of walking, as well as the specific geographical and historical contexts in which these walks take place, have not yet been tackled by ecocritics.

The first section of this chapter focuses on the history of walking in Turkey, by offering a brief glimpse into the nomadic cultures of Anatolia, and then shifts the focus to contemporary literary walkers. In particular, I examine rural walking narratives to show that characters, who embark upon difficult journeys in isolated natural settings, often confront immense sociopolitical pressures. In these works, nature hardly comes to the fore as a place for peaceful retreat. I showcase my argument by presenting an analysis of Ayhan Geçgin's *Uzun Yürüyüş*, a novel that, as previously suggested, contemplates the entanglement of natural and political spheres.

The second section turns toward the mountainous geographies of Turkey to demonstrate how socioeconomic conditions reinscribe mountains as places of conflict and rebellion. I examine Yaşar Kemal's epic novel *İnce Memed I* (1955) (*Memed, My Hawk* 1961) to revisit the trope of the brave bandit who takes to the mountain to revolt against the tyranny of landlords. The Taurus Mountains in Southern Anatolia become a site of war between state-supported landlords and Memed, the legendary defender of peasants' rights. I follow the footsteps of Memed and others who navigate the mountains—Yoruks, outlaws, and itinerant poet-singers—to shed light on the social and political struggles that take place in this region.

The third section shifts the focus from the Southern to the Eastern Anatolian mountains to remember a tragic history inscribed on the highlands: the 1915 deportation of Armenians under the Ottoman Empire. I examine three autobiographical narratives written by Mıgırdiç Margosyan, Yervant Odyan, and Vahram Altounian. They all construct verbal maps to trace the routes of forced exile and portray the severe conditions in which Armenians are marched toward the southern provinces of the empire, crossing remote mountains and deserts. Their mapping practices unveil the spatial dimensions of imperial politics and reveal the transformation of Anatolia's natural environments into historically charged spaces.

The fourth and final section examines contemporary migration flows. It follows the routes taken by undocumented Middle Eastern and Asian migrants, who enter Turkey from the eastern border and journey toward Europe via the Mediterranean Sea. I discuss Hakan Günday's novel *Daha* (2013) (*More* 2016), which places human smugglers at the center of the narrative to elucidate the perilous journeys of migrants as they travel over land and on water. Günday portrays how the natural environment acquires geopolitical significance as Turkey's remote mountains, forests, and seas turn into dark alleys used as migrant smuggling routes.

This chapter invites readers on myriad journeys: from northwestern urban centers such as İstanbul and Bursa to Mount Ararat in Eastern Anatolia; from the Taurus Mountains in the south to the Euphrates River in the east; and from the southeastern border with Iraq and Syria to the Mediterranean coast. As I map the movement of different communities in multiple directions, I reveal how the complex relationship between environment and politics is continually being redefined.

On Foot: Nomads, Rural Walkers, Drifters

The history of human mobility in Anatolia can be traced to the eleventh century, when nomadic Oghuz tribes first arrived from Central Asia. In the centuries that followed, many descendants of Oghuz Turks led nomadic lives in Anatolia. More than a million Turcoman nomads lived their lives moving between winter camps in the Mesopotamian plain and summer quarters on the plateaus of Central Anatolia (Kemal 1999: 3). Movement was a fundamental aspect of the lives of these nomadic tribes also referred to as *yörük/yürük* (Yoruk),[1] denoting those who walk, a derivation of the Turkish verb *yürümek* (to walk). Traversing different landscapes with their livestock and few belongings, and setting up their tents by this river and that mountain, they were experts at adapting to seasonal cycles.

Toward the eighteenth century, however, nomadic communities, who were exempt from paying taxes and carrying out other duties, began to receive less tolerance from the Ottoman Empire. This was, in part, because the Ottomans "responded to the new world of expanding trade networks and territorial states by initiating a series of measures intended to improve the empire's security ... A key component of this shift in priorities was the growing interest on the part of Ottoman officials to count, register, and ultimately, settle the nomadic and other itinerant groups" (Kasaba 2013: 17). In order to rule out "the territorial and political uncertainty that came with nomads" (17), the empire began to force the nomadic tribes to settle on one piece of designated land. The transition to sedentary life yielded radical changes in the culture and lives of the Yoruks.

Yaşar Kemal's 1971 novel, *Binboğalar Efsanesi* (*The Legend of a Thousand Bulls* 1976), recounts this gradual disappearance of nomadic life in Anatolia. Taking place in Çukurova, the novel oscillates between the 1800s and the 1900s. Kemal sheds light on significant historic events such as the clashes between the Ottoman army and the Turcoman Yoruks, who were defeated in 1876. He notes how, after the defeat, the nomads were no longer allowed to go to the mountains, as army soldiers were stationed on the roads "*leading into the Taurus mountains from the Chukurova plain. Not a soul was to be allowed to pass either from the plain into the mountains or from the mountains down into the plain. And so the huge plain became a death-trap for the Turcoman nomads*" (Kemal 1976: 70). For Kemal, the nineteenth-century folk poet Dadaloğlu's couplet best captures "the pain of rebellion and of the defeat": "The lord signed the decree that sealed our fate; so be it. / But if the decree belongs to the Sultan, the mountains belong to us" (Kemal 1999: 109–10). Following the defeat, nomads lost freedom of movement, and the natural environment became a politically appropriated site inaccessible without imperial permission. As Kemal recounts, many nomads lost their lives due to heat and epidemics, while others settled in one place, started paying taxes, and were summoned for military service.

At the same time as it offers a historical overview, Kemal's novel also foregrounds the story of a specific nomadic group, the Karaçullu tribe, which has, for centuries, pitched their tents in the Çukurova Plain during the winter and in the Aladağ Mountain during the summer. One of the last tribes to be spotted in Çukurova by the mid-twentieth century, they face myriad difficulties when forced to adapt to sedentary life. In addition to searching for a piece of land on which to settle, the Karaçullu tribe must also defend itself from the attacks of nearby villagers who demand "money, sheep, rugs, whatever they could get" (Kemal 1976: 116) from the nomads. As a nomad boy, who worries about his tribe, says, "There's no place in the whole wide world they can go to, nowhere at all for them to pitch their tents. As soon as they set foot somewhere it's money, money all the time … And all for the right to winter on a patch of dry arid land, on an abandoned knoll!" (112). As nomads try to build a new life in the "abandoned knolls," their tribe gradually breaks up and is dispersed across

Anatolia: "*In every province we abandoned a part of us, in every clime, in every tract of land. Discarded tents, forgotten, left to rot away ... Into a thousand sources we split*" (269).

As recounted in *The Legend of a Thousand Bulls*, nomadic lifestyle largely came to an end in Anatolia, although scattered groups of Yoruks can still be spotted on the Taurus Mountains today. The transition from nomadic to sedentary life entirely changed the way that people relate to the physical environment. This change is also reflected in language. The Turkic word *yurt*, for example, was used by nomads to refer to the places where they were temporarily encamped as well as to portable tents. Ironically, this word, which originates from a culture whose essence comprises movement and temporary dwelling, today carries connotations of territorial and national belonging. In modern Turkish, *yurt* refers primarily to one's country, and the expression *yeri yurdu olmak*[2] implies having an established dwelling place, a home, or a homeland, alluding to a sense of attachment. By contrast, the expression *yersiz yurtsuz*, with the negating suffixes *-siz/-suz* ("without"), is used to describe people without a home(land), implying a state of displacement and being on the move. The phrase has mainly negative connotations in mainstream society; leading an unsettled life is often deemed problematic due to the uncertain nature of movement. As I discuss shortly, this suspicion toward movement seems to have endured from imperial times to this day.

In what follows, I shift my focus to contemporary narratives of walking to demonstrate that the natural environment is still politically inscribed and unlicensed movement is still not tolerated. Walking narratives in Turkey can be categorized as urban and rural. Urban walking narratives have been examined by several critics so as to highlight the relationship between movement, urban space, and sociopolitical life.[3] This discussion, however, focuses on rural walking narratives, which have received little scholarly attention. When we look at characters who navigate rural environments, we can observe that class and its correlation with setting play a vital role in these narratives where the protagonists are often peasants, laborers, exiles, and outlaws. In rural accounts, nature is often politically charged and the bodies that move in it are deeply impacted by the sociopolitical context in which they are implicated. For example, in Yaşar Kemal's short story "Bebek" (2004a) (Baby), which takes place in a remote, poverty-stricken village, the story begins and ends with a long walk.[4] İsmail walks a lengthy distance to get to a village where he can find a nursing mother for his son whose own mother, a peasant, dies due to the strain of overwork. Nature is a difficult site woven with illness, hunger, labor exploitation, and other economic and social injustices. Walking is a matter of survival.

Another example is Yılmaz Güney's film *Yol* (1982) (*The Road* 1982), where a young man named Seyit Ali takes leave from prison to visit his home in a remote mountain village and is pressured by his family to "honor kill" his wife for betraying him. Unwilling to do this, he flees with his wife and son, and they set out on foot to cross the snowy mountains of Siirt in Southeastern Turkey. During their journey, Seyit Ali's wife freezes to death, as he suspects, leaving him in remorse after he tries unsuccessfully to rescue her. The film shows that a mountain or a remote village can be more imprisoning than an actual prison. Walking is an obligation for these characters who are placed under immense familial and social pressures, and the mountains stand for the ethical conflicts and physical obstacles they face.

As we can see in these rural walking narratives, nature scarcely comes to the fore as a romantic pastoral setting or a site for peaceful retreat. Unlike American or European literature, Turkish literature does not have a strand that focuses on the solitary man's immersion in the wild. Neither is there a tradition of walking narrative as a form of nature writing—reflected in the works of such authors as William Wordsworth and Henry David Thoreau—or as a form of philosophical inquiry—captured in the works of such thinkers as Friedrich Nietzsche and Jean Jacques Rousseau. Rural accounts of walking in Turkish often portray the dialectic between freedom and oppression, and the simultaneous desire and failure to flee society.

A contemporary novel that successfully captures this dialectic is Ayhan Geçgin's *Uzun Yürüyüş* (2015b) (The Long Walk). As previously mentioned, the protagonist is an unnamed young man who leaves everything behind to embark upon an epic walk that takes him from his home in İstanbul to the remote mountains in Eastern Turkey. The novel, which comprises two parts—"City" and "Mountain"—begins with his declaration of why he starts this journey:

> Şehrin dışına çıkmak, geniş bir ova, sessiz bir dağ eteği bulana kadar arkaya bakmadan yürümek. Sonunda, diye düşündü, her şeyi unutmak, insan olduğumu bile unutmak istiyorum. Kendimi parça parça, ip ip geriye doğru sökeceğim. ... Bu benim yok olma alıştırmam olacak. (15)

> To step out of the city, to walk without looking back until I find a vast plain, a quiet foothill. Ultimately, he thought, I want to forget everything, even the fact that I am a human being. I will unravel myself thread by thread, bit by bit. ... This will be my exercise in annihilation.

Tired of the constraints of urban life, he seeks to find a quiet corner out in nature to forget everything he has ever learnt. His desire to exit the urban environment to enter a natural one is tied to an inside/outside dichotomy that we find in most of Geçgin's novels. The fear of not being able to get out of the city, out of society, out of one's life is a recurring motif in *Kenarda* (2003) (On the Side), where Geçgin refers to a city without an exit, resembling a trap (Gürbilek 2020: 75). In *Uzun Yürüyüş*, the protagonist similarly looks for an "exit door" (Geçgin 2015b: 53) to get out of the city and to move forward. Instead of going around in circles and standing still in a "kımıltısız bir şimdi ve burada" (17; motionless now and here), he wants to keep moving until he finds an ideal place to stop, while also questioning whether such a place truly exists. As he notes, "Bir yer sorunu bu. Daha doğrusu, belki bir yersizlik sorunu" (17; This is a question of place. Or rather, a problem of placelessness).

In terms of its philosophical tone, Geçgin's novel can be compared with poet and philosopher Oruç Aruoba's *Yürüme* (1992) (Walking). Aruoba perceives movement—literally and figuratively—as a manifestation of intellectual restlessness and a philosophical quest. He elaborates on the continuum between the wandering body and the ruminating mind. Especially in the second part of the book titled "yer, yön, yol" (place, direction, path), Aruoba describes the person that embarks upon a journey as someone who "yerleşikliğinden rahatsız" (70; feels uneasy about settling) and is willing to follow an undefined path (102). For Aruoba, "*yeri-yurdu* olmaması gereken kişi" (106; the person who ought not to have an established dwelling place) finds freedom in erring,[5] that is in both wandering without direction and making mistakes. Geçgin's novel is reminiscent of Aruoba's work in that they both present walking as a philosophical revolt against the social script and a deliberate choice to stray off course. Geçgin's protagonist also embraces the state of being *yersiz yurtsuz*; he voluntarily uproots himself and sets out on a walk toward the unknown. One main difference between the two works is that Aruoba alludes to an ideal of freedom, which is deliberately absent in Geçgin's novel.

In *Uzun Yürüyüş*, the protagonist's journey begins in İstanbul, where his backpack is stolen, ridding him of undesired possessions. Drawing on an ethos of self-reliance, he learns to improvise to find food and shelter, spending the night on the street, on the seashore, in a park, and in a garbage collector's makeshift home. Although he has numerous adventures, two specific moments in the story mark significant turning points. The first is when he wakes up in a hospital in extreme pain, unable to remember how he got there. The doctor tells him that he was found among *çapulcular*[6] (marauders) and was beaten by the police. The author infers that the protagonist crossed paths with the protestors during the 2013 Gezi Resistance,[7] which was primarily a reaction to the increasing privatization of the urban environment, the sense of confinement that came with it, and the immense need for nonmonetized public spaces. The incorporation of Gezi into the narrative not only adds political context to the novel, but it also creates a contrast with the protagonist's ideal of finding a remote land unimpacted by modern capitalism and police violence. This is something he briefly discusses with the doctor who responds:

> Issız bir yer bulabileceğine gerçekten inanıyor musun? Genç bir çift tanıyordum. Yıllar önce doğanın içinde yaşayacağız deyip bir dağın yamacına, bir ormanın içine küçük, taştan bir ev yapmışlardı. ... Kendilerini istemeye istemeye köylülerle birlikte hem bir maden şirketine hem de HES'e karşı bir mücadelenin içinde buldular. Oysa istedikleri sakin bir yaşamdı. (Geçgin 2015b: 69)

> Do you really believe you can find a remote, untouched place? I used to know a young couple. Years ago, they built a small stone house in a forest at the foothill of a mountain to live reclusively in nature. ... They unwillingly found themselves in a struggle led by villagers against both a mining company and a hydroelectric power plant. All they had asked for was a quiet life.

The stories of others seeking the same thing before him act as an omen for the protagonist. The doctor's questions underwrite both the myth of pristine wilderness and the trope of the modern subject who discovers himself through immersion in the wild. Although the book mimics the generic protocols of wilderness narratives and philosophical quests, Geçgin points to the difficulty of lifting the self outside the social and political context in which one is embedded, even when one lives reclusively on a mountain.

At the start, the protagonist thinks that escaping the city and societal obligations may make him feel "lighter," but it turns out that he cannot easily relieve himself of the burden he has been carrying around. As Geçgin describes him, "Yola çıkarken bedeninin bir soğan zarı gibi tek tek soyulacağını sanmıştı, ama aksine bir ağaç kütüğü gibi kat kat kabuk bağlamış, katılaşmıştı. Bu beden ... fazla ağırdı" (88–9; When he started his journey, he thought his body would be peeled off, layer by layer, like onion skin; but, on the contrary, it was coated with layers of crust and solidified like a tree trunk. This body ... was too heavy).

The tension between lightness and gravity of existence grows even more prominent as the protagonist walks eastward and reaches the mountains in the second part of the book. There, he expresses the desire to become as light as thin air and to disappear among the clouds: "Gözlerini dağlara dikti. ...

Dağın zirvesi, boşluğa bir adım, sonra bir bulut" (105; He fixed his gaze at the mountains. ... The mountain peak, a step into emptiness, then a cloud). However, these introspective moments are suddenly interrupted by the arrival of the gendarmes[8] asking him for his identity documents. Staring at the mountains, he says, "Beni yine buldular (95; They found me again). The reader realizes that he has arrived at the mountains in Eastern Turkey, where the armed conflict between the Turkish state and the Kurdish guerrillas[9] has turned nature into a special security region inaccessible to civilians. Unauthorized movement is dangerous, and even criminalized, when it occurs on these mountains, which have historically been sites of rebellion against the state and remained under military surveillance.

For example, during the height of the Turkish-Kurdish conflict in the 1990s, Mount Ararat was only accessible to the Turkish military, and was intermittently closed and reopened for civilian climbers. It was declared a second-degree military zone in 2000 and remained closed to civilian access until 2004, when it became a national park ("Ağrı Dağı" 2019). These changes regarding a mountain's status demonstrate that "the mountain" both refers to "a brute fact—to a material reality" and is "a social construct," "a category of knowledge" (Debarbieux and Rudaz 2015: 2–3). Likewise, the eastern and southeastern mountains of Turkey are both material realities and politically constructed spaces. In literature, they are often portrayed as sites of war and exile, as evident in Bejan Matur's poetry book, *Son Dağ* (2015) (The Last Mountain). Matur writes about mothers waiting for their sons to return from war in the mountains while "dağlar büyüyor acıyla" (85; mountains grow taller with pain). Elegiac poems recount numerous stories that take place against the backdrop of "Vadilerin uğultusu" (18; wuthering valleys), "ağaçları inatla köklenen orman" (60; a forest whose trees perseveringly take root), and "dağlardaki kar kuyuları" (81; the wells of snow in the mountains).

The second part of Geçgin's novel, titled "Mountain," takes place against the background of similar landscapes as in Matur's book. The Turkish-Kurdish conflict inevitably begins to impact the protagonist's movement. When the gendarmes see the protagonist walking in the mountain, they suspect that he must be either mad or running away from the law. When he says that he has merely embarked upon a long walk, he is slapped by the Sergeant Major who says, "Yürüyüş parkuru mu lan burası ...?" (Geçgin 2015b: 97; Is this a damn walking parkour ...?). Since no one in his sane mind would simply take a walk on these mountains, he becomes a suspect and is taken to prison. There he meets another detainee who talks about the increasing number of police stations on the mountains and alludes to the real and symbolic walls built as a result of the war. Where the mountains are sites of armed struggle and surrounded by (in)visible political walls, an arbitrary outing is misconstrued as a suspicious activity.

After he is released, the protagonist clandestinely continues his walk on the mountains where the sound of military planes mix with the sound of foxes. He respectively encounters a young girl, who has lost her family while running from the war, and a Kurdish guerrilla. When the protagonist tells him that he is on his "hicret"[10] (146; hejira), the Kurdish man replies, "İnsan dağa niye çıkar? Özgür değilse çıkar, özgürlüğü için çıkar. ... Ama kanımca senin yolun çarpık bir yol olmuştur. Neden? Çünkü tek başına özgürlük olmaz meçhul adam" (147; Why would anyone take to the mountains? He would if he is not free, he would for his freedom. ... But I am afraid your path is a crooked one. Why? Because you cannot achieve freedom on your own, mysterious man). The man then goes on to talk about "halkların özgürlüğü" (freedom of the peoples), but the protagonist cannot relate to his words and wonders whether he is part of a "people" (147). For him, a solitary path is not necessarily a crooked one, or, at least, not the only crooked one. So he continues to walk, observing everything that occurs around him without judgment, merely gathering impressions.[11] He grows increasingly estranged from people, ideologies, and even language, as he chooses silence over human voices that pain him (13). The notion of *hicret* he mentions speaks to this alienation as it implies a sense of physical and mental detachment. The protagonist wants to be entirely defamiliarized from who he is, and this begins with erasing one's name. This is why he remains nameless throughout the story. When he occasionally introduces himself to strangers, he uses a different name each time, such as Erkan or Mahmut (29, 60).

At the beginning of the novel, when he first begins his walk, the protagonist mentions two types of wind blowing from opposing directions, one moving him forward and the other slowing him down (16). This tension between a symbolic tailwind and headwind is sustained until the very end of the novel. On the one hand, walking in wilderness is presented as a movement forward, a liberating practice at self-erasure by being immersed in nature's rhythms. Describing his walk as "sürükleniş" (23; drifting), the protagonist meanders along an indeterminate path, without a definite point of arrival.[12] Mountains seem like an ideal place for escaping the confines of selfhood and for cultivating an existential void. As he says, "bir yer bulduğumda artık yürümeyeceğim ... yatacağım, kafamdaki düşüncelerin yavaş yavaş, teker teker açlıktan ölüşlerini izleyeceğim" (78; when I find a place, I will stop walking … I will lie down and watch my thoughts slowly disintegrate, one after another).

On the other hand, this philosophical quest for finding a liberating expanse is constantly interrupted by social and political factors—such as the Gezi Resistance and the Turkish-Kurdish conflict—that pressure him at every turn. The further the protagonist travels away from polis/politics, the more he spirals back into it, which dismantles the nature/society dichotomy he had initially presumed. He cannot remove himself from the historical context in which he is imbricated, even in secluded mountains. As another character says, "dağlar bile özgür değildir, tutsaktır. Tüm doğa tutsaktır" (148; not even the mountains are free, they are captives. All of nature is captive). Seen in this light, as Geçgin remarks, compared with the strollers in the urban fiction of Yusuf Atılgan and Sevgi Soysal,[13] his fictional walker resembles someone pacing in prison (2015a).

The story of the protagonist, who oscillates between these two realities, ultimately closes on an ambiguous note. At the end, we find him standing alone on a wartorn mountain, which embodies the dialectic between freedom and captivity, singularity and collectivity, remembrance and forgetting. He stares into the expanse, toward an uncertain future. Even if there is no uncharted natural territory and no escape from society, Geçgin infers, there is still room to breathe and start over: "Manzara şimdi yine boş, yine insansızdı. Açık gök altında dağlar donmuş dalgalar halinde alçalıp yükseliyor[du] … Başı döner gibi oldu, sanki manzarayı ilk kez görüyordu. Söylediği hiçbir şey yoktu ama geride tuttuğu bir şey de yoktu." (Geçgin 2015b: 150; The landscape was now empty, unpopulated, again. Under the open sky, mountains undulated like frozen waves … He felt dizzy; it was as if he was seeing the view for the first time. There was nothing he intended to say and nothing he held back.)

Taking to the Mountains: *Mecbur, Eşkiya, Âşık*

Anatolia lies between two great mountain ranges that run parallel to the northern and southern coasts of Turkey: the Northern Anatolian Mountains in the north and the Taurus Mountains in the south. Several other mountains, small and large, are scattered across Anatolia. There is, as a result, a rich tradition of musical and literary narratives that portray mountains variously as obstacles separating lovers, sites of conflict and war, places of escape, and sacred spots for meditation. Sabahattin Ali's poem "Dağlar" (1931) (Mountains), which alludes to the sense of freedom experienced in the mountains, as opposed to the sense of entrapment felt in the city, and the folk song "Erzurum Dağları Kar ile Boran" (2002) (Erzurum Mountains in Snow and Storm),[14] where the speaker writes a woeful letter to his beloved from a remote, snowed-in mountain, are only a few examples of these mountain-inspired genres. There are also several cultural expressions and sayings in Turkish that allude to the sense of distance and insurmountability evoked by mountains. To give a few examples, *dağlara taşlara* (literally "to the mountains, to the stones") is an expression meaning "may it be far away from us," used in reference to a misfortune one wishes to avoid. *Arada dağlar kadar fark olmak* (a mountain of difference in between) implies two things that are worlds apart. *Dağları aşmak* (crossing the mountains) and *dağları devirmek* (overturning mountains) both allude to overcoming a nearly impossible obstacle.

While the abstract idea of mountains has always been a powerful notion in Turkey, few authors have actually written about them in more concrete ways that mirror the actual motions of life there. Mountains in Turkey have borne witness to myriad forms of human mobility as well as political struggles among different groups throughout recent history. Perhaps no other author has written about mountains and the communities that navigate them in more detail than Yaşar Kemal. This section focuses on Kemal's novel, *İnce Memed I* (1955) (*Memed, My Hawk* 1961),[15] and follows the footsteps of outlaws and itinerant poet-singers traversing the mountainous geographies of Southern Turkey, to demonstrate that socioeconomic conditions have reinscribed mountains as places of conflict and rebellion.

Born in the village of Hemite, near the plains of Çukurova in Southern Turkey, Kemal grew up close to the Taurus Mountains that separate the Mediterranean coastal region from the Central Anatolian Plateau. His family migrated to Çukurova from the eastern city of Van after it was occupied by Russia in 1915. Following a difficult journey that lasted a year and a half, Kemal's parents arrived in Hemite, where they were the only Kurdish household in a village of settled Turcoman nomads (Kemal 1999: 3). The first stories Kemal ever heard about the Taurus Mountains came from itinerant performers: *âşıks*,[16] folk poet-singers who perform their songs on *saz*, and *dengbêjs*,[17] Kurdish singer-storytellers. Traveling across Anatolia, witnessing a number of events later captured in their poetry and music, these folk artists were often regarded as the spokespeople of society. Moreover, *âşıks* and *dengbêjs* belong to an oral tradition, which can be seen as an art form always on the move. Rather than being solidified through writing, their recitations are orally passed on from one generation to another. While growing up, Kemal learnt to sing epic tales and ballads and to play *saz* with the itinerant poet-singers and story-tellers, who visited his village, such as Âşık Rahmi and Abdal-é-Zeyniki. By the age of nine, Kemal gained fame as "Âşık Kemal" or "Kemal the Bard" (Kemal 1999: 9–10). He also observed that mountains hold a central place in both *âşık* and *dengbêj* traditions, which preserve the unofficial oral histories of mountain communities.

We find several reflections of these oral traditions in Kemal's novels. In *Memed, My Hawk*, for example, there is an *âşık* named Poor Ali, who owns both a *saz* and a gun, suggesting that he is both a poet-singer and a rebel. He often climbs to a mountain top to find inspiration. When he sings, it is "as if the sound did not come from within him, but from a thousand years away, from afar, from the mountains, from the Chukurova, the sea, laden with the salt-tang of the water, the resin of the pines, the scent of the wild mint" (Kemal 1961: 282). In *Ağrıdağı Efsanesi* (1970) (*The Legend of Ararat* 1975), we encounter several *dengbêj*s who sing on top of Mount Ararat and whose songs reflect a deep engagement with the natural environment. As Wendelmoet Hamelink observes, "Someone who is not surrounded … by the mountains of the welat (the homeland), and by its nature, is regarded as less capable of being a good dengbêj: the geography where the dengbêj is born and lives determines the sound of his voice—it is said that a voice from the plains sounds different from a voice from the mountains" (2016: 306). The physical environment of Anatolia, particularly its mountainous topography, occupies center stage in the performances of *âşık*s and *dengbêj*s.

Mountains and the people who navigate them, from *âşık*s to *dengbêj*s to *eşkıya*s (bandits),[18] occupy an important place in Kemal's work. He writes about famous bandits, including his mother's uncles, such as uncle Mahiro, the most famous outlaw in Anatolia, Iran, and the Caucasus. Another uncle, whose story he often recounts, used to be the leader of a famous band. This uncle was captured and thrown into Van prison but managed to escape only to return again to save his friends. When he returned, he was caught by the police and killed. A legend then ensued about him: allegedly, the officers were so impressed by his courage that they opened his heart and found four hearts instead of one. As Kemal notes, there are at least two versions to this story: the legendary version about the bravery of the four-hearted brigand and the real version about the execution of a prisoner whose clothes were hung on a tree to set a trap for his family (Kemal 1999: 5–6). Growing up in a geography where harsh realities turn to memorable legends, Kemal turns childhood experiences into novels enriched with legendary tales and folk poetic traditions.

Of all of Kemal's novels that shed light on mountains and brigandry, the four-volume *İnce Memed* is perhaps the most memorable one. I focus particularly on the first volume, *Memed, My Hawk*, which follows the protagonist (Slim) Memed from childhood to late adulthood, from being a young peasant to a famed brigand hero. The novel opens with a detailed description of the Taurus Mountains, whose slopes rise from the shores of the Mediterranean Sea, and the scrub of Çukurova, "whose green expanse seems boundless, wilder and darker than a forest" (Kemal 1961: 5). From the onset, it is suggested that this region is a wilderness that may be dangerous to traverse. We then meet the protagonist: a young boy named Memed who grows up in a mountain village where peasants are enslaved by the villainous landlord Abdi Agha. Having lost his father, Memed lives with his mother and works on the land owned by the Agha, who is very cruel toward him. One day, after a conflict with the Agha, Memed first runs to another village where he takes shelter in the house of a family friend named Süleyman and then heads toward the mountains. Süleyman remarks that a young boy would never take to the dangerous mountains if he was not obliged to do so, out of fear for Abdi Agha: "See what goat-bearded Abdi has done to this child ... Sick of his life, he rushes off into the mountains, among the birds of prey and wolves!" (21). This is the first instance in the novel where Kemal alludes to the mountain as a site of escape and rebellion and foreshadows Memed's future as a brigand.

Although the Agha's men ultimately find Memed and punish him and his mother by nearly starving them to death, Memed never stops thinking about the mountains. While growing up, he hears several stories about brigands, including the legendary Big Ahmet, whom everyone both loves and fears: "Big Ahmet ... had been able to foster the two feelings together among the mountain people. Otherwise he would never have been able, as an outlaw, to survive a single year in the mountains" (56). Forced to become a brigand due to an injustice committed toward his family, Big Ahmet is known for his heroic deeds, such as bringing medicine to the sick and flour to the poor (57). Memed realizes that mountains can be home to outlaws who are commemorated for being brave and solid like a mountain.

The plot thickens when Memed grows up and falls in love with a girl named Hatçe, who is about to wed the Agha's nephew, Veli. Memed and Hatçe decide to run away, but during a confrontation, Memed kills Veli and wounds the Agha. Wrongly accused of shooting Veli, Hatçe is sent to prison. Memed, once again, hides in Süleyman's house, thinking, "Well, it's done. It was my fate. ... I'm certainly not going to give myself up to the police. I'll take to the mountains" (96). Realizing that Memed has no other option than to flee to the mountains, Süleyman takes him to Mad Durdu, a brigand from his family, but also warns Memed not to stay with Durdu for too long for he is a thief who would sooner or later get shot. According to Süleyman, there are certain rules brigands must follow to survive in the mountains. He advises Memed to behave with dignity, to become a leader while not treating others like slaves, and to never harm the poor (106). "There's no difference between the mountain and a prison" (98), Süleyman adds, alluding to the dangers of living the life of an outlaw. This statement sets the tone for the entire novel, which portrays the mountain as a difficult geography where many bloody conflicts take place, including the escalating conflicts between Memed and the Agha's men. Süleyman's words also echo Geçkin's novel in that both works portray the mountain as an embodiment of the dialectic between freedom and imprisonment.

Soon after he joins Durdu's band, Memed endures many sleepless nights. As Durdu says, "When a man first comes to the mountain, he can't sleep. One feels a strangeness in one's heart, a feeling of helplessness, as if one were alone in the world" (105). Later, Memed experiences this sense of estrangement when he is wounded during an armed conflict and takes shelter with a nomadic tribe. Kerimoğlu, the leader of the nomadic Saçıkaralı tribe, invites Memed to his tent, which has such beautiful "embroidered bags of dazzling colour" (140) that it brings tears to Memed's eyes. As the nomads feed and clothe them, Memed feels a "strangeness within himself:" "His whole chest was covered with cartridge-belts. ... 'So I've become a brigand, eh?' he thought. 'And from now on, all my life I'll be a brigand!'" (141). Because of the heart-warming treatment he receives, Memed feels temporarily alienated from who he has become. Since there is no escaping his situation, he decides he must at least choose what kind of a brigand he will be. A turning point in the novel occurs when Memed sees Durdu rob the nomads and humiliate the leader, Kerimoğlu, in front of his family.[19] As a result, Memed commits to being a virtuous brigand and leaves Mad Durdu's band.

From this point onward, Memed's decision to stay in the mountains is driven by political motives. Although he initially takes refuge there for personal reasons, he soon takes it upon himself to defend peasant rights and to revolt against both Abdi Agha and the entire system of land ownership. He dreams of the day he will gather the elders of the Dikenli Plateau around him and tell them, "There'll be no more sharecropping for any Agha. The fields are yours too and you're free to sow as much as you like. As long as I'm on the mountain, everything will be all right" (243). While we follow the footsteps of Memed navigating a mountainous geography, we also find out who else wanders the Çukurova region. In the last years of the First World War, following the defeat of the Ottomans, Çukurova was filled with war deserters, brigands, and thieves. This was a period when a class of newly enriched people—landlords (or Aghas)—was coming into existence and grabbing land away from the peasants. Every Agha hired a band of brigands to pressure the poor, through bloody fights if necessary (231-3). Ensuring the reader that he does not intend to romanticize brigandry, Kemal asserts that people like Big Ahmet and Memed are rare among the countless brigands that handle the Aghas' dirty work.

As Memed begins to have violent clashes with the Agha's men, the Taurus Mountains turn into a war zone. The sparsely populated mountains—with the forests lining the lower slopes and the rugged, rocky terrain of the higher elevations—turn into an ideal geography for war. After his men repeatedly fail to capture Memed, the Agha asks the government to send an army to catch the "brigand [who] is ruling the mountains" (320). Against a state-supported Agha, Memed receives the support of the local villagers, such as the elderly man named Big Osman, who coins the term "Memed, my hawk" (275), likening Memed to a wild bird of prey that dwells high on the mountain top and is seldom captured. Several other analogies involving mountains are used to describe the strength of Memed who is said to be "as firm as a mountain" (282), "a giant of a man," whose "eyes flashed in the darkness of the night," and whom the "bullets can't harm" (251).

Critic Berna Moran compares Memed with the figure of the noble bandit in world literature using Eric Hobsbawm's taxonomy of bandit typology in *Bandits* (2001) (Moran 2003). Moran contends that Memed could be categorized as a noble bandit because he takes to the mountains as the result of an injustice committed against him; he takes from the rich and gives to the poor; he only kills someone to defend himself; and he is respected by the simple folk (104). Yet despite these similarities, Moran argues, *Memed, My Hawk* is more closely linked with the *eşkiya* stories narrated in Anatolia, such as Hasan Kıyafet's *Gominis İmam* (1969) (Communist *Imam*), Timur Karabulut's *Çepel Dünya* (1971) (Filthy World), and Ömer Seyfettin's *Yalnız Efe* (1918) (The Solitary Zeybek) (105-6). Unlike the "conservative" noble bandit type, Memed gradually evolves into a utopian revolutionary and confronts a deeply rooted economic structure (113). Furthermore, he is not alone in his confrontation. When Hatçe goes to prison, she befriends an older woman named Iraz who attacked the man that killed her son, Rıza. Rıza was a young man like Memed who fought the feudal system. As such, Rıza's story "is a projection, or *paradeigma*, of the story of Memed" (Tharaud 2012: 574). Kemal insinuates that there are other men out there, who rebel against the economic-political system and the inequalities it perpetuates.

According to Kemal, men like Memed are examples of what he calls *mecbur adam* (the obliged man). Kemal describes *mecbur adam* by way of an anecdote:

> Paris'te Nazım Hikmet'e sordum. "Yahu," dedim, "sen bir Marksistsin. O koşullarda parti kurulamayacağını bilmiyor muydun? Niye uğraştın bu kadar?" "Mecburdum," dedi. Che Guevera bakan olmuş, bilmem ne olmuş, hep dağa gidiyor. Mecbur çünkü. Dünya öküzün boynuzunda değil, mecbur adamın sırtında duruyor. (Kemal 2000: 109)
>
> In Paris, I asked Nazım Hikmet: "You are a Marxist. Didn't you know that you could not establish a party under those circumstances? Why did you try so hard?" "I was obliged," he said. Che Guevara became a Minister[20] and whatnot, and always takes to the mountains. Because he has to. The world is not balanced on the bull's horn; it weighs on the back of the obliged man.[21]

Obligated to follow a path of his own making to rebel against a system he wants to dismantle, *mecbur adam* partakes in an existential and political struggle. He runs "to escape oppression, to save face or escape humiliation" (Tharaud 1999: xxii). Indeed, throughout the four volumes of *İnce Memed*, we see Memed take to the mountains to struggle against the feudal structure, because he has no other choice and he does not place the responsibility on anyone else's shoulders.

Toward the end of *Memed, My Hawk*, the enchanting mountains, covered in knee-high "purple hyacinths" and "little violets [that] glisten like tearful eyes" (Kemal 1961: 321), bear witness to the biggest armed struggle. After Memed saves Hatçe and Iraz from imprisonment, they all take shelter in a mountain cave. When the gendarmerie find the cave and open fire, Hatçe gets shot and dies after giving birth to Memed's son and Iraz goes to Antep with the baby. Memed is unharmed and manages to find and kill Abdi Agha. The novel ends with Memed taking to the mountains again: "He turned his horse towards Alidagh, galloped through the village like a black cloud and was gone, lost to sight" (351). In the remaining three volumes of *İnce Memed*, Kemal continues to explore similar issues in similar topographies. Although the figure of the tyrant changes, the system that upholds tyranny remains intact and Memed continues to fight the Aghas, surviving until the end of the fourth volume. As Memed continues to navigate the mountains, legends about him circulate from village to village through the storytelling of itinerant poet-singers. He becomes such a legendary figure in Çukurova that villagers do not recognize the real Memed of flesh and blood even when they meet him, because they think that such a humble-looking man cannot be the renowned brigand. As Sergeant İlyas adds, everyone has a different Memed in their hearts (Kemal 1994: 505).

Combining the real and the legendary, *Memed, My Hawk* elucidates an unofficial history inscribed on the secluded Taurus Mountains and captured in the folk songs of *âşıks* and *dengbêjs*. Kemal demonstrates that Turkey's mountainous geographies have long been invisible war zones where socioeconomic injustices are played out between different groups. In his writing, both the natural environment and those who move through them are always politically burdened. Even a seemingly personal issue often has grave social repercussions, proving that taking to the mountains does not offer an opportunity for escaping society. Instead, it throws one right back at the center of political conflict, perhaps in less visible sites, with better hiding spots, but impacted by history nevertheless.

Topographies of Exile

The largest region of Turkey, and far from the sea, Eastern Anatolia has an equally diverse topography and demography. Turkey's highest mountain, Mount Ararat, and largest lake, Lake Van, are located here. Several other mountains, plateaus, rivers, and lakes make Eastern Anatolia into a unique region, which can easily be disconnected from the rest of the country due to the heavy snowfall that makes mountain roads impassable in the winter.[22] The region has also historically been inhabited by an ethnically and religiously diverse population—including Armenians, Kurds, Alevis, Jews, Orthodox and Catholic Syriacs, Zazas, and Muslims. In the final years of the Ottoman Empire and the early years of the Turkish Republic, the tensions between the government and some of these communities resulted in numerous conflicts, wars, and displacements that still have repercussions in contemporary Turkish society and politics. Due to this complicated history, Eastern Anatolia has become a politically charged geography.

Mount Ararat is perhaps one of the most politically and culturally symbolic sites in the region. Located in Turkey,[23] near the border with Armenia and Iran, and visible from almost the entire city of Yerevan, Mount Ararat is particularly important for Turkish-Armenian history: It stands as an emblem of their broken coexistence and the history of forced exile.[24] The purpose of this section is to revisit this history inscribed on Eastern and Southeastern Anatolia. I examine the deportation of Armenians under the Ottoman Empire at the beginning of the twentieth century, by analyzing three autobiographical narratives penned by Mıgırdiç Margosyan, Yervant Odyan, and Vahram Altounian.[25] All three construct verbal maps of the deportation routes to reimagine the topographies of exile and shed light on the transformation of Anatolia's natural environments into political spaces.

To give a brief historical overview, during the Ottoman Empire, the great mountain plateau of Eastern Anatolia was largely inhabited by Christian Armenians. As Ronald Grigor Suny writes, "Some 2 million Christian Armenians lived in the Ottoman lands, most of them peasants and townspeople in the six provinces of eastern Anatolia" (2015: xviii). Following a series of events that gained momentum in the late nineteenth century, however, Armenians were forced to abandon the area. A major turning point occurred when the eastern territories of the Ottoman Empire came under the threat of invasion by Russian forces, who tried to persuade the Ottoman Armenians to ally with them. While most of the Armenian deputies in the Ottoman Parliament proclaimed their devotion to the Ottoman Empire, Armenians in the East were largely in favor of Russian rule (93–4). The Ottoman authorities thus saw not only the Russians but also the Armenians as a threat to the empire's integrity (79). As a result, the conditions of Armenians in Ottoman society started to change drastically.

In early 1915, at the brink of the Ottoman Empire's collapse, the Ottomans lost an important battle on the Caucasian front at Sarıkamış. Young Turks[26] attributed the loss to Armenian treachery and disarmed the Armenian soldiers in the Ottoman army. Next, in April 1915, several Armenian leaders and intellectuals residing in İstanbul were arrested and sent from the city (Suny 2015: xix). In May 1915, the Ottoman Council of Ministers issued a law publicly known as *Tehcir Kanunu* (Deportation Law),[27] which "gave the army the right to deport not only in the case of resistance by means of 'opposition and weapons', but even if the army should 'sense treason'" (Dündar 2010: 84–5). Small-scale deportations of the Armenian population had already begun, from places such as Dörtyol (Hatay) and Zeytun (Maraş) to the inner provinces of Anatolia (72). However, over time, they became larger in scope, resulting in "the deportation of Armenians from cities, towns, and villages in the East, ostensibly as a necessary military measure to ensure the security of the rear. Soon Armenians throughout the country were forced to … leave their homes" (Suny 2015: xix). Thousands of Armenians were ordered to march southward, toward Syria and Iraq, then parts of the Ottoman Empire: "Mountains, valleys, rivers, and deserts were the topographies through which hundreds of thousands of uprooted people moved in convoys guarded by Ottoman soldiers and gendarmes" (xx). Historians estimate that between six hundred thousand and one million Armenians lost their lives on the marches; many of them were killed, while others died due to exhaustion, starvation, and epidemics (Suny 2015: xx–xxi; Dündar 2010: 151; Akçam 2006: 183).

In the following pages, I turn to three 1915 narratives that recount Armenians' exile toward the Syrian Desert and I examine the significance of the physical environment and geographical imagination in these accounts. Each narrative offers a unique perspective: Margosyan—the only one who did not experience 1915 first-hand—is a contemporary novelist recounting his father's deportation from Heredan; Odyan is a journalist whose memoir tells of his own exile from İstanbul in 1915; and Altounian is a young boy whose diary notes offer a glimpse into his family's deportation from Bursa the same year. I begin by focusing on the work of Mıgırdiç Margosyan, who was born in 1938 in the Hançepek District of Diyarbakır, also known as *Gavur Mahallesi* (the Infidel Quarter), inhabited by non-Muslims.[28] It was his father Sarkis, born in Heredan in 1911, who got deported along with his family in 1915. Sarkis was only four when his family received the order to leave their home. As Margosyan relates, his father never talked about 1915 when he was a child, but most adult conversations that young Margosyan overheard during social gatherings ended with one particular question: "Kirvem, sen kaflede nerede kayboldun?" (Alpman 2015; *Kirvem*,[29] where in the cafila[30] did you get lost?).

In his 2006 memoir-novel titled *Tespih Taneleri* (Rosary Beads), Margosyan tells the story of the cafilas through a narrative that oscillates between his own childhood and his father's. Although it is written in the Diyarbakır dialect of Turkish, the book makes recurring references to other languages spoken in Margosyan's hometown, namely Armenian, Kurdish, and Zaza. The story begins with Margosyan being sent to the Karagözyan Armenian Orphanage in İstanbul at the age of fifteen so that he can learn his native Armenian language. Raised speaking Turkish and Kurdish, Margosyan does not speak proper Armenian until he moves to İstanbul. Wondering why he is sent to the orphanage, he soon realizes that linguistic education is, for his father, one of the primary means of reconnecting with Armenian identity.

The narrative then moves back in time to tell the story of Sarkis, Margosyan's father. After receiving the deportation order, Sarkis's family gradually falls apart. While some family members die on the road, others lose contact with one another. Sarkis's mother Saro Nene leaves her daughter Yeğisapet with a Muslim family and her son Apraham with a Zaza *hadji*, loses her son Sarkis by a fountain, and walks to Urfa with her two other children who die during the journey. In the meantime, Sarkis is adopted by a Zaza Agha from Siverek, who converts him to Islam and renames him Ali. Several years following the deportation, Sarkis manages to reunite with his mother and sister, who decide to reclaim their Armenian identities by using their real names and practicing Christianity again.

While recounting his father's story, Margosyan also relates his own childhood memories of his father. He recalls that Sarkis did everything in his power to reclaim the past by keeping the Armenian community united: He counted the Armenian houses in Diyarbakır "ğhane ğhane" (2006: 129; house by house), finding consolation in calculating the number of survivors and in recording who came from where: "Sıveregliler ... Sasonlilar ... Çüngüşliler ... Hayneliler ... Kulplilar ..." (130; The ones from Siverek ... Sason ... Çüngüş ... Hani ... Kulp ...). Like Sarkis, Margosyan also creates a verbal cartography of the myriad places that Armenians left behind and the various routes they followed: "'kafle'ler halinde hangi meçhule doğru yürüdüklerini bilmezken ... terk ettikleri diyarlardan, Bakırmaden'den, Pertek'ten, Harput'tan, Muş, Bitlis, Erzincan, Sivas, Tokat, Erzurum'dan ..." (156; they walked in cafilas toward an unknown fate, leaving behind Bakırmaden, Pertek, Harput, Muş, Bitlis, Erzincan, Sivas, Tokat, Erzurum ...). For both father and son, compiling a list of the abandoned cities is an important means of evoking the memory of a fragmented community, echoing a Kurdish elegy sung by Margosyan's mother Ğhıno: "Heredan, Heredan, Heredan, baba ocağı, ana kucağı ... Tüm bir kuşak, çoluk çocuk, senden koptu, koparıldı, parça parça, berdan berdan" (Alpman 2015; Heredan, Heredan, Heredan, family home, mother's bosom ... An entire generation was separated, torn apart from you, piece by piece).

As indicated in the title, *Tespih Taneleri* (Rosary Beads) portrays the dispersion of the Armenian community through the metaphor of rosary beads scattered across different directions. While depicting the cafilas' "meçhule doğru uzayıp giden uzun yürüyüş" (Margosyan 2006: 417; long, drawn-out walk toward the unknown), Margosyan also includes detailed descriptions of the natural environments they traverse. He mentions the marches that take place "tepelerin ardında, derelerin kenarında, derin vadilerde, sarp kayalık yarlarda" (417; beyond the hills, alongside creeks, in deep valleys, by steep cliffs). He foregrounds certain locations more so than others, such as the Tigris River, which originates in Eastern Anatolia and flows southeast through Iraq. The river is presented both as an essential part of Margosyan's daily life while growing up—it is where he goes swimming and fishing—and an important location where the cafilas were gathered prior to the march. These recurrent emphases on the physical environment owe to the fact that both Sarkis and Margosyan commemorate 1915 by mapping and archiving the places where the deportations took place. This is also why Sarkis often puts his son's knowledge of history and geography to test: "'Hele söle bağhım Margos ... Birinci Cihan Herbi ne zaman başladı, ne zaman bitti? ... Bızım Dicle çayi nerden çığhi, nereye tökıli?'" (98: 'Tell me Margos ... When did the first world war begin and end? ... Where does our Tigris stream originate and where does it flow into the sea?')

Creating a verbal map of the deportation routes is an essential feature of many 1915 accounts[31] that make a point of highlighting the geography of exile. During *tehcir*, many Armenians were displaced from the villages, towns, and cities, which they had historically inhabited, and sent to the more remote provinces. Several Armenian intellectuals and politicians, who resided in urban centers like İstanbul, were sent to the inner and southern parts of Anatolia. The Armenians in the eastern provinces were marched toward the southern provinces and the distant deserts in contemporary-day Syria, where several concentration camps were set up in places such as Meskene, Dipsi, Hamam, and Der Zor (Suny 2015: xix). Unfolding over a vast topography, forced exile converted most of Eastern and Southeastern Anatolia into a territory in motion, where widely dispersed cafilas moved in various directions. The physical environment became an extension of imperial politics.

Many survivor narratives thus foreground the natural environments that became politically instrumentalized during deportations. They pay attention to the climatic conditions and physical characteristics of the places that the exiled were sent to, such as the desert province of Der Zor. One example of these narratives is the İstanbul-based journalist Yervant Odyan's memoir, "Anidzyal Dariner," which was originally published as a series in the Armenian newspaper *Jamanak* in 1919. The memoir was published as a book many years later, first in English (*Accursed Years: My Exile and Return from Der Zor, 1914-1919* 2009) and then in Turkish (*Lanetli Yıllar: İstanbul'dan Der Zor'a Sürgün ve Geri Dönüş Hikayem 1914-1919* 2022). The books were supplemented with a map provided by Ara Sarafian, which traces Odyan's exile from İstanbul to Der Zor—the final stop of the deportation route in the Syrian Desert—and his return to İstanbul. Recreating the geography where the exile took place, the visual map complements Odyan's verbal mapping in the text.

Like many influential figures in the Armenian intellectual circle, Odyan feared being arrested in April 1915 (Beledian 2009: xi). Although he initially avoided arrest by hiding, he was ultimately captured and sent to Konya by train along with other Armenian journalists, such as Sebuh Aguni. In his memoir, Odyan remarks that he only realizes the gravity of his situation when he arrives at Pozantı, a district of Adana, for the railroad ends there and the exiled must walk the remaining distance to the next station in Tarsus. He writes, "So the real torture for the deportees began at Bosanti [Pozantı]" (Odyan 2009: 72). It is after this point that the narrative continues with a focus on the conditions on the road and in the camps: the Kuleg station near Tarsus, where Odyan witnesses the rapid spread of dysentery and other illnesses among camp-dwellers; the anticipation of the trains that arrive from Osmaniye twice a day and carry off thousands of people toward the Syrian Desert; and the severe conditions in which the convoys cross mountains on foot to reach Islahiye (79, 99).

In the text, the physical landscape embodies the dialectic between life and death, bios and thanos. The deported constantly circulate information about the possible places they could be sent to and the significance of these different locations. For example, when he is in Hama, Odyan is informed that those "who didn't accept Islam would be immediately put on the road and marched to the desert of Havran" (114). This piece of news drives several Armenians to convert to Islam, including Odyan, who changes his name to Aziz Nuri. Another example is Odyan's recurring encounters with the Euphrates River, which rises in Eastern Anatolia and flows southeast across Syria and through Iraq. The first time Odyan sees the river is when they pass through the camps in Meskene. They stop by the river, where they bathe and drink water, which is a moment he describes as "pleasant" and "refreshing," especially given "the high temperatures" in the area (137). However, later, the same river becomes a boundary between life and death when they depart for Miadin in Eastern Syria and hear that if sent "across the river" (to the eastern side of the Euphrates into Mesopotamia), they may be killed by "a Bedouin tribe [the Shavis] well known for their brigandage" (152). Indeed, as he dreads, Odyan is soon deported to the other side of the river, to a village named El Bousera. Fearing for his life, he escapes El Bousera and walks toward the Euphrates River, but he has such a terrifying experience with the Arab tribes in the desert that he decides to return to El Bousera, risking imprisonment. During this exhausting walk, on the verge of getting lost, the Euphrates River becomes his compass:

> For the first time since I was deported, I was overwhelmed by a sense of hopelessness and abandonment. ... In the distance on my left I could see some trees by moonlight. This was a sign that Euphrates was there. ... I went once

more to the bank of the Euphrates, washed, drank some water and, turning to my right, went into the desert. (167–8)

This second encounter with the river is crucial: the western side of the river represents a failed escape, the eastern side signifies a desperate return to an unknown fate in the desert, and the river itself presents a limit, as well as a temporary respite, in between the two possibilities.

The changing significations embodied by geography show that the map of hope is one that is in flux, constantly shifting as Odyan moves from one point to another. Different locations appear on his mental map as potential places of refuge or danger. For example, when he is in Der Zor, Odyan considers various routes of escape. He first hears about Armenians who take shelter with the Yezidis on the Sinjar Mountain, a "'four-days' travel through the desert from El Bousera" (157). Later, when still in Der Zor, Odyan decides to flee to Aleppo, where he has social connections. However, when he is caught by the authorities and informed that he will be sent to Diyarbakır, he loses hope and asks to be sent back to Der Zor instead, because, as the police confirm, "Of all those who were exiled to Diyarbakır individually, none ever arrived" (241). As Odyan continues to navigate unknown territories, he is occasionally surprised by the turn of events, such as the time he is temporarily asked to be a translator for the military in Der Zor. Following three years of exile, Odyan ultimately survives 1915 and returns to İstanbul.

Another survivor account comparable with Odyan's in terms of its verbal cartography is "Vahram Altounian'ın Güncesi" (2014) (Vahram Altounian's Diary). Written in Turkish using the Armenian alphabet, this is Vahram Altounian's account of his family's deportation from Bursa to the Syrian Desert and covers a period of four years (1915–19). The diary was first published in 2009, in French translation, as part of a book prepared by his daughter, Janine Altounian.[32] This book was then translated into Turkish and published in 2014 under the title *Geri Dönüşü Yok* (No Possibility to Return). The books include two maps: the one prepared by Krikor Beledian shows the route that the Altounian family followed from Bursa to Der Zor, and the other prepared by Raymond H. Kévorkian shows all the deportation routes and the main locations for transit centers and camps. Combined with verbal narrative, these visual documents help readers trace the long distances traversed by Vahram Altounian and his family.

Vahram Altounian was only fourteen years old when his family received the deportation order. His two older brothers Manuk and Harutyun had already gone to France, and Vahram and his brother Hayk got deported along with their parents Abraham and Nahide in August 1915 (Beledian 2014: 13n3). Stretching from Bursa to Konya to Der Zor, their exile took them to several different sites that assumed symbolic meanings after 1915. The diary is annotated by Beledian's footnotes,[33] which explain the historical significance of the geographical locations mapped by Altounian. For example, when going from Pozantı (Adana) to Islahiye (Antep) variously on foot and camel-back, the Altounian family passes by a mountainous topography, where the Taurus and Amanos Mountains create a rough terrain (Altounian 2014: 15). As Beledian notes, many Armenians died in this mountainous area, especially along the Osmaniye-Islahiye line that runs through Hasanbeyli (2014: 16n13).[34] To give another example, after Altounian's family leaves Akhtarin, a transit camp in Northern Syria, they go to Al-Bab, which lies to the southeast. Once they arrive there, a horseman advises them to escape the southbound convoy and to take shelter in a nearby village. Al-Bab ("door" in Arabic) was considered an entryway into the Syrian Desert in the south and thus seen as a boundary that should not be crossed (Beledian 2014: 19n27).

Altounian's diary is only thirty-six pages long, but, as Zeynep Uğur observes, "The deportation's trajectory is noted in an extremely fastidious manner, especially given the fact that the journal is written after everything happened" (2016: 209). The descriptions of the places, where the Altounian family temporarily stops, take up most of the space in the narrative. This, as Uğur adds, "can be considered a reaction against the loss of the author's homeland" (209). When describing these places, Altounian's narrative oscillates between lengthy accounts and absolute silences. The city of Rakka, which was reached by crossing the Euphrates River, was considered a relatively safe place where the exiled could stay in houses and caravanserais and it is depicted in detail (Beledian 2014: 24n41). By contrast, other locations are mentioned only in passing. For example, the time Altounian's father dies near Hamam and the time spent in Der Zor represent two lacunae in the text. According to Beledian, these silences are an essential part of Altounian's narrative as they point to the limits of language in expressing trauma (2014: 23n40).

During the deportations, Vahram Altounian loses contact with his brother Hayk[35] in the desert, but he and his mother eventually survive 1915 and return to Bursa in 1919, after following a route in reverse direction: departing from Rakka, reaching Aleppo, and traveling from Adana to İstanbul to Bursa (Altounian 2014: 29–33). That same year, they move to France, are reunited with Vahram's two older brothers, and start a new life there. However, it remains questionable whether, as Beledian states, one can ever have a new *memleket* (homeland) or integrate into a new life "after the desert" (2014: 36n72).[36] As manifest in the demarcation—life *before* and *after* the desert—geography is an essential reference in unveiling the tragedy of 1915.

Of other survivors, some continue to live in Anatolia and convert to Islam, while others flee outside the Ottoman territories and form large diasporas in Armenia, Russia, France, and the United States. Some of those who live in Armenia name the hills of Yerevan after the Anatolian cities where they used to live: "New" Malatya, "New" İzmir, "New" Sivas (Temelkuran 2008: 34). As the French-Armenian film director Serge Avedikyan states, "ailesi Anadolu kökenli olanlar için … geri dönmek diye bir mit vardır" (2021: 188; those Armenians, whose families are from Anatolia … live by the myth of returning there).[37] At times, their longing is combined with a nostalgia for Mount Ararat, as in the case of the Armenian poet Silva Gabudikyan, whose family migrated from the Turkish city of Van to the Armenian capital Yerevan. Gabudikyan notes that "Ulaşamadığımız bir dağdır Ararat. … Hepimizin kalpleri onun dibinde gömülüdür" (Temelkuran 2008: 103; Ararat is a mountain we cannot reach. … Our hearts are buried in its depths). To this day, Mount Ararat stands tall between Turkey and Armenia as the reminder of a shared wound and "*Garod*, özlem …"[38] (Margosyan 2006: 462; *Garod*, longing …). As Margosyan writes, if we can one day perceive Ararat as a conjoining zone, and not a separating limit, between Turkey and Armenia (2006: 116–17), maybe then we can begin to reconcile with this traumatic history engraved on Anatolian mountains, deserts, and rivers. Perhaps then, the same topography, where thousands of people were once exiled from their homes, can be reinscribed with new meaning.

Migrating down the World's Throat

Over the last decade, Anatolia has increasingly become an important migratory route. A large number of migrants from the Middle East and Asia arrive at the eastern and southern borders of Turkey with the hope of either settling in this country or moving on to Europe. Their journeys in Turkey begin on land, at the border, and often continue on the Mediterranean Sea. This section examines what happens between these two points. I focus on the myriad natural environments that migrants traverse to discuss how these sites are redefined as geopolitical routes of population flows and what symbolic meanings they embody.

My focus will be on contemporary author Hakan Günday's novel *Daha* (2013) (*More* 2016), which portrays the lives of undocumented migrants that enter Turkey with the help of human smugglers. The narrator of the novel is a young boy named Gaza. Having lost his mother at birth, Gaza is raised by his father Ahad who smuggles people from several countries including Uzbekistan, Afghanistan, Pakistan, Iraq, and Syria to Europe via Turkey. While recounting a story of migrant smuggling as seen from a child's perspective, Günday also presents Turkey's remote mountains, seas, and forests as transit routes used for sustaining informal channels of migration. He demonstrates that political and economic factors greatly determine how the physical environment is perceived and utilized.

The novel opens with the sea. Gaza's father tells him about the time he mercilessly killed a migrant in order to take his lifejacket after their boat capsized: "These guys are from the desert, what do they know of swimming! You see them once, and then they're gone. ... I don't even know how I swam, but I made it over to the guy ... I grabbed the buoy and yanked it out of his hand ... Then a wave came and carried him off" (2016: 2). His father passes this "life lesson" about survival to his son because Gaza needs to begin working as a smuggler and must overcome his "naiveté." The first chapter of the book then recounts Gaza's descent into smuggling and his consequent "transformation into a dreadful monster" (55) while working with other men who bring him "to the end of humanity and back" (16).

It is no arbitrary decision to start the novel with the scene on the Aegean Sea, which is a reenactment of the shared fate of contemporary migrants whose clandestine journeys often end abruptly in water. Once home to epic journeys and discoveries, the Mediterranean Sea has now become a "Mediterranean Seametery" (Abderrezak 2018: 147).[39] Contemporary politics has turned this ancient sea into a wounded body of water.[40] The opening scene, however, does not only portray physical drowning; it also alludes to the myriad ways in which migrants drown in the economic and political system. Günday calls attention to this "swallowing mechanism" in the following passage, which elucidates the significance of Turkey's role in irregular migration flows:

> A country whose geopolitical significance was discussed daily by politicians on TV. ... Turns out geopolitical meant ... the huge Bosphorus Bridge, 1,565 km long. An enormous bridge passing through the lives of the country's inhabitants. An old bridge, one bare foot on the Eastern end, the other shoe-wearing foot on the Western; all kinds of lawlessness passing over it. It all went

straight through our bellies. Especially those referred to as *the immigrants* …
We did what we could … to make sure they wouldn't get stuck in our throats.
We swallowed and sent them on their way. Wherever it was they were going
… (2016: 8)

Günday refers to the geopolitical importance of the Bosphorus Bridge, which connects the Asian and European continents, to allude to the stereotypical description of Turkey as a bridge between the east and the west. There is also a critical pun in the original language: The word for "Bosphorus" in Turkish is "Boğaz," which means "throat" as well as "strait." Paying attention to Turkey's role as a country of transit, Günday presents the Bosphorus Bridge as the throat of global politics and economy. Each time the world swallows, migrants are sent down this throat, toward "wherever it was they are going." Turkey's transcontinental lands, seas, and bridges allow the global *swallowing* mechanism to work efficiently. Günday draws the reader's attention to the mutually constitutive relationship between geography and politics. From the perspective of global politics, Turkey's geography is pivotal due to its role as a crossroads of migratory movements.

The continuum between geography and politics is also evident in Gaza's outlook on the world. He perceives world geography in terms of smuggling routes: "The regular presence of Near-Middle-Far Asians in my life meant I now had the ample geographic knowledge of a Gypsy" (2016: 18). For him, the land extending from Near Asia to Europe is merely a transnational network of trade routes, much like the ancient Silk Road. It is a line of transportation for importing and exporting the "*goods* [that] came from the Iran border three times a month, were joined up with the ones from Iraq or Syria if there were any and sent to us" (13; my emphasis). At the same time, Gaza highlights Turkey's role in global economy by alluding to the geography of human trade—particularly the distances migrants cross to get to their destination—as a puzzling math problem. While contemplating "how you could go in one hole in the East and come out another in the West," Gaza ironically remarks that "Turkey is the only difference between the East and the West. I don't know which one you'd have to subtract from the other to leave Turkey, but I do know for sure that the distance between them is equal to Turkey" (8).

Like his perception of geography, the way that Gaza relates to the natural environment is also mediated through human smuggling. When migrants arrive from the Middle East at the Turkish border, a smuggler named Aruz picks them up and brings them to a forest near Kandalı, a fictional town by the Aegean Sea. This is where Gaza and his father transfer migrants into their trucks and drive them to the coast. During these repetitive journeys from the border to the forest to the sea, the nature of Anatolia is depicted in claustrophobic terms. Gaza describes the places they pass by in the following words: "leafless" and "lifeless" forests, where the "dark tree trunks melted into one another" (165); the Derçisu creek that leads to the "cursed" (41) woods where they bury bodies; and the Aegean coasts that look like they have "been gnawed on by wolves" (44). For Gaza, the forests, valleys, creeks, and the sea are remote sites ridden with violence. All kinds of crime go unnoticed in these isolated spaces used as migration routes. Gaza witnesses terrifying incidents that strip migrants of their humanity: murders, lynching, sexual and psychological abuse, to which he too falls prey. The suggested violence is also evident in the name of the town where they live: Kandalı, originally spelled as Kandağ (blood mountain), is described as "a flowerpot ... where anything that overgrew would dry up and croak before long" (39).

Pointing to the difficulty of surviving such a ruthless environment, Gaza remarks, "I hated nature! Everything eating everything else! ... Wasn't there some other way?" (180). For him, human smuggling is a journey through hell, and the natural environment where this journey occurs is a dark place thoroughly touched by the human hand—with various atrocities happening to migrants in the foreground and mountain wars going on in the background.[41] Seen from this perspective, the circumstances in which migrants find themselves during their journeys to Europe are not always better than the ones in the war-torn countries they flee in the first place. This dark and oppressive tone is sustained throughout the novel as migrants pass through a series of connected exteriors (forests, valleys, coastal towns, and seashores) as well as disconnected interiors (sheds, trucks, underground reservoirs, and pontoons).

During the various routes that lead them to the Mediterranean Sea, migrants find themselves confined to many enclosed spaces where they are temporarily held until their next destination. For example, Gaza's father turns a water reservoir into a waiting room for thirty-three Afghan migrants, who need to pay more money or give up a kidney to depart toward their next destination. Soon the reservoir becomes a matrix of political experiment in dictatorship with Gaza playing at the "deity" (79), surveilling the migrants through a camera—as if conducting a lab experiment—and taking notes on their changing behavior. Soon violence ensues and the waterless water reservoir becomes as suffocating as the Mediterranean Sea where many migrants lose their lives. Gaza's cold-blooded tone is reflected in Günday's wordplay, which builds terrifying shortcuts from everyday metaphors to an enduring violence that keeps readers on their toes.

For example, when talking about the fees migrants must pay for transportation, he says, "The *determined fee* required for *unrestricted roaming* was whatever came from the heart. It included the heart. Or the kidneys, plus expenses, or whatever…" (13).

Another example of the enclosed interiors is the truck that belongs to Gaza's father and causes the death of many migrants. The first incident occurs when Gaza turns off the air conditioner in the back of his father's truck, causing the death of an Afghani man named Cuma (Friday). The second incident occurs when Gaza and his father have an accident while driving a truck full of migrants. Gaza survives the accident, but everyone else dies, including his father. Gaza is stuck under the pile of bodies for several days, unable to move. These examples show that although migrants are promised *unrestricted roaming*, those who depart from an undesired location toward a more promising one often lose their lives or end up in conditions that arrest their mobility. In this sense, the novel mimics the spatial hierarchy of contemporary politics: migrants' trapped position in enclosed spaces resemble the condition of thousands of migrants stranded in a legal limbo. Even though migration is associated with mobility and the media frequently uses aquatic metaphors involving fluidity—such as the "sea of refugees" or the "flood of immigrants"—migrants' movement is extremely restricted. With little control over their motions, they are hidden, transported, and sent away, like goods.

For Gaza, the vast natural expanse of Anatolia, where the smuggling takes place, represents a landscape of captivity.[42] Forced to work for his father, Gaza feels just as trapped as the migrants. When he grows up, he tries to escape this feeling of entrapment by traveling across the globe and by seeking an explanation for the brutalities he witnessed throughout his life. During his travels, he partakes in different forms of collective violence, thinking that siding with the attacker rather than the attacked may cure his fear of humans. A major turning point occurs when he joins a racist group in Britain that attacks an Arab boy. After everyone else suddenly disappears, Gaza is left alone with the boy who cries in fear. Unexpectedly, Gaza too has a breakdown and screams, "I'm scared too! Do you understand me?" (369). He then begins weeping uncontrollably, "weeping for Felat … for Cuma … for all those dead Afghanis … for my mother … for myself" (370). Unarmed in the face of an innocent child, Gaza decides to change the course of his life and travels to Afghanistan to see "the place all those people had come from, passing through the reservoir in Kandalı to get to the West" (379). At this point, the novel begins to map, in reverse, the routes taken by migrants. Departing from Turkey and crossing over to Afghanistan,

Gaza navigates the exact same locations that migrants pass by. While spatially moving in the opposite direction, he also figuratively travels backward in time, confronting his past. He whispers, "Forgive me for the awful things I did!" (385) to a group of migrants he encounters on his way.

Throughout *More*, Günday insinuates that although the journey from the Middle East to the West is seen as a passage from oppression to liberation, it is in fact full of peril. At the conclusion of the novel, Gaza endures a similarly dangerous journey that ends in the same way the journeys of many migrants end: abruptly and arbitrarily. He arrives at the Bamiyan Valley in Afghanistan to redeem himself for killing Cuma. While standing where the Buddha statue, destroyed by the Taliban in 2001, used to stand, an armed fifteen-year-old boy shoots him from a distance. The fact that Gaza is randomly killed by a little boy resembling his younger self highlights the uninterrupted continuity of the system Günday critiques all along. There is no justifying why children are dragged into migrant smuggling and war zones, or why migrants are forced to risk their lives while crossing borders. Individual lives are lost one after the other, but the system that *overlooks* these losses—in both senses of the word as "holding a commanding position from above" and "failing to notice"— remains intact.

Moreover, Gaza's death in a valley enclosed in the central highlands overtaken by the Taliban is a final example of how nature has become a war-ravaged landscape. Gaza describes the moment prior to being shot as follows: "I was on one of the slopes leading down into the valley. I ran and ran without a care. I weaved between boulders. I weaved between trees. … I stopped. Looked at the horizon. Spread my gaze over the mountains and hills corrugating the horizon and the vast emptiness stretching out toward it" (397). What is initially described like a calming moment in the vast nature suddenly turns out to be a murder scene when a boy, holding a rifle, appears from behind the trees and shoots Gaza. Like the historic Mediterranean Sea resignified as "seametery" in light of contemporary migrations, the historic Bamiyan Valley, an important natural and cultural heritage site, is reinscribed as a place of conflict and terror.

Günday's novel is encyclopedic and branches out in multiple directions. Ultimately, however, it sheds important light on the lives of undocumented migrants who traverse Anatolia in search for a home. Günday occasionally adds that migrants are pawns in a game played by politicians in both Turkey and the West. He remarks, for example, that "Since it was especially difficult to get bloodstains out of the carpets of the European Parliament and the White House, they didn't let the fighting inside their homes. … [but] they … saw no harm in grappling inside other people's houses" (72). "Other people's houses," in this case, include both the wartorn Middle East that migrants flee and the Anatolian-Mediterranean landscapes, where migrant smuggling from the many easts to the many wests takes place. Following a long and winding route stretching from the Middle East to Turkey to Europe, and vice versa, the novel uses a cartographic narrative to trace migration paths.

Günday's *More* aligns with the previous works discussed throughout this chapter as they all call attention to the relationship between movement, environment, and politics. As seen in the constellation of fictional and historical works examined here, nature is not merely a material reality unimpacted by human activity but is often politically charged. Mountains, deserts, valleys, forests, and seas variously become places of war, landscapes of exile, and routes for migration. Taking readers on different journeys, this chapter demonstrates that the distance between nature and society is but an "ideological construct" (Morton 2013: 27). Tracing the routes of myriad people—rural walkers, itinerant poet-singers, outlaws, deported populations, and migrants—reveals that when moving through nature, we are also wandering the terrain of history. As we witness the difficult histories of countless communities inscribed on less visible sites, we are reminded, once again, that the natural environment is continually reorganized, instrumentalized, and endowed with new meaning in connection with changing sociopolitical circumstances.

Notes

1 As historian Halil İnalcık writes, "nomadic groups of various origins were assembled under the name 'yörük' because of their common way of life" (2014: 471).
2 In Turkish, "yer" means "place," and "yurt" variously refers to "home, homeland, dormitory, or dwelling place."
3 One example of these urban walking narratives is Adalet Ağaoglu's 1971 radioplay, *Köpeğin Ölümü* (The Death of the Dog). Written after the 1971 military coup, the play follows the footsteps of the female protagonist who walks alone on the street after midnight and is followed by two policemen that accuse her of being a spy, if not a "bad" woman. Other urban narratives follow in the European tradition of *flânerie*, and trace the footsteps of strollers who anonymously wander the modern city with no other purpose than to observe contemporary life. The protagonist of Yusuf Atılgan's novel *Aylak Adam* (1959) (The Loiterer), for example, is such an

idler and observer strolling İstanbul. There are also female *flâneurs* in Sevgi Soysal's *Yürümek* (1970) (Walking) and Leyla Erbil's *Tuhaf Bir Kadın* (1971) (*A Strange Woman* 2022). However, unlike their male counterparts, they cannot move about the city without being seen and judged (Özsoy 2012: 319).

4   As he notes in his conversation with Alain Bosquet, when he first began writing, Kemal went on long walks and was convinced that he could not write without walking. He was accustomed to taking long walks from the time he worked in the rice fields and as a water inspector along the Savrun River. While writing "Bebek," Kemal also walked for days to think about the plot. His walks in rural environments found their way into this short story (Kemal 1999: 117–18).

5   The Latin root of "err" is *errāre*, that is "to stray; to wander; to fall into error."

6   The term was initially used by the Prime Minister Recep Tayyip Erdoğan to refer to the protestors during the Gezi Resistance and was later appropriated by the protesting collectives.

7   The İstanbul Metropolitan Municipality run by the AKP had granted permission to turn a public park in Taksim Square, Gezi Park, into a shopping mall and to reconstruct the Ottoman-era Artillery Barracks that once occupied the site. Environmental activists organized a campaign in early 2013, applying unsuccessfully for a court order to stop the construction. Soon after the destruction of the park began on May 27, 2013, activists were joined by thousands of protestors who occupied İstiklal Street (the main street in Taksim) and other adjacent boulevards. What began as a local environmental protest soon turned into a nationwide uprising in reaction to AKP's neoliberal policies and authoritarian rule.

8   An armed general law enforcement organization that maintains security, generally in rural areas.

9   Namely, the Kurdistan Workers' Party (PKK).

10 A word with religious origins, "hicret" refers to a journey undertaken to escape a dangerous situation, an exodus.

11 Geçgin's protagonist is reminiscent of Oğuz Atay's protagonist in "Beyaz Mantolu Adam" (1995) (The Man with the White Coat), who also observes his surroundings without passing judgment. Atay's unnamed protagonist silently navigates the city, wearing a white coat. He is incessantly followed by people who misconstrue his silence, accusing him of being mad (15), deaf (18), perverse (25), a tourist (17), and a drug addict (18). He projects a ghostly presence through a silent walk that mirrors and negates the faulty judgments of others.

12 Geçgin's emphasis on "drifting" can be seen in connection to his problematization of "volition" in the same passage. The protagonist notes that he pretends to have a volition and to be in control of his movements when he is actually being moved by external forces, as if he were floating on water (2015b: 23). In an interview,

Geçgin makes a similar remark: "Belki bizler iradi varlıklar olduğumuza çok fazla inanıyoruz" (2015a; Perhaps we unjustifiably believe that we are volitional creatures).
13 See my earlier note on Atılgan and Soysal (n3).
14 "Boran" is the name of a wind blowing from the northeast.
15 *Memed, My Hawk* is the first volume of the tetralogy titled *İnce Memed*, which was published between 1955 and 1987.
16 I refer to *âşık*s as "itinerant folk poet-singers" and "bards," because the English editions of Kemal's work use both of these translations. *Saz* is a long-necked string instrument used by *âşık*s, whose songs and poems carry a variety of themes. Sometimes they are more spiritual in tone, addressing the ephemeral world and the love of God, as in the case of the thirteenth-century devout Islamic Sufi mystic Yunus Emre. Other times, they give voice to the existential and political struggles of the marginalized communities. As ethnomusicologist Ulaş Özdemir observes, Alevite *âşık*s like Hasan Hüseyin Orhan and Âşık Veysel (nineteenth and twentieth centuries), Bektashi *âşık*s like Neşet Ertaş (twentieth century), and Armenian *âşık*s such as Aşuğ Zeki (Sarkis Nurluyan) (nineteenth century) have all preserved the unofficial histories of minority cultures (2017).
17 Combination of *deng* (voice) and *bêj* (derivative of "to say"), *dengbêj*s recite epic songs with or without musical instruments.
18 The word *eşkiya* can be translated as both "bandit" and "brigand," although these two words have slightly different connotations. Whereas Edouard Roditi, the translator of *Memed, My Hawk*, uses "brigand," Barry Tharaud, a prominent critic of Kemal's works, uses both "bandit" and "brigand" interchangeably.
19 It is revealed later in the novel that Durdu is ultimately captured and killed by the same villagers he once robbed (Kemal 1961: 338), thus confirming Süleyman's observation that in order to survive in the mountains, one must never attack or humiliate the innocent.
20 Che Guevara was appointed as the Minister of Industries in Cuba in 1961.
21 Nazım Hikmet revisits an old saying—"The world is balanced on the bull's horn"— and reconfigures it as "The world weighs on the back of the obliged man" in reference to people who shoulder the responsibility to resist economic and political injustice. Hikmet's words also echo an earlier poem he wrote, "Ellerinize ve Yalana Dair" (Of Your Hands and Lies): "The world is not balanced on the bull's horn / this world is balanced on your hands" (1949). The poem addresses the people whose honest, laboring hands carry all the burden of a world that runs on exploitation and lies.
22 Orhan Pamuk's novel *Kar* (2002a) (*Snow* 2004) sheds light on the disconnection and the complicated history of this region. Taking place in Kars near the Armenian border over the three days that heavy snow cuts off any communication with the rest of the country, *Snow* portrays the increasing tensions among an ethnically and religiously

mixed population. As the local *Border City Gazette* proclaims, "ALL ROADS TO KARS CLOSED. The snow that has been falling for two days has now cut all our city's links to the outside world. … heavy snowfall will continue for three more days. And so for three days, the city of Kars will have to do as it used to do during the winters of old—stew in its old juices" (Pamuk 2004: 31–2). Left on their own to resolve their issues and mend their wounds, locals spend three days facing a difficult situation where they are caught between Islamic extremism and a farcical military coup.

23 Mount Ararat became part of Turkish territory with the 1921 Kars Treaty.
24 Prior to the events of 1915, a large Armenian population was living in Eastern Anatolia, where Mount Ararat is located. After they were displaced from their homes in 1915, the mountain acquired great symbolic value for the Armenian community as it represented the lost homeland. The fact that Mount Ararat is visible from many points in the Armenian capital Yerevan further enhances its symbolic significance.
25 All three works—by Mıgırdiç Margosyan (1938–2022), Yervant Odyan (1869–1926), and Vahram Altounian (1901–1970)—came from Aras Publishing, an İstanbul-based press founded in 1993 by Armenian intellectuals, including Mıgırdiç Margosyan and Hrant Dink, a journalist and an advocate of the Turkish-Armenian reconciliation who was assassinated in 2007.
26 Ottoman politicians associated with *İttihat ve Terakki Partisi* (the Committee of Union and Progress).
27 *Tehcir Kanunu* was a temporary law officially called "Sevk ve İskân Kanunu" (Law of Relocation). *Tehcir* can be translated as "forced migration" or "forced exile," but "deportation" is the most common term used in the critical scholarship in English. See Suny (2015), Dündar (2010), and Akçam (2006).
28 See Margosyan's *Gavur Mahallesi* (1992) (*Infidel Quarter* 2017).
29 The word "kirve" derives from the Kurdish language and refers to a person who plays an important role in a boy's circumcision ritual. Currently, the word is used in Eastern Anatolia to connote a very close friend, someone who is considered family.
30 Margosyan uses the word "kafle" (cafila), spelled in the Diyarbakır dialect, in reference to both the marching convoys of deportees and the events of 1915 at large.
31 A contemporary example of these accounts is Nazım Alpman's documentary, *1915 Tehcir Yolu* (1915 Deportation Route), which chronicles the geography of deportations from Merzifon, a district of Amasya in the Black Sea Region, to Vakıflı Köy, a village in Hatay in Southern Turkey. Alpman places emphasis on symbolic locations such as Mount Moses in Hatay, which was home to thousands of Armenians that refused to leave when they received the order for deportation. Another important mountain mentioned in the documentary is Mount Judi in Şırnak, where Armenians took shelter in 1915. The family of Rakel Dink—Hrant

Dink's wife—took refuge there along with members of the Armenian Varto clan, spending decades isolated from the world (Dink 2015).

32 Teacher, writer, and translator of Sigmund Freud's works from German to French.

33 Beledian translated the diary notes into French and prepared the footnotes.

34 Odyan witnessed some of the tragedies that befell the marching convoys between Osmaniye and Islahiye and wrote about them in his memoir (2009: 121).

35 Although Vahram Altounian does not mention it in his diary notes, as Beledian adds, Hayk Altounian was ultimately reunited with his family (2014: 25n44).

36 Beledian notes that "Çölden sonra memleket olmaz" (2014: 36n72; One cannot have a homeland after the desert).

37 Avedikyan explores this nostalgia in his film *Retourner à Sölöz* (2021) (Back to Sölöz).

38 "Garod" in Armenian and "özlem" in Turkish both mean "longing."

39 See Marco Martinelli's play *Rumore di Acque* (2010) (Sound of Water), which sets a good example for Abderrezak's notion of "Seametery." The play is "a litany, a funeral oration" (Notti and Treu 2018: 132) for migrants who lost their lives in the sea. The main character is a general, who looks over a pile of waterlogged documents that belong to drowned migrants and cruelly notes, "On every big boat / minimum one cadaver / you're not going to tow it to land / toss it back in the sea / there's a funeral for you / No more efficient cemetery than that / economical / cozy little space down there" (Martinelli 2010: 13).

40 Contemporary works that respond to these perilous journeys over the Mediterranean Sea often carry "Homeric echoes" (Notti and Treu 2018: 131) or allude to the exodus in *The Odyssey*. One example is the Chinese artist Ai Weiwei's artwork titled "Odyssey" (2017–18), which draws on Homeric references to elaborate on the current political crisis.

41 Although the Turkish-Kurdish war is only a background motif in the novel, Günday includes it as a way to offer a more comprehensive panorama of contemporary politics in Turkey.

42 Gaza cannot easily rid himself of this feeling of captivity. After the previously mentioned truck accident, he is sent to an orphanage, where he is molested by the dormitory manager, and then to a mental hospital, prior to taking the decision to leave Turkey and to travel abroad.

4

Animals

Writing the More-Than-Human

Bilge Karasu's tale, "In Praise of the Fearless Porcupine," begins with a chance encounter between the narrator and a porcupine strolling down an Ankara boulevard. Impressed by the animal's courage to navigate the city, the narrator remarks, "This was a porcupine worth writing about. ... It deserved a eulogy, a *procupineade*" (2003: 64). Not quite knowing how to compose a eulogy, he waits until he sees the porcupine a second time. He convinces himself that the second encounter occurs with the same animal for, as he notes, "The rest of my story depends on this very certainty" (63). The narrator then sets out to tell the porcupine's story in the first-person-singular, recounting numerous adventures that the animal allegedly experiences amid reckless cars, humans, and dogs. Every now and then, he stops and says, "I thought and decided. The porcupine must have spoken thus" (65).

So far, the tale may read as the reiteration of an all too familiar anthropocentric fable: a man voicing an animal he barely knows. Yet the author intentionally uses this technique to make an ironic, metafictional commentary on the anthropocentric fallacy at work in literary representations of animals. Rather than merely positioning himself as an invisible narrator and making the porcupine speak through his absence, the narrator repeatedly confesses that he "invents" this fine story and must cover over any incoherence so that he can compose a credible *procupineade*. Toward the end of this autobiographical sketch, the porcupine says, "When approached, I roll myself into a ball and erect my quills; that's all I know, all I know for certain. That's the way we porcupines[1] are" (69). Ultimately, the only thing that the porcupine can ever be certain of is his species' inward/outward movement: folding inwards to protect themselves from danger and folding outwards to open themselves to the world. That this is his only certainty undermines the legitimacy of the narrator's projections onto the animal thus far, proving the narrator to be an unreliable mediator. Moreover, the inward movement of the porcupine can be seen as a resistance to the narrator's absolute reading of the animal. The animal curls up in a ball and erects sharp spines to protect himself both physically (from attacks) and symbolically (from an oppressive reading).

Karasu's porcupine finds good company, perhaps even an alibi, in Derrida's "*Che cos'è la poesia?*" (1995a) (What is poetry?), where the philosopher considers the question of the animal alongside that of writing. Derrida compares the voyage of a humble hedgehog crossing the highway with the poem's voyage: Just as the hedgehog rolls up in a ball for protection upon sensing the danger on the road, thus ironically exposing himself to accident, the poem too retreats to avoid being run over by some great discourse, which exposes it to that same risk (1995a). The poem's retreat, as Timothy Clark puts it, "is the hedgehog's movement inwards/outwards both to and from an ineluctable vulnerability. ... This double bind *is its mode of existence*—this risk" (1993: 49–50).[2] Both the animal and the poem are engaged in an inward/outward movement that, at once, protects them from the risk of an absolute reading and exposes them to this risk. For Derrida, then, if there is such a thing as "thinking concerning the animal," it "derives from poetry" (2008: 7).

Karasu's porcupine and Derrida's hedgehog provide an opportunity to think simultaneously about irreducible animal alterity and the risk of human (mis)reading. Despite being literary animals at the service of their writers, they resist translation and challenge the restrictive economy of human language. It is in reaction to this economy that Derrida proposes the neologism *animot*, which shifts our attention from the undifferentiated category of "Animal [*l'animal*] in the general singular, separated from man by a single, indivisible limit" to the plural *animaux* (animals), while also emphasizing the suffix -*mot* (word) to highlight "the limits of a language confined to human words and discourse" (47, 104). Like Derrida, Karasu also ponders the limitations of anthropocentric language and seeks new narrative forms to accommodate animal alterity.

This chapter follows a similar trajectory and examines human-animal encounters in contemporary literature to question the relationship between writing and animal life. I ask whether it is possible to use language as a medium for thinking and writing about animals without erasing their otherness. How can we write about the more-than-human world without committing representational violence? Can we include animals in literary narratives without using them to confirm our deep-seated presumptions about the human? How can literature complicate the human/animal boundary by revisiting the ideological fixations about both the human and "the animal, through whose difference and inferiority *Homo sapiens* habitually defines himself, as if gazing into a kind of weird anti-mirror" (Garrard 2014: 243)?

Over five sections, the chapter gradually transitions from prose to poetry, and from a critique of animal representation to a discussion about the challenges of reading animal alterity. In the first section, I cast light on the street animals of Turkey and examine violent human-animal encounters as a way to consider the precarity of animal life. I then analyze two contemporary novels, by Kemal Varol and Faruk Duman, to address various forms of physical and symbolic violence that animals are exposed to in life and in text. These writers not only call attention to animals' physical vulnerability—via a problematization of animal use in warfare and of hunting—but also touch upon the issue of representational violence. They inquire into the capacity of literary narrative to preserve animal alterity and to question the human/animal divide.

The second section moves from a local engagement with animals to a global dialogue concerning animal representation and draws on critical theory to unsettle the foundations of anthropocentric thought. I revisit the question of liminality by examining the unnameable humanimal bodies in Bilge Karasu's tales. If the human always defines itself in relation to an inferior nonhuman other that he claims to read so well, I ask, what happens when the self and the other become illegible? I then demonstrate how Karasu's modern fables obscure species and gender boundaries.

In the remaining three sections, I shift my attention to poetry. Moving away from the predominant focus on prose in critical animal studies in Turkey, I underscore poetry's potential for altering how we perceive and write about animals. The poets I study do not conceive of language as a transparent tool for representing animals, but celebrate the possibility of a writing "beyond the *logos*, a-human, barely domestic" (Derrida 1995a: 297). The third section examines İlhan Berk's poetics of illegibility and his unique method for preserving the complexity of the living world. The fourth section explores such motifs as humanimal embodiment and poetic transformation in the works of Birhan Keskin and Elif Sofya. The fifth section analyzes the use of aurality in Deniz Gezgin's echopoetic work, which foregrounds more-than-human sounds to disrupt speciesist language.

The constellation of writers I engage with problematize the human/animal hierarchy by seeking a language that builds affective bonds between humans and animals. As Latife Tekin remarks, "İnsanın öteki canlılardan üstün olduğu düşüncesinden sıyrılanlar dili yenileyebilir ancak" (2009: 115; Only those who rid themselves of the opinion that humans are superior to other beings can revitalize language). The literary works included in this chapter not only present a revised understanding of animals vis-à-vis humans but also revitalize language in order to make space for more-than-human otherness.

Alterity, Representation, and Violence

In 2017, the İstanbul Research Institute organized an exhibition titled *Dört Ayaklı Belediye: İstanbul'un Sokak Köpekleri* (*The Four-Legged Municipiality: Street Dogs of İstanbul*), displaying photographs and travelogues about the street dogs of İstanbul from the nineteenth to the twentieth century. As curator Ekrem Işın notes, street dogs have populated the city since the years of its conquest. As a result, they became prominent symbols of the Ottoman-Turkish street culture (2017). Leading fairly demarcated lives, they grew attached to specific neighborhoods where residents offered them food and shelter (Schick 2010: 27). Their attachment to chosen territories intrigued foreign travelers who wrote that "köpekler padişahlar gelse bile yerlerinden kımıldamazlar" (Işın 2017; dogs would not move even at the sight of the Sultan). This carefree canine existence, according to the dog-narrator in Orhan Pamuk's *Benim Adım Kırmızı* (1998) (*My Name Is Red* 2002b) is what distinguishes them from dogs in the West: "In the lands of the infidel Franks, the so-called Europeans, every dog has an owner. These poor animals are paraded on the streets with chains around their necks ... Dogs who roam the streets of Istanbul freely in packs and communities, the way we do ... such dogs are beyond the infidels' conception" (2002b: 14).

According to Dr. Paul Remlinger, the head of the Imperial Bacteriology Institute in İstanbul from 1900 to 1910, the number of dogs in İstanbul in the early twentieth century was approximately sixty to eighty thousand (Remlinger 1932: 26; Schick 2010: 28), thus making them the "second population of the city" (de Amicis 2005: 80). However, this second-largest population was also subjected to slaughters and displacements. The most drastic episode took place in 1910 when thousands of dogs were gathered from the streets of İstanbul and sent to the nearby island Sivriada (Hayırsız Ada). While this was justified at the time as an issue of public health, critics pointed out that the increasing urbanization and greater intra-city mobility changed the way that dogs were perceived (Schick 2010: 30). Street animals were seen as incompatible with the modernized city structure and intermittently erased from the urban landscape. This was sometimes done openly: In 1987, Mayor Bedrettin Dalan announced that the municipality had bought twenty-five dog-slaughtering vehicles (Alkan 2016: 618). Today, the dog population is controlled through different mechanisms. They are collected from İstanbul's central neighborhoods and abandoned in the city's outskirts, where they lead less visible lives (Yıldırım 2019: 221).

In his essay titled "Cinayetin Azı Çoğu" (The Measure of Murder: Too Much, Too Little), Bilge Karasu responds to a 1987 article published in the newspaper *Milliyet* regarding the burning of hundreds of dogs and cats by a veterinary manager in Bursa for "public hygiene" reasons. Karasu condemns this self-appointed right to kill animals and writes, "İnsanlar, şehirlerinde rahat etmek için dirim ortaklarını teker teker yok etmenin ne kadar ilkel bir 'çözüm' olduğunu, iş işten geçmeden anlayabilecekler mi?" (1994b: 51; Will people realize, before it is too late, what a primitive "solution" it is to extinguish their companions in life, one by one, for the sake of being more comfortable in their cities?). Similarly, in another essay, "Bir Hayvanla Yaşamak" (Living with an Animal), Karasu notes that violence may involve hundreds of animals wandering the streets or a single animal kept as a house pet. He gives various examples, including a couple who terminate the life of their "strange-looking puppy" once they find out the animal is actually an aguti, a rodent species (1994a). These are cruel reminders that our companions indoors and outdoors are treated like property and easily disposed of when they become "burdensome."

Literature also has its share in this violence. In urban narratives, animals are often represented in one of three ways. Those animals that evoke positive emotions in humans—such as street cats, birds, and dolphins—appear in numerous works, from poems to urban novels.[3] "Less lovable" creatures like insects and mice are typically portrayed negatively and are less represented in general.[4] Finally, there are those animals whose presence is never acknowledged, but they frequently lurk in the background like specters, because somebody is always consuming meat, wearing leather products, and using animal-tested cosmetics without making the connection to animal life. These are the "absent referents," that is animals "made absent through language that renames dead bodies before consumers participate in eating [or wearing] them" (Adams 2010: 66).

Animals often have more visibility in rural narratives, where the "livestock" that partake in humans' daily routines make recurring appearances. Yet despite their visibility, they, too, embody an asymmetrical role relative to human characters: They often provide labor or yield products for human consumption, such as meat, milk, and wool. Wild animals in these narratives sometimes have better luck and run free, only to be observed from a distance; yet, at other times, they are captured or hunted. For example, Abbas Sayar's novel *Yılkı Atı* (1970) (*Yılkı* Horse) takes place in rural Anatolia and recounts a tradition where villagers capture wild horses in the spring to put them to work but abandon them in the wild during the winter. These temporarily tamed horses have a hard time coping with extreme colds, hunger, and the attacks of other animals when they are abandoned in the wild again.

In life and in text, animals are variously perceived, used, and represented according to a taxonomy created by humans. We decide which ones become pets and which ones become food, whose extinction is to be tolerated and whose is to be protested, whose presence arouses affection and whose causes distress. There is not even sufficient accountability for crimes against animals. As noted by Mine Yıldırım, the cofounder of Dört Ayaklı Şehir (Four-Legged City), an organization dedicated to animal justice, violence against animals is considered a "misdemeanor" under Turkish law and is decriminalized (2019: 227). The precarious lives of animals are yet to be taken seriously and come under protection.

How can literature problematize the physical and symbolic violence inflicted on animals? I focus on two contemporary novels that tackle this question. Kemal Varol's *Haw* (2014a) (*Wûf* 2019) and Faruk Duman's *Ve Bir Pars, Hüzünle Kaybolur* (2012) (And a Leopard Sadly Disappears) are both modern fables that critique animal cruelty in warfare and hunting, respectively. These writers also address the problem of representational violence, but they do so in unique ways. Whereas Varol's darkly comic narrative highlights the gap between how animals see themselves and how they are seen by humans, Duman's dreamlike narrative focuses on a wild animal that is both physically and symbolically difficult to capture.

Let us begin with Varol's *Wûf*, which is told from the perspective of two dogs, Mikasa and his grandson. These two narrators are both symbolic "spokesdogs" of recent history and material creatures of flesh and blood exploited by political institutions. While the main story is retrospectively told by the grandson, we intermittently access Mikasa's adventures through his own telling in present tense. The story follows Mikasa's footsteps from his youth, when he first runs away from home as a puppy, to adulthood, when he is captured to be sent to the Gendarmerie Canine Training Center. After graduating from the center, by a twist of fate, clumsy street dog Mikasa becomes a military dog in Arkanya, an imaginary place that alludes to the southeastern city of Diyarbakır in the 1990s, a time when the Turkish-Kurdish conflict was at its height. Varol himself grew up in

Diyarbakır in the 1980s, under an extended state of emergency, and he chose this period of intense political turmoil as the setting for the story. While recounting Mikasa's life, the novel also offers a glimpse into the lives of several dogs lying wounded in shelters, trained in military centers, and used in war zones.

Admittedly, most literary works that "voice" animals have less to say about animals than they do about humans. To give an example, written from a feline point of view, Oya Baydar's novel *Kedi Mektupları* (1992) (Cat Letters) is an allegorical work that recounts various sociopolitical conflicts experienced by Turkish cats and their human companions while living in exile in Germany. As Nina the cat playfully notes, "Hanımımın yazdığı öyküde, kedilere ilişkin dişe dokunur yeni birşey yok, ama insanları yakından tanımak ve anlamak isteyen kediler için yararlı bir yazı" (231; In the story she wrote, my lady-owner says nothing worthwhile about cats, but it is a useful piece for cats that want to understand humans better). Nina reminds us that treating animals as allegorical figures to comment on human societies often ends with what Susan McHugh calls "a magic tragic": "Reading animals as metaphors, always as figures of and for the human, is a process that likewise ends with the human alone on the stage. Now you see the animal in the text, now you don't" (2009: 24).

While McHugh makes an important observation that applies to most animal allegories, I propose that Varol's novel is an exception to the rule. Although *Wûf* is, in part, intended as a political allegory, it does not simply treat animals as metaphors and should not be discarded as yet another example of "magic tragic." The novel touches upon many issues concerning animal life and testifies to the tragic fate shared by humans and animals alike. Animals are not merely symbolic tools that allow the author to offer commentary on political history. Of flesh and bone, variously loved and harmed, animals are as real and vulnerable as humans. While the formal choice of making an animal speak human always runs the risk of turning him or her into a "stand-in, ventriloquist dummy" (Wolfe 2011: 103), Varol takes this risk only to show that more-than-human nature is also heavily impacted by political circumstances. Like the birds that weed out land mines and borders from the soil in an Elif Sofya poem (2014: 15), Varol's dogs are both participants and sacrificial figures in a history inscribed by humans.

The title of the novel is also telling: The original title *Haw* is a pun on "hav," the barking sound in Turkish. Using an onomatopoeic word for a title, Varol calls attention to the process of translating animal sounds into human language, but he does not leave it at that. The letter "w" does not exist in the Turkish alphabet; it is borrowed from the Kurdish alphabet to create a Kurdish pronunciation of the Turkish onomatopoeia.[5] The resulting combination is an emphasis on the politics of language within the context of the Turkish-Kurdish history as well as a critique of the transparency of animal speech in literary representation. Contrary to conventional fables and allegories, where the language of speaking animals typically remains unquestioned because it is undoubtedly *generic* human language, Varol calls attention to the specificity of the political and linguistic context that shapes the animal representation in his novel.

Wûf opens with Mikasa being brought to a dog shelter after losing his legs during the war, a story that unfolds gradually in the book. His grandson notes, "My grandfather, drenched in blood, was rushed to the shelter. Taking him for dead, they'd tossed him like an empty sack to the side of the narrow mountain pass" (Varol 2019: 11). After a long healing period, Mikasa gathers the strength to talk about his adventures: joining a gang of street dogs, falling in love with Melsa (a dog guarding the building of a political party), and being captured by the men who bring him to the Gendarmerie Canine Training Center. The time that Mikasa spends at the training center marks a significant turning point in the story. Soldiers try to turn him into a skilled military dog when all that Mikasa cares about is being Melsa's lover:

> I was a mutt off the streets, the others German shepherds with nobility mixed into their blood. While they immediately found the objects they were given to sniff, it was harder for me to find the thing than finding, say, *Melsa*. ... "This one'll never amount to shit," the trainer kept saying. "He's not much of a patriot." (87)

Captured against his will and forced to participate in human conflict, Mikasa is trained by being kicked after each mistake (89). One day, he finally succeeds in recovering a toy duck hidden underground and he graduates. He is then sent to a police station in a mountainous region called Arkanya, where there is civil war between Northerners and Southerners. Although Varol never states it explicitly, the Northerners allude to the Turkish military and the Southerners allude to the Kurdish guerrillas. Mikasa becomes a military dog for the Northerners. He is expected to detect mines, a task, as we know by now, for which he is ill-suited.

At this point, the novel shifts to war fiction and Varol uses black comedy to depict Mikasa's transition from a street dog to a military possession. Unable to escape his fate, Mikasa slowly loses all agency and observes the objectification of his existence: "My days were dull replicas of one another, like the photocopies of my dark fate stored in the army's files. I was bound. I was registered inventory. I was a liability. And I wasn't going anywhere" (100). Mikasa's name is changed by the soldiers to an assigned serial number, "SK: 107" (90), which symbolizes his existence as a military tool. He is then renamed "Bubi" (Varol 2014a: 123),[6] which alludes to *bubi tuzağı* (booby trap), a name he acquires for successfully identifying an explosive. Once a modest street dog, Mikasa now finds himself in the midst of the war in Arkanya, crying and praying that he adapts to his new role: "'God willing', I said, 'I'll go a mutt and come back a wolf'" (Varol 2019: 77).

When portraying the time Mikasa spends in Arkanya, Varol alludes to the Turkish-Kurdish conflict and sheds light on the havoc wreaked by the war on both sides instead of taking an ideological stand (Varol 2014b). He portrays both humans and animals dreading their own death. Each time Mikasa goes to the mountain with the soldiers, time seems to stop as they walk on a land covered in "canisters of methane, plastic explosives, nails, ball bearings" (Varol 2019: 174). While trying to locate mines, Mikasa thinks, "I paused. I came to a stop and so did my tail. The soldiers following me stopped in their tracks. The clouds hung in the sky, and the cars driving alongside us came to a halt. The nearly-dried-up river ceased flowing ... It felt at that moment like a crooked tick in some soldier's notebook[7] waited in suspense to be scratched" (174). Since death always lurks in the background, the novel conveys an elegiac tone. As evident in the epigraph from Georges Perec's *A Man Asleep*, which Varol includes in the novel, the fate of humans and animals on both sides—Northerners and Southerners—is predetermined by the powers that be: "Everything is ready for your death: the bullet that will end your days was cast long ago, the weeping women who will follow your casket have already been appointed" (Perec 1990: 155; Varol 2014a: 183).[8]

Indeed, the book ends with the death of humans and dogs that share the same inescapable fate. During another outing on the mountain, numerous mines go off, causing major explosions. As Mikasa notes, "I'd pointed to the wrong spot. ... I turned and took one last look at The Girls.[9] Then at the Southerners on the mountain peaks. They were all about the same age and all afraid to die. ... Suddenly, there was a fierce explosion" (Varol 2019: 179–80). Mikasa deliberately mislocates the first mine because he wants to kill the man who hurt his beloved Melsa, but then he inadvertently fails to locate the other mines buried in the vicinity. Following the explosions that kill several animals and humans, Mikasa realizes he has lost his hindlegs. He passes out, and, as we already know from the first chapter, he is taken to an animal shelter.

While *Wûf* primarily serves as an allegory of the war, it portrays more than a human tragedy. It is possible and productive to read this story *also* as the story of animals caught in the web of political history inscribed by human agents. As discussed in the previous pages, where and how animals live, if they are allowed to live at all, is often decided by men. Dogs are abandoned on the streets, killed when seen as a surplus, subjected to dog fighting, and put into use for many other purposes, including warfare, depending on their breed. It is thus worth paying attention to the appropriation of animal life by human institutions in this novel, even if this may be the author's secondary concern. After all, *Wûf* is not the same kind of allegory as George Orwell's *Animal Farm* (1945), where all kinds of animals are engaged in all kinds of acts to convey a political message. Rather it focuses on the actual natural and social environments where dogs serve humans in countless ways. It is filled with dogs that are variously starved, rescued, trained, abused, and wounded in the cities and the mountains. Varol considers it important to document the precariousness of animal lives.

Another contemporary fable that pays attention to the violence committed against animals is Faruk Duman's novella *Ve Bir Pars, Hüzünle Kaybolur* (2012) (And a Leopard Sadly Disappears), which is dedicated to the last Anatolian leopard shot in Beypazarı, Turkey, in 1974. Duman critiques humans' self-appointed right to kill animals, by focusing on a wild animal that is both physically hard to capture and symbolically difficult to comprehend. *Ve Bir Pars* is narrated by a young man who returns to an unnamed town where he grew up after completing his military service. He often goes on long walks in the forest and encounters a leopard that only a few people claim to have seen. Wearing his late father's boots, which give him inner strength, he returns to the forest to pursue the leopard. The novella focuses primarily on this relationship between human and animal, but there are other stories taking place in the background. For example, the protagonist falls in love with a childhood friend, Ceren, whose father does not want them to be together. Following a series of conflicts with Ceren's father and brother, the lovers finally run away together.

At the beginning of the novella, the narrator encounters the leopard for the first time during an outing in the forest. Thrilled and scared, the narrator describes this significant moment in the following words: "Neredeyse ayak ucuma kadar geldi, ben heyecandan, korkudan ölmek üzereydim. … Sonra usul usul doğruldu, çizmelerim az ötede bağcıkları çözülmüş halde duruyordu. Gidip bunları tek tek önüme bıraktı. … Ve siste kaybolup gitti" (Duman 2012: 38; [The leopard] nearly reached my feet, I almost died out of excitement, of fear. … Then he slowly stood up. My untied boots were a bit farther. He fetched them and left them in front of me one by one. … And disappeared into the fog). The leopard's willingness to return his father's boots suggests an unspoken understanding between the two, which will be manifested again at the end of the novella.

After this first encounter, we find out, through the narrator's reminiscing of the past, that the narrator has actually known of the leopard's existence for a long time. His younger brother Resim was killed by "ormanda bir şey, bir canavar" (16; something in the forest, a monster), presumably the leopard. Similarly, the legendary Hunter Kemal was killed by an animal he encountered in the woods for the first time, which we again presume is the leopard. Since the leopard cannot be easily spotted in wilderness, the locals refer to him as an enchanting yet elusive creature, whose presence is felt but never seen. For example, when people recount Hunter Kemal's encounter with the animal, they note that he saw an otherwise invisible wild creature: "görünmez bir şeyi ... görmesi, bu herkese nasip olacak değildi" (83; not everyone had the chance to see ... an invisible thing). This sense of invisibility attributed to the leopard is further accentuated by Duman's repeated references to the forest fog. Each time the leopard appears, he quickly disappears again into the foggy forest, where he moves like "gölge" (a shadow) and "karaltı" (a silhouette) (16). Unlike other male characters in the novella—including Hunter Kemal and Ceren's hunter father who want to kill the leopard—the narrator wants to see the animal alive. He is immensely intrigued by the existence of this creature and takes a critical stance against hunters whom he holds accountable for the numerous animal lives they have taken (33).[10]

Duman deliberately attributes a spectral quality to the leopard to subvert the roles of the human as the seeing/knowing subject and the animal as the seen/known object: the narrator—like everyone else entering the forest—is watched over by an animal he can barely see.[11] This can be construed as a reaction to the fact that humans have, for centuries, written about animals claiming to see them clearly, but few have addressed how animals may be seeing them in return. Derrida, for example, alludes to several thinkers who have "seen, observed, analyzed, reflected on the animal, but who have never been *seen seen* by the animal" so as to problematize the asymmetrical gaze of the human and prioritize the "bottomless gaze" of the animal (2008: 13, 12).[12] Similarly, Duman prioritizes "görmüş geçirmiş bakış" (2012: 39; the seasoned gaze) of the leopard who *sees* everything in the forest and moves around as if he has created the rivers and the trees: "Eserinin içinde yürüyen biriydi o" (39; [The leopard] was someone walking inside his creation). Both physically difficult to see and symbolically hard to grasp, the leopard retains alterity by never being entirely accessible to the protagonist, who searches for himself in the abyss of the animal's gaze.

Duman's emphasis on animal gaze is also manifest in the local myth about a sinister "eye" that supposedly surveys the forest, watching everyone. The "eye" belongs to the forest as much as to its many inhabitants, including the leopard, who is described as a fragmented body with multiple eyes: "Pars, parçalanmış bir hayvandır. Geceleri ormanda dolaştığı zaman. Vücudunun her bir parçasını, orada onun adına gözlerini dört açsınlar, diye ormanın dört bir tarafına bırakırdı" (68–9; The leopard is a fragmented animal. When he wanders the forest at night. He leaves a part of his body in every corner of the forest so that they can keep watch on his behalf). The forest has a thousand eyes, some of which belong to the leopard, and others belong to the sentient creatures that live in the forest. The novel focuses so intensely on the more-than-human agents of the natural world that eventually not only the gaze but also the motions and sounds of animals come to the fore, such as the chirping of skylarks and the groaning of bears (23, 35). As Duman observes elsewhere, "Dili doğa doğurmuştur" (2014a; Language was born from nature), and one cannot write about nature without lending an ear to its polyphony. He thus portrays a forest full of seeing, moving, and vocalizing animals and living organisms in constant transformation.

Duman's novella has a fable-like tone. He incorporates several elements that reflect his intention to portray the encounter between human and animal outside a realistic framework: local myths and legends, references to fairy tales like the Grimm Brothers' *Rapunzel*, and a constantly (dis)appearing and almost surreal animal. *Ve Bir Pars* offers a dreamlike reading experience as it oscillates between the past and the present, reality and fantasy, and flashbacks and imaginary dialogues.[13] The language contributes to this dreamlike atmosphere: stripped of grammatical protocols, Duman's sentences often begin with conjunctions and end with linking verbs, resembling incomplete thoughts. The novella also ends on a rather uncertain and surreal note. The narrator and Ceren run away from her father, taking shelter in the foggy forest. The leopard offers them protection by standing between the lovers and the father. As the lovers leave, they hear the sound of two bullets from a distance, implying that the leopard may have been killed by the father, Hunter Hasan.

As previously suggested, *Ve Bir Pars* is dedicated to the last Anatolian leopard shot in Turkey and can be read as an ode to an extinct species. Leopards—real and fictional—may be difficult to capture, but they are always exposed to this risk, just as they are always exposed to the risk of becoming mere symbols in the service of humans. Duman thus draws attention both to physical violence against animals by critiquing hunting and to representational violence by using an animal that is immensely difficult to see and describe. At the outset of the novella, Duman inserts an epigraph from Jorge Luis Borges's parable "Inferno, 1, 32," which acts as a warning against the risk of animal representation:

> From the twilight of day till the twilight of evening, a leopard, in the last years of the thirteenth century, would see some wooden planks, some vertical iron bars

... something suffocated and rebelled within him and God spoke to him in a dream: "You live and will die in this prison so that a man I know of may see you a certain number of times and not forget you and place your figure and symbol in a poem. ... You suffer captivity, but you will have given a word to the poem." (Borges 1964: 237; Duman 2012: 11)

If literature often captures, or "takes captive," its object, then Duman shows what a delicate task it is to write animals, given this risk. *Ve Bir Pars* asks whether it is possible to bring animals into being with language without reducing them to objects of misrepresentation. Duman's solution to this problem is to deliberately make the animal into a creature that evades sight. In other words, he revisits the problem identified by McHugh in an ironic and pointed manner: "Now you see the animal in the text, now you don't" (2009: 24). Through the figure of an invisible and illegible leopard, Duman shows that animal alterity may, in part, be preserved, by "derail[ing] absolute knowledge" (Derrida 1995a: 299) about the more-than-human world.

Eating and Being Eaten: Unnameable Bodies, Liminal Beings

Animals have always been subordinated to humans according to a definitive limit, which has been variously scrutinized by Western critics. While Cary Wolfe critically remarks that "the full transcendence of the 'human' requires the sacrifice of the 'animal' and the animalistic" (2003: 6), Giorgio Agamben draws attention to the "anthropological machine of humanism," which defines the human "through the [hierarchical] opposition man/animal, human/inhuman" (2003: 37).[14] The fact that "humanity" has always been imagined in relation to "animality" shows how deeply entangled the two concepts are. This section focuses on Bilge Karasu's book of modern fables, *Göçmüş Kediler Bahçesi* (1979) (*The Garden of Departed Cats* 2003), to show how Karasu revisits and complicates the human/animal divide through a discussion of liminality.

The Garden of Departed Cats is told from the perspective of a traveler and writer in an ancient Mediterranean city, where a traditional game of human chess is held between armed tourists and locals. During his stay in this city, the narrator is intrigued by a man, also a writer, whose face he describes "as beautiful as death" (Karasu 2003: 23). After spending several days growing attracted to one another, the two men eventually find themselves playing in the opposing teams of the lethal game of chess. Following a self-destructive move in the game, the narrator dies in the arms of his beloved. From this point on, the beloved repositions himself as the actual narrator-author of this story that he claims to have completed on behalf of the dead man.

Each brief interaction between the two men comprises a chapter of the book. Interleaved between the thirteen chapters are twelve, loosely connected fables. The loving and deadly encounter between the two men is the thread that connects the chapters to the fables, which also contain other characters that variously love, annihilate, and get tangled with one another. Most of the fables have mutually vulnerable human and animal characters that love and are loved, eat and are eaten by, hunt and are hunted by each other. The book is filled with uncanny love stories, and "love means—literally or figuratively—eating and nothing else" (7). Karasu's tales not only transgress species boundaries but also blur the edges between self and other, reality and imagination, life and death.

I focus on two tales from the book.[15] The first tale, "The Prey," is a three-legged story of love and annihilation that revolves around a fisherman, the sea, and an *orfinoz*—a made-up fish species that is neither *orfoz* (grouper) nor *orkinos* (bluefin tuna). The fisherman catches the *orfinoz* and places his hand in the mouth of the fish only to find that the fish swallows his whole arm. Unable to take back his hand and row the boat, he floats with the currents until they are lost in the depths of the sea. Asking, "Who is the prey? The fish or the fisherman?" (12), the story subverts the typical structure of domination. The reciprocal act of eating deconstructs the human/animal, subject/object hierarchies and functions symbolically as a loving and lethal act that exposes the mutual vulnerability of both parties. This tale is interrupted by a series of alternating, connected tales that foreground a similar prey–predator dynamic, but the prey and the predator are never stable ontological positions. All of the characters—whether they are humans, animals, or mythical creatures—move between these two positions.

In "The Prey," the themes of affection and destruction are most evident in the encounter between the fish and the fisherman. While his hand is caught by the *orfinoz*, the fisherman recalls a childhood memory about holding a snake by the neck: "The snake doesn't resist, it simply administers the child his punishment: swinging its entire body like a flaming whip, it bloodies his arm, wrist and hand" (12). The boy, who keeps smiling despite the pain, concludes, "We are friends now" (12) and lets go of the snake. In a similar fashion, the fisherman now develops a bond with the fish as the two, "one inside the other" (14), sink toward the depths of the sea. Ultimately, they reach a rock, which suddenly

> begins to split in two. He knows that only those who have befriended the snake and spoken to the seagull can enter through this narrow opening to kneel down and press their cheeks against the feet of death. ... The outcome of this encounter is always uncertain; one can emerge from the darkness and return to earth, having learned something; or one may never emerge. (14)

Entering through the opening in the rock symbolizes a form of death, an act of "annihilation" (14), as well as an opportunity for change, a gateway into a better understanding. As Karasu notes, the opening is only accessible to those who have truly loved and surrendered to another. In this and other tales, love is depicted as the ultimate space of relation to alterity. In love, one finds oneself torn into a thousand pieces. This deconstruction is the first step toward being able to then construct something new. As the fisherman states, only if they are "torn to pieces" can they be "reborn" (17) into some other form.

In this story, the object of love is an animal, an "other" in its most radical form. Loving this radical other marks the beginning of an unpredictable ontological relationality. As they are sinking, the fisherman and the fish begin to merge as one unnameable[16] body. A growing sense of uncertainty overwhelms the fisherman,

> [who] is searching for a name, perhaps for himself, perhaps for the fish, or perhaps for the creature formed out of the two. As though surrounded by mirrors that multiply endlessly, he looks, he sees, and the more he looks the more he sees: one, a hundred, a thousand creatures that he has never seen before. A man whose arm is the body of a fish; a fish whose mouth holds a human head; a man swallowed by a fish; a fish and a man coupling; a man who is a fish who is a man; a fish, a man, self-coupling ... Endlessly. (16)

A queer body emerges from the dissolving boundary between human and animal, male and female, real and mythical, alive and dead. The uncanny existence of this creature alludes to "a liminal transformation" (Haraway 1991: 177). When loving/eating,[17] Karasu's indecisively humanimal characters navigate permeable boundaries, always searching for a new name. As Haraway notes, "In eating we are most inside the differential relationalities that make us who and what we are" (2008: 295). These relationalities assume myriad forms in the tale, where the loss of self-enclosed subjectivities—their "relentless annihilation" (Karasu 2003: 19)—sheds light on liminal becomings.

The presence of entangled agents—who variously nurture and destroy one another—reflects Karasu's conception of nature:

> Baktıkça baktıkça bizi ürkütmeğe başlayan bir doğa; bütün karışıklığı, karanlığı, besleyiciliği, öldürücülüğü ile. İnsan, içinde erir bu doğanın; tel tel, ip ip sarmaşıklar boğazına, çevresine dolanır, bir koza gibi kapatır onu. İnsan bu kozayı delip kelebek olur çıkar mı ortalığa, köklerin boğuculuğundan kurtulur mu, bilinmez. ... Bir sürekli başkalaşım içindeki bir petek görünümündedir bu doğa, her gözünde ayrı bir işin—sık sık da kanlı bir işin, yemek gibi, yenmek gibi bir işin—görüldüğü bir petek. (Karasu 1991: 30)
>
> Nature begins to intimidate us the more we look at it, with all its complexity, darkness, its ability to nourish and to kill. The human is doomed to dissolve in it; tendrils and tangles of ivy wind around his neck and body, and enclose him in a cocoon. It is uncertain whether the human can breach this cocoon and come out as a butterfly and save himself from the suffocating roots. ... Nature resembles a honeycomb in constant metamorphosis: a honeycomb with a different and often bloody affair—such as eating and being eaten—going on in each cell.

Resembling Timothy Morton's dark ecology whose "essence is unspeakable" (Morton 2016: 110), Karasu's dark nature is an unnameable web of mutually (de) generative relationalities. For this reason, *The Garden of Departed Cats* is filled with human and animal bodies that are variously nurtured and torn apart by one another. They are often in a state of metamorphosis. As Özlem Öğüt Yazıcıoğlu and Ezgi Hamzaçebi remark, the images of "bleeding, disintegrating, or decaying bodies, serve a twofold function ...: On the one hand, they underscore the fragility and mortality of corporeal existence, as shared by human and animal alike. On the other hand, they point to affective encounters between humans and animals, triggered by an awareness of this shared existence" (2019: 138).[18]

Affective encounters between human and animal bodies are also present in the third tale from the book, "A Medieval Monk," where a hybrid animal, "half jerboa-half mongoose" (Karasu 2003: 44), lives in the folds of a monk's sash. The animal crawls inside the sash during a night the monk spends in a mountain cave. Just like the fisherman in "The Prey," the monk bonds with an animal that hurts him. During times of hunger, the creature digs into the monk's bowels: "No one but the monk knows the claws, the teeth that rip through his robe and scrape and pierce his flesh" (44). The animal both becomes a part of the monk's body and remains a creature with his own conflicting desires. Although monks typically practice asceticism to transcend the physical realm, the "pinkish-furred animal with flesh-eating incisors and claws" (44) is a creature who knows only how to interact physically. Their coexistence despite this irresolvable contradiction reveals the "aporetic nature of his [the monk's] affective relation to the animal" (Öğüt Yazıcıoğlu and Hamzaçebi 2019: 146).

"A Medieval Monk" takes place between two different time dimensions. It begins with the medieval monk arriving at a present-day caravanserai that accommodates a group of travelers who "belong to another time" (Karasu 2003: 44). Although the doors of the caravanserai are closed, one of the men inside can see the monk standing outside, and finds a "gap in the wall that will open years from now" (46) to let him in. Once the monk steps in, the man watches him, listening to the monk's whispers, which resemble "hieroglyphs" (47) that must be carefully deciphered. The man offers the monk food and watches in astonishment as the latter "brings the bun not to his mouth, but to his sash" (47) to feed the hidden animal. Tempted to decode the mystery of the monk, the man then decides to draw a picture of him "in the air": "The picture takes shape little by little; the monk who stands within the drawn lines becomes two-dimensional" (48). The monk's material body gradually turns into a two-dimensional image, an artistic reproduction, captured within an imaginary frame and laid on the ground. Wanting to add his signature, the man draws out "a long skewer-like object that resembles a carver's knife. Pressing it against the monk's bare flank, he begins to sign" (48). As the signature presses itself against his flank, the monk "starts emitting ear-splitting noises and coughs. … The coughing turns to vomiting. … he spits blood, dark clots of blood, then his lungs, piece after piece, dark and bloody" (48).

The grotesque spilling out of the monk's internal body parts is a reaction to the man's attempt to decipher him and to capture his dynamic existence within the confines of a static two-dimensional image. Karasu insinuates that representation is violence. As manifest in the lethal signature, the attempt to read and represent the other always runs the risk of wounding the other. Another act of violence is committed against the animal: the man reproduces only the image of "the monk chewing his bread" (48) and not the animal in his sash, which forces their separation in the aesthetic reproduction. Displeased by the suppression of animal alterity, the monk vomits onto the frame, spoiling the representation. Similarly in "The Prey," the fisherman fears being separated from the fish. When he speculates about his friends' failure to see the fish eating his arm, he adds that this may be preferable, because "this is what I fear: that they may take you away from me" (20). Building on such notions as "tangling one with another" and "intertwining, becoming enwrapped" (220) throughout the book, Karasu resists the forced disentanglement of the human from the animal and the animalistic.

Concerned both for the animal and "the animal-like fragility of his own embodied existence," the monk has an intense physical reaction, which may be understood as "abjection" (Öğüt Yazıcıoğlu and Hamzaçebi 2019: 152). Abjection occurs when distinct boundaries are complicated by "fragile borders (borderline cases) where identities (subject/object, etc.) do not exist or only barely so—double, fuzzy, heterogeneous, animal, metamorphosed, altered" (Kristeva 1982: 207). The heterogeneous body of the monk reacts to the man's simplistic deciphering, "it abreacts" (3), vomiting things dark and bloody. Following this incident, the animal abandons the monk's sash and enters the other man's sash instead. Alarmed, the man attempts to kill the animal, which causes the animal to rip open his body. The man dies and the animal returns to the sash of the monk, who knows how to coexist with this creature. At the end, the monk walks away from the caravanserai, feeling the animal's warm furry back as "the most positive evidence of reality" (Karasu 2003: 51).

In his storytelling, Karasu frequently underscores such acts as cracking, opening, and ripping. Bodies ripped open and the crack on the wall of the caravanserai in "A Medieval Monk" (51, 46); the opening in the split rock in "The Prey" (14); and the metatextual commentary on the tale that "rips suddenly" in "Midnight's Tale"[19] (237) all allude to the process of tearing a hole in the visible surface to invite a closer look at the possibilities that lie beyond. As Karasu writes, "somewhere in the habitual flow of life, a fairy tale is always born when this flow, when this fabric of habit is suddenly ripped apart" (254). Only when the habitual is broken and the familiar surface of reality is disrupted do firm boundaries begin to dissolve, revealing relationalities, liminal embodiments, and illegible identities that defy naming.

Like the composite body of the fisherman and the fish transfigured into a thousand creatures, the heterogeneous body of the monk and the jerboa-mongoose evades decoding. These queer, unnameable bodies are as elusive as the "departed cats" that give their name to the book's title, but which appear only a few times in the text.[20] Against speciesist hierarchies, Karasu elaborates on humanimal entanglements that destabilize dualistic ontological categories. He invites the reader to rethink human-animal relations and proposes that we "stop placing man on a pinnacle … Then, perhaps, we'll understand the real worth of man—we'll give him the respect that is due him as something significant only together with animals, plants, water, mountains, and stones" (Karasu 1994c: 132).

Poetics of Illegibility: Reading Like an Entomologist

The question of illegibility central to examples of contemporary prose analyzed thus far, from Duman's novella to Karasu's tales, is critical to the work of a renowned poet, İlhan Berk. A member of *İkinci Yeni* (the Second New),[21] an informal group of second-generation modernists writing in the 1950s, Berk radically expanded the horizon of Turkish language via the immense attention he paid to more-than-human existence. According to him, "Doğa gizlenmeyi sever. Doğası gereği" (2006a: 115; Nature loves to hide. Due to its nature).[22] Yet despite the fact that nature retreats from us, we continue to be drawn to it, for "Dünya bir metin. / Bunu okuyoruz" (40; The world is a text. / We read it). Reading even the smallest life forms with utmost care, Berk claims, "Bir böcekbilimci gibi baktım her şeye" (36; I looked at everything like an entomologist). He simultaneously points to the necessity of reading the world-text and to the impossibility of an absolute reading.

Although Turkish poetry has frequently included animals, they have often been treated as objects of representation tackled via a transparent language. Berk's poetry is distinctive in that he takes neither the objectification of animals nor the transparency of language for granted. He thinks critically about how we perceive and write about animals, dwelling on such issues as politics of naming and semantic indeterminacy. For Berk, poetry plays a vital role in enhancing our relationship with the nonhuman world. As Michael Malay remarks, "poetic seeing might offer non-instrumental modes of relating to animal others. To see animals poetically is not to re-embed the other into what we know, but to acknowledge—even in the act of describing—the ways that elude us" (2018: 18). Similarly, when writing about animals, Berk tries to see them through an inquisitive, poetic lens and calls attention to "the ways that elude us." He is thus reputed as "'görme'nin şairi" (Ergülen 2012; a poet of "seeing") as well as a poet deeply skeptical of optic illusions.

Berk's writing post-1950 is increasingly philosophical and experimental, and it is influenced by thinkers such as Edmund Husserl and poets like Stéphane Mallarmé and Guillaume Apollinaire. Berk reinvigorates the poetic language by experimenting with imagist and visual poetry, found and concrete poetry, modernist minimalism, phenomenology, and surrealism. He dreams of breaking the deadening habit of signification and of writing a sentence, where "Anlam her seferinde görünüp yitecek, varlığı böyle bir koşula bağlanacak" (Berk 1992: 137; Meaning will, each time, appear and disappear. Its existence will depend on such a condition). For Berk, "Dil, yalnızca anlamla sınırlı değildir" (2007b: 78; Language cannot be reduced to meaning). Meaning momentarily enters the poem only to flee it, leaving behind a constellation of traces. What interests him is the ambiguity of language and the dark, invisible side of poetry (1994a: 108), which allows us to navigate untrodden territories.

Berk's poems cultivate a space for what is not yet known or said (Berk 1994b: 175). This, he observes, is only possible via questioning the limits of "us" (reason or logos), which he finds inadequate for understanding either nature or poetry (1997: 51). If "the Word, logos, does violence to the heterogeneous multiplicity of the living world by reconstituting it under the sign of identity" (Wolfe 2003: 66), then Berk's poetry accommodates this heterogeneous multiplicity by tapping the creative potential of language beyond the semantic economy of logos.[23] Poetry, he argues, allows for a constant revision of the significations we attribute to the more-than-human world while exposing our limitations in accurately reading it. Berk thus works toward what I call a poetics of illegibility, a poetics that acknowledges the indeterminacy of language and stays with the difficulty of reading animal alterity given this inherent uncertainty.

As previously discussed, illegibility—as a method for preserving animal otherness—is already present in Duman's and Karasu's works to varying degrees. Duman writes about a semi-visible leopard whose constant (dis)appearance makes it challenging for humans to capture or to define the animal. In Karasu's tales, the emphasis on liminality dissolves the firm boundary between human and animal, shedding light on unnameable bodies. In Berk's work, however, illegibility is an even more crucial tool for thinking about more-than-human nature. It is a fundamental aspect of his poetics. When writing about nature, Berk celebrates "the loss of the [human] subject's sovereignty" (Berk 2009a: 8) and abandons the human desire to codify animals through names. Noting that "Adlandırmak ölümdür!" (2007a: 190; Naming is death!), he yearns for a world not yet schematized through logos: "Adını bir türlü usunda tutamıyordu bir kuş. ... Adlarla gördüğümüz dünya, dünya değildir" (190–1; A bird could not possibly keep his name in mind. ... The world we see through names is not a world). Similarly in his poem, "İm Ad Değildi Daha" (Sign Was Not Yet Name), he writes, "Eskiden bir ustura, bir su kovası, bir at yan yana gelebiliyordu. / Dünya anlaşılmak için değildi" (2007a: 210; Once upon a time, a razor, a water bucket, a horse could come side by side. / The world was not meant to be understood). Prioritizing "image" over "meaning," Berk asserts that "İmgenin ('varlığın gölgesi') gücü belirsizliğindendir" (1996: 16; The power of the image ["the shadow of existence"] derives from its indeterminacy). An acknowledgment of this indeterminacy is the first condition of opening oneself to the world.

Ultimately, Berk develops a poetic methodology, which pays close attention to the endlessly unfolding world of animals and plants. In "Ecology," he writes, "I'm beginning to inspect [the woods] from several angles / I tear off a wormwood leaf, then its juice / seeps into my hand. I twist off a branch / from its stem. I count the rings / of a long thin willow branch" (2009b: 44). The poet reads the natural world, which surrounds him, like an ecological text with an ever-evolving texture.[24] He does not want to eradicate its complexity by presenting a fully comprehensible and potentially reductive narrative about it. Instead, when writing, Berk tries "to draw near to the subject from all sides; but never fully grasp it: only *to circle it*. To start going round again just when you draw near" (Berk 2009a: 8). His poem, "There Have Been Trees I Have Made Friends With," sets a good example to this self-admitted failure to comprehend the complete nature of things:

> "I filled silence with names." Codified things. I have known the
> sky's and the trees' infancy. There have been trees I have made
> friends with. There still are. I didn't understand the Milky Way. Nor
> numbers. ...
> The relation between a pebble's name and its shape
> has not been proved. ...
> Fine. Mystery is everything.
> ... Recognition impedes
> reason. *The World is ours*! Said the snails, talking among themselves.
> I can't say I understand that. Nor that I don't understand. One
> should read the snails.
>
> (2006b: 54)

The poet first alludes to the desire to "fill silence with names." He then calls attention to the impediment of reason and recognition, and he observes everything around him (sky, pebble, tree, snail) by admitting the difficulty of an accurate reading. He points to the discrepancy between sign and referent, word ("pebble's name") and object ("pebble's shape"). The poem closes with the significance of paying attention to small, seemingly inconsequential, life forms such as snails. Tiny creatures like ants and silkworms make repeated appearances in Berk's poems as agents playfully exposing the limits of human language and epistemology. Like the snail in the poem above, who declares, "*The World is ours!*" a wood louse in another Berk poem reclaims the world, challenging humans' dominion over nature: "A wood louse / says we know the world. / Says / water / says / herb / passes on" (Berk 2008: 42).

Often the animals we encounter in literature tend to be the larger and more familiar ones, such as dogs, horses, and dolphins. By contrast, Berk pays attention to small creatures that few poets care to write about. One other example is his long poem about a snail.[25] The poem is composed of two parts, which present two different perspectives on the animal, as seen from outside and inside. Part I focuses on the snail's external appearance and on how the animal is perceived by the poet:

> From out-
> side it looks as if it inscribes a circle but when time comes to close
> > back in from whence it came suddenly it retracts both ends of the line
> > and darts inside.
> A bungalow.
> Spherical.
> Shape of shapes.
> You see it resembles nothing other than itself.
> But if we must compare it to something, then let's say a restless
> > water drop.
> ...
> > When you touch its shell with your forefinger:
> > -Ping!
> you'll hear a sound.
>
> (2009a: 49)

Berk pays close attention to embodiment as he tries to understand the existence of this creature, whom he calls "a clever puzzle" (50). He describes the bodily form of the snail in minute detail, observing the animal's movement, sound, and pace. As Aaron Moe notes, animals are "makers" that participate in *poiesis* through numerous bodily movements, gestures, and vocalizations; attentiveness to another species' bodily *poiesis* can lead to innovative breakthroughs in poetic form (2014: 11). Berk pays attention to the bodily *poiesis* of the snail so as to compose a poem that takes its matter from the animal's physical constitution and unique abilities. While he humorously addresses the poetic urge to compare the shape of the snail with other, similar shapes, he quickly adds that the animal ultimately "resembles nothing other than itself." Berk deliberately makes this move, because using too many analogies runs the risk of diverting the poet's attention from the physical reality of the animal to its metaphoric representation. Moreover, Berk wants to keep an open perspective when writing about animals, and analogies may turn the poem to a limited field of play between similar concepts. So he gathers a list of brief, inconclusive analogies (e.g., bungalow, water drop) that disrupt the logic of comparison to create an impressionistic narrative.

Part II of the poem moves from the outside to the inside:

> From in-
> side, then we'll start from the shell's mouth, from that intractable
> place. ...
> Isn't everything there?
> Lungs (they almost take up all the space), heart ..., intestines (stretch-
> ing from one end to another) ..., brain (with its cover not opened yet),
> tongue (that comes and goes), tentacles (always at the ready, and isn't that
> where its eyes are?) etc.
> It will look from there at this place we call the world: Retracting
> its antennae, purveying every inch of the ground it passes, with one
> foot slowly (slowly? In one minute it can cover 1.12m–1.85m) ...
>
> (2009a: 51)

Initially the poet's gaze penetrates the snail, offering an almost anatomical sketch. Berk studies the physiology of the animal and the inner organs as if under a magnifying glass. Gradually, however, the animal emerges as a "seeing subject" and looks at "this place we call the world," sensing it through his tentacles. Ultimately, how the poet perceives the snail and how the snail perceives the environment become inextricably linked. The inside/outside, subject/object limit is not insurmountable, as seeing is bound up with being seen.

As evident in this poem, Berk makes frequent use of parentheticals. He inserts them into the poem for various purposes: to offer additional commentary, to provide an interlude, or to question an assumption. For example, in Part II, Berk writes that the animal purveys "every inch of the ground it passes, with one / foot slowly." He then pauses and immediately inserts a parenthetical remark that questions the accuracy of the characteristics, such as slowness, that humans typically attribute to snails: "(slowly? In one minute it can cover 1.12m–1.85m)." Berk opens parentheses in numerous other works. This can be seen as an influence of phenomenological thought on his poetics. Berk shows familiarity with the process known as *epoché* or bracketing, a feature of Husserl's method of phenomenological reduction. Husserl proposes putting one's judgments about the natural world in brackets so as to neutralize one's prior beliefs and presumptions about it (2012: 59, 225). *Epoché* thus refers to "the suspension of all pre-constituted ideologies ... in order to gain access to a pre-conceptual experience of the world (being-in-the-world implies that we experience the world *before* we can come to know it)" (Picchione 2016: 15). Many modernists have utilized bracketing as a tool for poetic experimentation, "to revisit the world anew and to unfold, through innovative linguistic modes, new possibilities of existence" (16). In like manner, Berk uses the bracket to suspend preconceived categories of thought, to re-examine the bracketed matter, and to perceive the world afresh. For him, bracketing is also useful in interrupting the flow of the poem and in incorporating a second text into the narrative (Berk 1994a: 87). Disruptive and defamiliarizing, it also serves as a method of writing under erasure, *sous rature* (Berk 2009a: 9).

When encountering the more-than-human world, Berk uses the phenomenological approach and "begins with what presents itself as evident to a consciousness that has tried to purge itself of all presuppositions" (Clark 2014: 277). Relying on experiential observation, he sees himself as a being-in-the-world whose environment is "a field of meanings" (Cooper 1992: 169) that presents itself to be heard, seen, and smelled with all the senses available to a person. Asserting that reason alone is not sufficient in comprehending the world, Berk engages in an embodied experience of it. An example in point is his series of bird poems:

> Yine dağlar arasına girdik. / Denizin alnı inip kalktı. / Şimdiki halde kuş seslerini dinliyoruz. (2007a: 35)
>
> We entered the mountains again. / The forehead of the sea rose and fell. / We listen to bird sounds in this current state.
>
> Gök boş ve sağdan uçtu kuşlar. (44)
>
> The sky is empty and birds flew from the right.
>
> Kuşlar geçiyorlar geçiyorlardı: Yüzünü aradım. (45)
>
> The birds were passing by, and passing by: I searched for your face.

All three poems utilize a minimalist language and concise imagery. In the first poem, Berk briefly references the sounds produced by birds while defining the ambience of the landscape in which he is immersed. The second poem describes the transient motion of birds that cut through the empty sky, while the last one focuses on the continuous flight of flocks as a background against which the poet searches for the beloved's face. Berk presents the birds and the sky as part of his physical and psychic landscape. He depicts a single fragment from a bird's flight or sound to convey how the physical surroundings impinge upon his consciousness. As he notes, "Ben varlığımı, çevremi anlatmadan doğrulayamam" (Berk 1994b: 44; I cannot confirm my existence without describing my environment). An awareness of the poet's experience cannot be divorced from an awareness of space and the other beings in it. Like Latife Tekin, who asks, "Kuşlar olmasa boşluğun derinliğini hissedebilecek miydik böyle?" (2009: 151; If it wasn't for the birds, could we feel the depth of emptiness?), the poet perceives his environment via the birds' bodily *poiesis*. Even when he cannot fully articulate their existence, the birds are there, just as he is.

In other poems, Berk pays attention to different aspects of animal embodiment. In the following one, for example, he lends an ear to the sounds produced by a crab:

I looked
to the voice

enveloping

the crab

(sounds
i
d
o
n
t
u
n
d
e
r
s
t
a
n
d).

(2008: 77)

Berk takes a moment to listen, inviting the reader to do the same. He then admits his failure in comprehending the animal's sounds. At the same time, he divides the phrase "I don't understand" into single letters and individual sound units vertically listed down the page to privilege the phonetic aspect of human language over its semantic value. This way, Berk draws human vocalization ever closer to animal sound, placing them on equal ground. Neither is more or less valuable than the other.

The question of sound is crucial for Berk, who critically asserts that more-than-human sounds, including those of animals and inanimate things, have been silenced. He writes, "Şeylerin ... neden susturulduğu, (başta taşlar, evler, köprüler, keçiyolları, kurşun kalemler, kağıtlar, vb. sonra da varolup da konuşmayan ağaçlar, otlar, hayvanlar, böcekler [sevgili böcekler], kuşlar, arılar) *sorulmalı*" (2006a: 26; One *must ask* why things ... are silenced (to begin with, stones, houses, bridges, goat paths, pencils, papers, etc., and then those things that exist but do not speak, such as trees, weeds, animals, insects [dear insects], birds, bees). In *Şeyler Kitabı* (2002) (*The Book of Things* 2009a), a book of meditations on various things from everyday objects to numbers to animals, Berk challenges the alleged silence attributed to the nonhuman world by foregrounding the importance of bracketing: "The silent world immediately calls out for a bracket. It questions everything: According to who?" (2009a: 7).[26]

Berk's poetry cultivates a space for silenced animals, ceaselessly questioning the limits of his knowledge and reasoning about nature. An awareness of these limitations is precisely what propels him to better comprehend the myriad inhabitants of the world. Seen in this light, his poetics shares resemblances with what Kate Rigby calls an "ecopoetics of negativity, in which it is not the adequacy of the poetic word but its perpetual falling short that directs us toward an earth and a world beyond the page" (2004: 12). This inadequacy gives way to a poetics that privileges *attentiveness*, whose Latin root (*tendere*), as Moe reminds us, implies a *stretching toward* another being, "suggesting an embodied action of the mind" (2014: 24). Such attentiveness has always been a decisive aspect of Berk's writing. Even in one of his earliest works, *Günaydın Yeryüzü* (1952) (Good Morning, Earth), Berk stretches his consciousness toward animals and other bodily natures, planting the seeds of an inclusive poetics: "Hanginiz aklınıza getirdiniz. / Benim bir gün insanlığımı / Bitkilere hayvanlara kadar / Bir gün tutup genişleteceğimi / Bütün bu dünyaya saracağımı sonra da" (1982: 15; Who would have thought / That I would, one day / Expand my humanity / To plants and animals / In an embrace of the world).

Humanimal Embodiment and Poetic Transformation

Contemporary poet Birhan Keskin's book *Yeryüzü Halleri*[27] (States of the Earth) begins with an epigraph by the eighteenth-century Ottoman poet Şeyh Gâlip Dede Efendi, whose work is imbued with Sufi elements.[28] The second line of the couplet reads, "Sen yoksun o benlikler hep vehm ü gümânındır" (Keskin 2005: 9; You do not exist, those selves are illusions),[29] which sets the tone for the entire book by positing the notion of an isolated self as a false ideal. The book comprises meditative poems whose speakers exercise self-abandonment in the search to find their reflections among the diverse creatures of the earth.

Keskin nostalgically recalls her childhood as a time when "Her şey, *bir* şeydi" (37; All was *one*) and alludes to such notions as *yekpârelik* (wholeness; oneness) throughout the book to highlight her desire to reclaim a sense of connection to the earth. The result is a series of poems that transfigure the poetic voice into a variety of creatures—a phoenix, an ant, a spider—and counter the human/animal divide by evoking "dünyaya 'yayılma hali'" (38; a state of diffusing the self throughout the earth).

The trope of transformation is crucial to this book. As Keskin remarks, "İnsan kendini sürekli olarak yeryüzünde bulunan bir sürü varlıkla eşleştirmek ve eşitlemek durumunda ... ki insan denen şeyin ne olduğunu anlayabilsin" (2006: 35; Human beings must constantly place themselves on equal ground with the myriad beings on this earth ... so as to understand this thing called being human). In *Yeryüzü Halleri*, the poetic voice is indeed divided into a thousand different creatures: "I understand as the earth talks inside me, / I'm a memory fragmented, / scattered to the world" (Keskin 2013: 51).[30] The poems expand from the center out in a spiral-like movement, oscillating between self and other, introspection and extrospection, human and nonhuman.

Keskin's poems often consist of two layers. On one level, they focus on the bodily *poiesis* of the animals in question. On another level, they rethink human experience in relation to animal embodiment. For example, in "Fish," Keskin writes, "Once I fell for the lure / ah my wounded tongue / I cannot speak" (2013: 39). She stages two parallel realities using language at once literally and figuratively, hence invoking the imagery of both a wounded fish and a wounded woman who has lost her voice. In this and other poems, animals represent a range of qualities that are abstracted and transferred into the human sphere. Another example is the poem titled "Denizkabuklusu" (Seashell): "O[31] beni sahilden, kendimi gömdüğüm, sertleşmiş ıslak kumdan aldı, / ... / tuzla, dalgayla boğuştuydum ben, ve hayvanım çıkmıştı benden. / Kendi içine kıvrılmış, rüyasını unutmuş / soğuk taş değil miydim artık ben? / O bana bir rüya verdi, inanamadım" (Keskin 2005: 14; They took me from the beach, from the hardened, wet sand where I had buried myself, / ... / I had wrestled with salt, with waves, and my animal had abandoned me. / Was I not cold stone now / enfolded into myself, having forgotten my dream? / They gave me a dream, I could not believe it). On a literal level, the poem recounts how a seashell, detached from the animal that lives inside, is washed up on the shore and remains buried under moist sand. Having lost the animal that holds it in place, the shell is but a hardened outer coat that is empty inside. On a figurative level, the poem conflates the physical hardness of the empty seashell with the emotional hardening of the speaker, who has lost her vitality and her dreams only to recover them through the caring touch of another. Keskin's writing intertwines human and nonhuman states of being in various ways.

Similarly, in the poem titled "Horse," it is unclear at which point animals exit the poem and humans enter, or vice versa: "Var idiyse eğer, ve yapılabilecektiyse ve yapılmadıysa / Atlarım bil ki bu sebepten dağa bayıra vurmuştur" (2005: 20; If there were a way, and it could be done and was not done / Know that this is the reason my horses have taken to the mountains). The poet does not explain what it is that could be or was not done. Rather, she foregrounds the urgent need to take flight in reaction to a distressing incident. Whether these lines refer to animals throwing themselves out onto the slopes or to the disillusioned speaker who retreats is deliberately left uncertain. Keskin enmeshes the images of both the animal and the human in such a way that denies priority to either. In a distilled, contemplative narrative, she moves back and forth between the two states of being, making it difficult to tell which layer is the bedrock of the poem.

Keskin makes use of two parallel poetic processes here: the construction of animal figures and metaphors through poetic language and the making of poetry through attention to animal bodies, movements, and characteristics. In other words, she draws attention to "the question of zoopoiesis, of the creation *of* the animal as much as the creation *by means* of the animal" (Driscoll 2015: 223). As a result, the animals in Keskin's collection—whether they are ants, horses, or penguins—have both symbolic and material presence. She engages in what Moe calls a "joint venture": "when a poet undergoes the making process of poiesis in harmony with the gestures and vocalizations of nonhuman animals, a multispecies event occurs. It is a co-making" (Moe 2013: 2). To give one more example, in "Karınca" (Ant), Keskin writes:

> Ruhumdaki sabır, kalbimdeki aşkla kurdum
> kor dantellerden bu yolu, ormanın altına
> yeter ki oku onu.
> ....
> Kışa girdik kıştan çıktık
> ama değişmiyor insan
> karınca duası diyorlar ördüğüm yola.
>
> (2005: 15)
>
> I built this trail of ember lace
> beneath the forest
> with patience in my soul, love in my heart.

If only you would read it...
....
We entered winter, came out of it
yet people do not change
"Ant prayer,"[32] they call this path I have woven.

Similar to the previous poems, the speaker of "Karınca" can be construed as both an animal and a human. On the one hand, the poem alludes to ants' ability to build elaborate trail networks that resemble lace work. It then juxtaposes their patient labor and progress through an infinitely unfolding world against the absence of someone who could accurately read the traces they leave behind. In a way, then, the poem reads like ants' revolt against humans, who never change and perceive ants as small and insignificant creatures. On the other hand, the speaker may also be a human, who sympathizes with the ants and expresses her own fear of being misread by an anonymous "you" that may not follow the traces she inscribes on her path with patience. She also feels just as small and inconsequential as an ant in the face of her own mortality. Keskin observes, "insan bu yeryüzünde sonlu olduğunu biliyor. İnsanın en büyük trajedisi bence bu. Öleceğimizi biliyoruz ve bu müthiş bir keder. Ama dağ bunu bilmiyor, karınca bilmiyor" (2002; humans are aware of their mortality on this earth. I think this is the biggest human tragedy. We know we will die and this is a formidable sorrow. But the mountain does not know that, neither does the ant). The speaker longs to forget this "sorrow" of "lingering in the world like an inn with two doors" (Keskin 2013: 51) and wants to partake in the rhythms of the earth. After saying "my human parts are aching hard," she stretches the limits of her mortal body and diffuses herself throughout the earth: "I became broader / now I'm far from myself" (35, 43).

Keskin seeks a revised understanding of the self through an embodiment of other beings. She uses the states of the earth to understand the many states of the self, and practices a "reversal of pathetic fallacy, she becomes a tree, makes a plain of herself" (Dalton 2013: 14). In this respect, Keskin's writing is "a fiercely personal writing, writing of the self, that consistently transmutes into something strange, experimental and bold in its use of elemental imagery" (14–15). As the poems bear witness to the constant transformation of the speaker's voice, ultimately, the limit between self/other, human/animal, autobiography/heterobiography becomes a dubious linguistic demarcation. Whether it is an animal that moves through the poet or a poet that moves through the animal remains compellingly uncertain.

A similar strategy is prevalent in the work of another contemporary poet, Elif Sofya. Daughter of a renowned animal rights activist, Sofya offers a critique of speciesism by unveiling various forms of violence inflicted on animals. She elaborates on the permeable boundary between human and animal, paying close attention to sites of collision and reconciliation as well as potential metamorphoses that emerge from within these sites. In her 2014 book, *Dik Âlâ*,[33] a constant transmutation of the narratorial voice into animal alterity reveals a strong sense of connectivity to nonhuman embodiment: "Bana iyi bak ben / Sonra hayvan olacağım" (2014: 33, Take a good look at me, I / Will then become an animal). The speaker persistently forms affective bonds with more-than-human beings. For example, the human speaker in the poem titled "Sincap" (Squirrel) offers her body as a safe habitat to an animal at risk: "Saklanıyor damarlarımda kızıl saçlı bir sincap / Bu sincabın icabına bakılacak diyorsun" (13; A red-haired squirrel hides in my veins / You say this squirrel will be done away with). Cognizant of the vulnerability of corporeal existence, the speaker offers shelter to the red-haired squirrel. At the same time, the fact that an animal hides in her veins suggests that it is not blood but a reddish animal circulating in her system. Ultimately, it is not only the animal but also the animal within that is under threat. Similarly, in the poem titled "Olasılık" (Probability), the poet refers to an unnamed body, remarking "yaralarından yavru ceylanlar çıkıyor" (38; baby gazelles rise from your wounds). That new life emerges from wound-inflicted bodies, whether this is the body of an animal or human, is a strong manifestation of resilience and resistance. In various poems, Sofya portrays her speakers' bodies as inhabited by other creatures to call attention to the fragile existence of humans and animals alike. Her ecopolitical critique thus consists of a language grounded in embodied experience.

Humanimal embodiment is also manifest in Sofya's use of pronouns, especially in various disguises of "I" and "you." Sometimes, resembling Keskin's work, there is an ambiguous doubling of the first-person singular, so that it contains both human and animal voices. For example, the poem titled "Bulutların Geliş Hızı Üzerine" (On the Moving Speed of Clouds) ends with the following lines: "Beni sorma / ... / Bilmediğim bir çengelde / hala asılı kaburgalarım" (65; Do not ask about me / ... / My ribs are still hanging / from a hook I don't recognize). Since the poem portrays environmental and political degeneration in an urban setting and hints at the approaching elections, the "I" may be a human being painfully alienated from his surroundings. Yet the allusion to the meat industry reveals that the speaker may as well be an animal whose suffering is normalized and whose life is reduced to a product for human consumption. Reminiscent of Karasu's unnameable bodies, Sofya's subjects oscillate between human and animal, creating blurred boundaries and a space of mutual vulnerability. A similar decaying urban atmosphere is also found in the poem "Uygarlaşma" (Civilization), where the speaker is "civilization" itself, recounting "kanlı bir ağız tarihi" (88; a bloody mouth history): "Beton bina, büyük müze, otoban / Hem temizim, hem de nezih, steril / Nasılsa gözden uzak çalışıyor mezbaha" (89; Concrete building, big museum, highway, / I am both clean and sterile / Out of sight is the slaughterhouse anyhow). Here the "I" is clearly an antagonistic voice engaged in an ironic monologue. The poem emphasizes the contrast between the eye-catching infrastructure development visible to the city-dwellers and the violence of the industrial slaughter facilities in the less visible margins of the city.

As evident in the phrase "bloody mouth history," Sofya often traces the continuum between physical violence (animal slaughter; bloodshed) and linguistic violence (politics of naming; history-making). She insinuates that the damage inflicted on animals can be both material and discursive. While critiquing the physical exploitation of nature, like Berk, she also condemns those who claim mastery over the natural world through language: "Beni sen bana bir ad taktığında yavaşça / ... / Çoktan boğmaya başlamıştın aslında" (Sofya 2014: 30; You had already begun to suffocate me / ... / When you slowly gave me a name). Instead of classifying and naming animals—as pet, game, or test subject—as it suits us, Sofya addresses the need for listening to birds' "dik yazılara sığmayan çığlıkları" (15; screams, which do not fit in vertical [human] writing).[34] In "Sevgilim" (My Beloved), she thus constructs a nonhuman voice of revolt in reaction to an adversary human "you:"

Bir yıkım krallığı kuruyorsun hızlıca
Irmaklara parmakların geçiyor
Hidroelektrikleniyor serbestliği suların
Kırlara kırılarak dağılırken hayvanlar
Dağların derisi yüzülürken
Kışkırtılmış kahkahalar boğuluyor yamaçlarımda
İçimde ağaçlar ve
çılgın çalgılarıyla kuşlar yürüyor.

(49)

You quickly establish a kingdom of destruction
Running your fingers through rivers

> Hydroelectrifying free-flowing waters
> While animals are scattered in pieces around the prairie
> And mountains are skinned[35]
> Provoked laughters drown in my slopes
> Trees and birds walk within me
> playing their wild musical instruments.

The speaker's body is populated by an assemblage of insurgent, more-than-human bodies that revolt against extensive ecopolitical destruction. While mountains are skinned like animal bodies, the speaker's body turns into slopes where trees and birds march in protest, playing their songs.

Throughout the book, the identities of "I" and "you" change constantly to accommodate different voices. In the end, however, the poet turns to herself to confront her own sense of complicity in the ongoing devastation of the natural world: "Bütün kuşlarını yere dökmüş / Bir gökle karşılaştım / Adıma bir hesap kesildi / Saçlarımdan başladı suçlarımın örgüsü" (98; I encountered a sky / that dropped all of its birds onto the ground / I was held accountable / The braid of my crimes started at my hair). In Turkish, the word "saç" (hair) alliterates with the word "suç" (crime). The speaker's sense of guilt spreads from her braids to her whole body, reflecting a sense of accountability that Sofya ultimately wants to evoke in every reader as a call to action against animal cruelty.

Echopoetic Journeys and Entangled Species

In the 2015 issue of the fanzine *cin ayşe*, contemporary author Deniz Gezgin calls attention to the need for a rewilded language that produces an echo of nature. She mentions the possibility of "hayvanca bir yazın" (2015: 31; an animalistic writing), which derives its material from the sonorous world of myriad species. Her poetic novel, *YerKuşAğı* (2017c) (EarthBirdMesh), is such an experiment in resonating the sounds and vibrations of the more-than-human world. It is written as a reaction to the devaluation of animal life in contemporary society, where, as Gezgin remarks, humans construct wildlife parks surrounded by barbed wire and keep animals in cages for display, encircling all of nature with an oppressive language (2017c: 77). *YerKuşAğı* dims human voices to lend an ear to animal sounds. As she notes, while writing this uniquely lyrical work, Gezgin bit her tongue so that she would not suppress the sounds of the creatures that entered her work (2017b). The readers are also invited to surrender themselves to the riveting rhythms of the book and to partake in a quasi-mythical, humanimal odyssey.[36]

YerKuşAğı recounts the journey of four characters: Moy, a young girl whose body is filled with animal sounds; Şuri, a wounded, oil-covered cormorant; Hagrin, a hybrid creature defined as an ivy with hooves; and Cice, a playful muntjac. What brings them together is their shared vulnerability in the face of human-induced violence and speciesist language. Variously silenced and injured, they embark upon a long walk toward *yokyer*,[37] which can roughly be translated as "a place that does not exist," "a nonexistent place," resembling "utopia" (no place). Gezgin also infers that *yokyer* is a "nonplace," meaning that it is less of a physical place than an ideal state of being. It symbolizes the possibility of what she calls "Can almadan yer bulmak" (Gezgin 2017c: 32; Finding oneself a place in the world without taking the life of another being).

Reaching *yokyer* requires a continuous metamorphosis that allows the characters to "beden beden dolaşmak yahut tümüyle sesle[38] bedenlenmek" (Gezgin 2017c: 41; embody each and every living being or to be embodied entirely by sound). The emphasis on sound and sonorous embodiment challenges the predominance of vision-centricity in animal narratives.[39] While many senses, from sight to touch, play an important role in human–nonhuman encounters, Gezgin's novel particularly foregrounds hearing and aurality. It can thus be considered an example of what Marilia Librandi calls the "aural novel" or an "echopoetic" experiment: "A written text founded on listening is first *a receiving text* rather than a producing one. By 'echopoetics', I refer to such a receptive capacity as an unconditional openness to the outside" (Librandi 2018: 9–10). Noting that "the ear is basically a receptive organ," Librandi calls attention to the significance of listening in comprehending the world and foregrounds a "poetics of resonances" (9). This is a useful framework for analyzing *YerKuşAğı*, which focuses on nature's polyphony. As Gezgin writes, "Rüzgar havaya sürtünür üfler, kayaya vurur horuldar, ağaca dolanırsa yapraklardan ses alır … sesin devri daimdir (2017c: 34; The wind brushes against the air and blows, it pounds on the rock and vibrates, it envelops a tree and gathers the sound of the leaves … the cycle of sound is everlasting). Perceiving sound as inseparable from movement (14), Gezgin pays close attention to the motions and ever-changing sounds of more-than-human nature.

The "auditory mode of writing" (Librandi 2018: 5) at work in Gezgin's novel is particularly manifest in the character of Moy, who lends an ear to extra-semantic modes of signification, timbres, and vibrations. Raised by her father, who is a hunter, Moy lives in a household full of mounted heads and taxidermied animals whose sounds she begins to hear as a child: "Henüz konuşacak yaşta bile değilken içine dolan çığlıkların … önüne geçemezdi" (Gezgin 2017c: 19;

She could not prevent ... the screams of animals from filling her head at an age she could not even speak). Moy feels the pain of animals, and she is considered a strange child for not being indifferent to their suffering. Unlike her father, who masters the Latin names of animals only to utter them while consuming meat at the dinner table, Moy never learns these names by heart. Instead she looks closely at animal book pictures to hear "her resimden onu içeri çağıran ötüşleri, horultuları, çığlık ve ıslıkları" (24; the chirping, snorting, screaming, and whistling that call out to her from every picture). Moy lives with the fear of eating, hence annihilating, the creatures she loves the most, such as Cice the muntjac. When she does not see Cice around for a long time, Moy always worries and says, "Ya onu yuttuysam? Ona sevgimden, iştahımdan, onunla ve o olmak istediğimden yapmışsan bunu?" (55; What if I swallowed Cice? What if I did it out of love and hunger, and because I wanted to be one with her and to become her?). Gezgin shares Karasu's concern with loving-eating-annihilating the other, but here it induces anxiety in Moy, who continuously witnesses her father hunt, eat, and drown animals in silence the minute he swallows them.

Moy, Şuri, and Hagrin meet one another after each of them experiences a life-altering event. Moy spends her childhood being heavily medicated due to health problems. Şuri is held captive by a man who wounds his wing and makes him suffer until he loses his voice. As Gezgin notes, "Ötüşe dönmek için zehri tükürmesi şart" (16; He must spit out the poison to be able to chirp again). Even after escaping captivity, Şuri's suffering continues for he is poisoned during a fire at an oil spill in an unnamed gulf. While inhaling toxic fumes, Şuri wonders whether it is worth escaping the fire since "başka bir yer yok, her yer aynı, ellenmiş. Ama bir canlı olageldiğinden yürüdü ... yokyere vardı. Ellenmemiş, çiğnenmemiş bir orası" (46; there is no other place, everywhere is the same: touched. But being a living creature, he walked ... and arrived at *yokyer*, the only untouched, untrampled place). *Yokyer* remains the only ray of hope in this world touched by the destructive human hand.

The story of Hagrin—hybrid of Ha and Rin—is even more complicated. Neither man nor animal, neither mortal nor divine, Ha is described as a multispecies creature, giving off an enthralling scent (69–70). Once captured and tortured by people, then saved by a circus owner named Dilbaz,[40] Ha ultimately escapes to the mountain. Rin is vaguely described as a woman who runs away from home after being captivated by Ha's scent from a distance. Once she finds Ha on the mountain, they begin to merge as one as their bodies entangle: "Bir uyandı böğürtlen gözlü bir çalıya sarınmış, bir dahakinde avucunda yeşil tüylü taşlar ... Kasıklarında sivri uçlu tomurcuklar yapış yapışken kolları dipte incecik bir köke dolaşık" (66–7; One morning they awoke to find themselves wrapped around a shrub with bramble eyes, next morning they grew green-furred stones in their palms ... While their groins were sticky with pointed flower buds, their arms were tangled with the thin roots of a tree). Ha and Rin emerge as the wise-natured creature, Hagrin, a combination of human, animal, and plant. Hagrin then joins the other characters in their journey across *yokyer*.

During this journey, each character is variously portrayed as "fallen," "wounded," "dead," "no longer": "Ha, Rin, Moy, Şuri, bütün düşenler, ölü diye üstü örtülenler" (73; Ha, Rin, Moy, Şuri, all those who fell, all those who are deemed dead and covered over). Seen in this light, the existential negation of the word *yokyer* (nonexistent place) also carries connotations of being a place for the "no longer." For example, it is insinuated that Moy ultimately loses her life (61). She falls from an ash tree, but when she falls, instead of hitting the ground, she discovers Şuri underneath her peeled skin and Cice tangled up with her (54, 30). She says, "Sen içimde bulduğum cansın Şuri,[41] ölüm müsün, dirim misin ne belli" (32; You are the life I found within me, Şuri, who is to tell if you are death or life?). Through a kind of rebirth, characters discover one another underneath each other's skin. Similar to the characters in Karasu's and Sofya's works, the characters in Gezgin's novel permeate and embody one another, metamorphosing into new forms.

Arriving at *yokyer* also requires an active forgetting of human language. Gezgin uses the child, Moy, to accentuate the difference between "sese gelmek" (acquiring sound) and "söze gelmek" (acquiring word). She writes, "Bütün yeni doğanlar sese gelir, sulardan duyup bildikleri şarkıyı mırıldanırlar. Bebekler de öyle böyle hayvandırlar. Kulaklarına kelimeler dolmaya, onları taklit edip de konuşmaya başladıkça suları can gibi çekilir" (33; All newborns acquire sound, they hum the song they learn from the water.[42] Babies are, in one way or another, animals. Once they begin speaking by mimicking the words that fill their ears, their water starts to withdraw like life). Gezgin insinuates that the echopoetic experience begins in the womb, but it gradually vanishes as infants—from Latin *infans* (nonspeaking)—acquire language. As children learn to speak, they lose their receptiveness to the sounds that surround them. Aware of this loss, Moy deliberately distances herself from human language in order to be able to hear and echo the pulsations of myriad other beings again. She captures the sounds of wild animals: "karnında deniz memelilerinin sesleri çalkalanıyordu" (58; the sounds of sea mammals swashed inside her belly). She echoes "yaprakların dilini, suyun huyunu" (63; the language of the leaves, the temperament of water). Her body becomes an archive of "sounding, speaking bodies" (Abram 1997: 86).

Inspired by Hagrin, "tüm seslerin yankısı ... Ne biçimsiz ne de tek biçimde" (Gezgin 2017c: 28; the echo of all sounds ... Neither formless nor with single form), Moy speaks less and less to embody the vocalizations and vibrations of more-than-human beings. It is through the act of listening that she grows closer to the animal other. In Librandi's words, "Hearing is what brings humans close to the animal because it is this that tears us from articulated human speech; the ear is an organ of sonorous alimentation, the organ most like an antenna designed to capture signals. It is where we are most other insofar as we cease enunciating in order to receive what comes to us from outside" (2018: 129).

In fact, Moy actively forgets all the letters of the alphabet and all the names she has ever heard. Only then does she begin to remember the smell of weeds and seeds: "Dili bu sayede kıvrık, tüylü, mavişin" (Gezgin 2017c: 73; Only in this way does her tongue turn curvy, feathery, bluish). Throughout the book, the word "dil" retains the double meaning it has in Turkish: tongue and language. Gezgin alludes to both meanings and brings them into a contrast. She presents the materiality of the tongue as an antidote to the discursivity of language. Often, the characters lick rock salt to feel their tongue more intensely, to prioritize its gustatory function over its role in speech production, and to be reminded of the corporeality shared by humans and animals alike. As Gezgin notes, an element that is both soluble and solvent, pure and purifying (2017b), salt "içinize sinen beşeri sökecek" (2017c: 16; will rid you of the human settled inside of you). The stress on corporeality and embodiment is also evident in the transformation that Moy experiences. Throughout the journey, she adapts the abilities of myriad species, mutating into an ever-richer being with sharpened senses. As she moves through different landscapes, her ability to see, hear, taste, smell, and touch is enhanced: "sesle, kokuyla, tenine değen türlü şeylerle donanıyor" (29; She is equipped with sound, scent, and various things touching her skin). Through sensory experience, Moy's body grows increasingly entangled with the natural elements surrounding her: animals, rocks, foliage, and water.

Indeed, the novel places repeated emphasis on entanglements, as evident in the unusual title *YerKuşAğı*[43] (EarthBirdMesh), which alludes to the tangle of the earth and the sky. Gezgin makes frequent reference to this tangle in the text (51, 67) and uses expressions that reverse expectations about what is down below and up above, such as "tüm tohumların döküldüğü bir gök yeri" (7; a sky-place where all the seeds are spilled). The earth–sky connection is also related to the reversal between Moy and Şuri. While Moy is elevated toward the sky and suspended there after falling from the tree, Şuri, who is supposed to fly over the oil-covered Gulf, falls on the ground. As Gezgin writes, "Sürüler dağılmış, düşenler yer kuş ağını boylamıştı" (44; The flocks dispersed, those who had fallen wound up in the earth bird mesh); "Biri [Moy] yerde olacağına göğe tırmanmış, öteki [Şuri] gökte uçacağına yere saplanmış. İki küçük yersiz beden, başka biçimde yaralı ve bir arada" (10; One of them [Moy] climbed up the sky instead of landing on the ground, the other [Şuri] is stuck in the ground instead of flying in the sky. Two small, displaced bodies, variously wounded and together). These playful reversals contribute to the making of *yokyer*, a nonplace where the earth and the sky, the human and the animal, are intertwined.

The four characters' journey "Yerden göğe, ot kökünden yıldız köşelerine" (8; from the earth to the sky, from the roots of the weeds to the corners of the stars) ultimately ends with a remark on the potential for transformation. They arrive at a sick tree, whose roots date back to an ancient era, and sit by its decaying body. They then notice a growing fissure on the surface of the earth. From within this chasm, they hear the noise of the people they are trying to leave behind and fear that people will catch up with them and force them to return from *yokyer* to "bir yer" (79; a place). They counter this fear with a note of hope as each character begins to see the world from the eyes of another vulnerable creature. Hagrin gazes at the world through the aching eyes of the sick tree. Moy sees everything through the eyes of Hagrin and Cice. As each character perceives the world through the gaze of another, the book ends with a final emphasis on co-becoming: "Birbirine dönüşen, birbirini dönüştüren şeyler zaman rotasından çıkar, samanyolu misali bir tozlu geçitten genişliğe varırlar" (73; Things that transform, and are transformed by, one another depart from the route of time, pass through a dusty passage resembling the Milky Way, and arrive at an expanse). Gezgin suggests that the journey leading to *yokyer* and to the "expanse" passes through an infinite metamorphosis of the self into alterity.

Interlacing past and present, myth and reality, *YerKuşAğı* is both a tale of all times and a tale that exists outside history. The story alludes to the possibility of another reality, where a sensitive child such as Moy, a mythic creature like Hagrin, a wounded cormorant like Şuri, an old species like the muntjac, and an ancient tree find their reflections in one another, gathering "her şeyden bir şey" (28; something of everything) they touch. As characters rewild their tongue and reattune their ears to the sonorous world of nature, they know that "Yerin halleri gibi sonsuzca halden geçerek yabanıl olunur" (Gezgin 2017a, Rewilding oneself is only possible via passing through infinite states, like the states of the earth). Resembling Keskin's and Sofya's poems, *YerKuşAğı* is a story of humanimal characters that endlessly evolve into one another.

The range of contemporary authors discussed in this chapter complicates the human/animal divide in myriad ways and critiques human exceptionalism by removing the human from the top of the hierarchical ladder to the inside of the ecological tangle. Experimenting in different genres, they all write against the physical and representational violence that animals are subjected to in life and in text. Their works build affective bonds between humans and animals, paying close attention to embodiment and interspecies entanglement. Instead of reiterating speciesist discourses and reducing animal alterity to a question of readability, they engage with liminality and illegibility to accommodate the heterogeneous multiplicity of living beings. In *Thus Spake Zarathustra*, Nietzsche remarks: "It is a beautiful folly, speaking: therewith danceth man over everything" (1999: 153). The writers included in this analysis are all cautious about the oppressive potential of human language. They are less interested in dancing over animals than in walking among them and invent a resilient grammar that draws human and more-than-human worlds ever closer to one another.

Notes

1 The quotations are taken from the English translation of Karasu's tale. The animal in the original Turkish tale is *kirpi*, which can alternatively be translated as "hedgehog," given the physical and behavioral attributes described in the tale (e.g., the animal's ability to roll into a ball).
2 As Timothy Clark notes, Derrida's essay responds to Friedrich Schlegel's "Athenaeum Fragments," no. 206, where Schlegel thinks of "the fragment form in relation to the idea of a transcendental poetry, a poetry that will have no empirical referent but would exist as the essential or the absolute poem ... 'entirely isolated from the surrounding world and ... complete in itself like a hedgehog'" (Clark 1993: 46; Schlegel 1971: 189). Unlike Schlegel's hedgehog-fragment, which represents an absolute closure upon itself, Derrida's hedgehog-poem can never fully close in on itself.
3 See the dolphins in Yaşar Kemal's *The Sea-Crossed Fisherman* (1985b), the cats in Gündüz Vassaf's *İstanbul'da Kedi* (2014) (Cat in İstanbul), or the pigeons in Nazım Hikmet's "Dört Güvercin" (2007) (Four Pigeons).
4 Nazmi Ağıl humorously addresses the negative perception of insects in his poem, "Doğayla Barışık" (In Peace with Nature), which depicts a family picnicking in "cennet doğa" (2005: 7; a nature paradise) until their meal is interrupted by bees and ants. Disturbed by these "intruders," the family members flee the very nature they

were previously enjoying and return to their home, where pest control workers have just completed applying chemical solutions to eliminate insects and rodents.
5 There is a similar pun in the English translation: *Wûf* is pronounced the same as "woof," but it borrows the long vowel "û" from the Kurdish alphabet to create a Kurdish pronunciation of the English onomatopoeia.
6 The pun on "Bubi" and *bubi tuzağı* is more clear in the original Turkish version. See Varol (2014a).
7 The notebooks where soldiers count down the days left for military service.
8 This epigraph appears at the beginning of the twelfth chapter in *Haw*, but it is omitted from the English translation.
9 "The Girls" refer to the young soldiers in Northerners' military (Varol 2019: 102).
10 Duman has long held an interest in the issue of hunting, taking it up in many other works, such as the collection of short stories titled *Av Dönüşleri* (1999) (Return from the Hunt) and the novel, *Köpekler İçin Gece Müziği* (2014b) (Night Music for Dogs). In these narratives, we encounter a critique of masculine hunter archetypes who are equally violent toward humans and animals.
11 There are only two instances in the novella where Duman alludes to a "mutual understanding" between the protagonist and the leopard, referring to the time they see each other for the first time and to the time when the leopard protects them from Ceren's father by standing in between them. Yet even in those instances, the protagonist has no access to the animal's inner being. On the contrary, it is the animal who knows all about the protagonist's past and offers help.
12 In *The Animal That Therefore I Am*, Derrida asks what his cat may be seeing when staring at him. Rather than inquiring whether the cat can comprehend him, he wonders whether he can ever comprehend the cat. Derrida's inquiry is, in part, a revision of Michel de Montaigne's question about the human capacity to imagine "the secret internal stirrings of animals": "By what comparison between them and us does he [man] infer the stupidity that he attributes to them? When I play with my cat [*ma chatte*], who knows if I am not a pastime to her more than she is to me?" (Montaigne 1957: 331; Derrida 2008: 6–7).
13 Duman sustains the tension between reality and fantasy until the end of the book, where he reveals that the protagonist's mother passed away months ago. This is a surprise ending for the reader who has, until then, witnessed several conversations between the narrator and the mother. This revelation repositions their conversations as imaginary or as flashbacks. At the end of the novella, the narrator describes his mother as a "belirsiz" (Duman 2012: 89; indistinct) figure who disappears into the foggy night, like the leopard.
14 See Agamben's discussion of "anthropogenesis" in *The Open: Man and Animal* (2003).

15 The Karasu tale that I discuss in the opening pages, "In Praise of the Fearless Porcupine," is the fourth tale in *Göçmüş Kediler Bahçesi* (1979) (*The Garden of Departed Cats* 2003).
16 The act of naming resurfaces in one of the interpolated tales in "The Prey" about a boy who brings his first prey before the elders of the clan. Just as the patriarch of the clan is about to name the boy, thunder strikes and "[t]he boy remains nameless" (Karasu 2003: 16).
17 The act of eating in Karasu's work stands in contrast to the notion of "sublimated eating," which Derrida finds in Hegel's historicism and defines as an assimilating act, where "spirit eats everything that is external and foreign, and thereby transforms it into something internal, something that is its own" (Derrida 2009). Karasu's human, animal, and humanimal characters never fully assimilate one another while eating or being eaten by each other. Instead, they coexist in a tension-ridden relationship that destabilizes several boundaries we presume to be intact.
18 In addition to the central story, an interpolated tale in "The Prey" also foregrounds the fragility of corporeality. In it, the Bey (the horseman) rides away from falcons and lances flying behind him while chasing a deer and a leopard. This manifold chase results in the death of the horse (mutilated) and the leopard (head soaked in blood), at which point the Bey wonders, "How could he have loved this leopard?" (Karasu 2003: 10). The reader is not given any explanation as to the background of this story, but only a glimpse into the mutually loving and destructive relationships between animals and humans.
19 Although this is the twelfth tale in the book, it is unnumbered and reads like a metatextual commentary on the writing of the tales. As stated here, the narrator-writer organizes the tales around the twelve hours of the day (Karasu 2003: 237).
20 The book's title and the multiple references to cats call for a brief explanation. The lethal chess game that locals play is called "The Game of Departure" (Karasu 2003: 55). The garden where the game is played is named "The Garden of Departed Cats" in reference to the cats that go there to die. In the tenth chapter, a cat crosses the playing field and disappears into the garden (174). In the twelfth chapter, the same cat is found asleep in this garden where the narrator is about to die, suggesting that they are both about to *depart* (233). Playful comparisons between cats and humans are also present in "Midnight's Tale," where the narrator compares loving a person with loving a cat (242), seeking a human reflection in the cat or a feline reflection in the human.
21 The phrase *İkinci Yeni* was coined by Muzaffer Erdost in 1956. Observing a difference in the poetry published in the magazine *Pazar Postası* after 1953, Erdost claimed that a new poetics was in the making (Messo 2009: 10–11). He loosely defined this poetics as abstract, devoid of meaning, and privileging individualism and formalism over social-political concerns. Erdost had in mind a unique group

of poets including Ece Ayhan, İlhan Berk, Turgut Uyar, Cemal Süreya, and Edip Cansever, who had varying opinions as to this categorization.

22 Elsewhere, Berk draws on a parallelism between nature and poetry, and writes that "[şiir] doğa gibi de gizliliği sever" (1997: 52; Like nature, [poetry] loves secrecy).

23 Berk's questioning of the relationship between language and logos may, in part, be seen as an influence of thinkers like Derrida, who contemplate "the borderline of the moment when the word has not yet been born, when articulation is no longer a shout but not yet discourse" (Derrida 1978: 240). Furthermore, Antonin Artaud's attempt to divorce writing from thought and his celebration of meaninglessness as a form of methodological madness (Berk 1998: 41) leave a strong imprint on Berk's poetics.

24 See my discussion of the "ecological text" versus the "book of nature" in *The Ecopoetics of Entanglement* (Ergin 2017).

25 Although the poem is about a "salyangoz" (snail), it is titled "Sümüklüböcek" ("Slug"), probably because, in colloquial Turkish, the word "sümüklüböcek" (literally "the slimy bug") was commonly used to refer to both snails and slugs, who secrete mucous gels.

26 Berk states that, unlike "Kierkegaard, Husserl and Heidegger [who] opened parentheses only for 'being'" (2009a: 144), he brackets all things silent. In contrast to Heidegger, who asserts that "man is *world-forming*," "the animal is *poor in world*," and "the stone (material object) is *worldless*" (Heidegger 2004: 17), Berk identifies a unique world in all three categories—humans, animals, and objects—and opens brackets for all of them.

27 *Yeryüzü Halleri* was first published in 2002. In 2005, it was published as part of an anthology titled *Kim Bağışlayacak Beni*, which includes five poetry books by Birhan Keskin. I use the 2005 edition in my discussion.

28 Sufism is a mystical form of Islam that stresses introspection and inward search for God. Abandoning one's ego is necessary to turn toward divine truth. Through contemplation, the Sufi practitioner seeks spiritual ascent and union with absolute being.

29 "Vehm ü gümân" can be translated as "suspicion" or "supposition." It has connotations of believing, suspecting, or worrying over something that may not be real.

30 Some of the poems from *Yeryüzü Halleri* were translated into English and published in the anthology titled *& Silk & Love & Flame* (Keskin 2013). The extracts in English are taken from this edition.

31 In Turkish, there is only one pronoun used for the third-person singular—"o"—which is gender and species neutral. I translate "o" as "they" to maintain the ambiguity of the referent.

32 The expression "ant prayer" has a double meaning in Turkish. In colloquial language, it is used in reference to illegible writing in very small font. In the Islamic faith, it refers to an abundance prayer, in which an ant prays for rain during a drought.
33 *Dik Âlâ* is rather difficult to translate into English. It derives from the expression "dik âlâsı," which conveys the excess or the extremity of an often unpleasant situation or characteristic. The title may be read as a reference to the extent of ecological and political degradation brought about by humans.
34 "Dik" can be translated as both "vertical; upright" and "hard-headed; obstinate," and "yazı" means "writing." "Dik yazı" is an unusual expression that makes critical reference to human language. It alludes both to the obstinacy of humans, who claim mastery over animals via language, and to the vertically inscribed letters of the alphabet.
35 While this line alludes to resource extraction—such as stone mining—in mountainous areas, Sofya uses the word "skinned" to evoke the image of "animals skinned alive."
36 Gezgin often invites readers on mythical journeys that reshape our perception of more-than-human nature. See her trilogy *Bitki Mitosları* (2007a) (Plant Mythoi), *Hayvan Mitosları* (2007b) (Animal Mythoi), *Su Mitosları* (2009) (Water Mythoi).
37 In the word *yokyer*, "yer" refers to "place" and "yok" is a morpheme connoting existential negation. The author variously refers to *yokyer* as "olmayan bu yer" (Gezgin 2017c: 75; this place which does not exist) and "yer olmayan" (67; that which is not a place).
38 The Turkish word "ses" can be translated both as "voice" and "sound." I use "sound" for the most part to accentuate the writer's emphasis on including the various sounds of nature, as opposed to prioritizing the human voice.
39 As discussed earlier, several texts on animals problematize the tension between human gaze and animal gaze, between seeing and being seen.
40 The word "dilbaz" is a pun on "cambaz" (acrobat), which derives from the Farsi word "canbaz." "Can" means "life" and "baz" is "player;" hence "canbaz" is someone who plays with his/her life. Since "dil" means language, "dilbaz" refers to someone who plays with language. Gezgin introduces Dilbaz as someone who can speak all the languages spoken in all the towns of the world.
41 The name "Şuri" means "breath" or "life."
42 Water of the womb (the amniotic fluid).
43 The title consists of three Turkish words: "yer" (place, ground, earth), "kuş" (bird) and "ağ" (mesh, net, web). As explained in the main text, I translate "yer" as "earth" to foreground the sky-earth relationship and "ağ" as "mesh" to highlight their entanglement. Alternatively, if read as one single word without capitalized letters—"yerkuşağı" (earth belt)—the title could be seen as a pun on "gökkuşağı" (literally "sky belt," meaning "rainbow").

Works Cited

Abasıyanık, S. F. (1952), "Bir Kaya Parçası Gibi," in *Son Kuşlar*, 35–8, İstanbul: Varlık Yayınları.
Abasıyanık, S. F. (1972), Letter to Yaşar Nabi Nayır, in Y. N. Nayır (ed.), *Dost Mektuplar: Mektuplarıyla Edebiyatçılarımız*, 88–91, İstanbul: Varlık Yayınları.
Abasıyanık, S. F. (1995a), "Coming of Age on Kaşıkadası," trans. A. Ö. Evin, in T. S. Halman (ed.), *A Dot on the Map*, 241–8, Bloomington: Indiana University Press.
Abasıyanık, S. F. (1995b), "Robinson," trans. M. Nemet-Nejat, in T. S. Halman (ed.), *A Dot on the Map*, 155–6, Bloomington: Indiana University Press.
Abasıyanık, S. F. (1995c), "The Stelyanos Hrisopulos," trans. J. LeBaron, in T. S. Halman (ed.), *A Dot on the Map*, 135–42, Bloomington: Indiana University Press.
Abasıyanık, S. F. (2002), "Sinağrit Baba" [1st print 1950], in O. Tapınç and S. Sönmez (eds.), *Mahalle Kahvesi*, 102–5, İstanbul: Yapı Kredi Yayınları.
Abasıyanık, S. F. (2004a), "The Armenian Fisherman and the Lame Seagull," trans. T. S. Halman, in T. S. Halman (ed.), *Sleeping in the Forest: Stories and Poems*, 139–42, New York: Syracuse University Press.
Abasıyanık, S. F. (2004b), "Eftalikus's Coffeehouse," trans. J. S. Jacobson, in T. S. Halman (ed.), *Sleeping in the Forest: Stories and Poems*, 88–92, New York: Syracuse University Press.
Abderrezak, H. (2018), "The Mediterranean *Seametery* and *Cementery* in Leïla Kilani's and Tariq Teguia's Filmic Works," in Y. Elhariry and E. T. Talbayev (eds.), *Critically Mediterranean: Temporalities, Aesthetics, and Deployments of a Sea in Crisis*, 147–61, Cham: Palgrave Macmillan.
Abram, D. (1997), *The Spell of the Sensuous: Perception and Language in a More-Than-Human World*, New York: Vintage Books.
Adams, C. J. (2010), *The Sexual Politics of Meat: A Feminist-Vegetarian Critical Theory*, New York: Continuum Books.
Agamben, G. (2003), *The Open: Man and Animal*, trans. K. Attell, Stanford: Stanford University Press.
Ağıl, N. (2005), "Doğayla Barışık," in *Kokarca Aramak*, 7–8, İstanbul: Adam Yayınları.
"Ağrı Dağı" (2019), Doğubayazıt Kaymakamlığı, June 11. Available online: http://www.dogubayazit.gov.tr/agri-dagi (accessed March 1, 2021).
Akbaş, M., and N. Bozok (2015), "*Aylak Adam* ve *Tuhaf Bir Kadın* Sokaklarda Gezinirken: Aynı Sokaklar[da] Farklı Deneyimler[le]," *Folklor/Edebiyat* 21 (81): 125–38.

Akbulut, B., F. Adaman, and M. Arsel (2017), "The Radioactive Inertia: Deciphering Turkey's Anti-Nuclear Movement," in B. Akbulut, F. Adaman and M. Arsel (eds.), *Neoliberal Turkey and Its Discontents: Economic Policy and the Environment under Erdoğan*, 175–90, London: I.B. Tauris.

Akçam, T. (2006), *A Shameful Act: The Armenian Genocide and the Question of Turkish Responsibility*, New York: Metropolitan Books/Henry Holt.

Akdenizli (Mavi Derinliğin Sırları) (2002), [Film] Dir. Orhan Tuncel, Cam. Haluk Cecan, Turkey: TRT.

Akgül, O. (2021), "Madalyonun Tek Yüzü: İklim Krizi ve 2021 Türkiye Orman Yangınları," *Greenpeace*, August 13. Available online: https://www.greenpeace.org/turkey/blog/madalyonun-tek-yuzu-iklim-krizi-ve-2021-turkiye-orman-yanginlari/ (accessed February 8, 2022).

Akkuş, A. T. (2018), "Buket Uzuner ile *Hava*'yı Konuştuk: İnsan, En Büyük Aşkı Tabiat'a İhanet Etti!," interview with B. Uzuner, *Yeşil Gazete*, October 13. Available online: https://yesilgazete.org/buket-uzuner-ile-havayi-konustuk-insan-en-buyuk-aski-tabiata-ihanet-etti/ (accessed December 17, 2019).

Alaimo, S. (2010), *Bodily Natures: Science, Environment, and the Material Self*, Bloomington: Indiana University Press.

Alaimo, S. (2013), "Jellyfish Science, Jellyfish Aesthetics: Posthuman Reconfigurations of the Sensible," in J. Macleod, C. Chen, and A. Neimanis (eds.), *Thinking with Water*, 139–64, Montreal: McGill-Queens University Press.

Alaimo, S. (2016), *Exposed: Environmental Politics and Pleasures in Posthuman Times*, Minneapolis: University of Minnesota Press.

Alessi, E., and G. Di Carlo (2018), *Out of the Plastic Trap: Saving the Mediterranean from Plastic Pollution*, trans. E. Başgül di Carlo, ed. B. Jeffreys, World Wide Fund for Nature Report, Mediterranean Marine Initiative, Rome, June. Available online: https://awsassets.panda.org/downloads/a4_plastics_med_web_08june_new.pdf (accessed July 4, 2022).

Ali, S. (1931), "Dağlar," *Atsız Mecmua* 7: 161.

Alkan, A. (2016), "Deportation as an Urban Stray Dogs Management Policy: Forest Dogs of İstanbul," *Lex Localis* 14 (3): 613–35.

Altounian, V. (2014), "Vahram Altounian'ın Güncesi," in *Geri Dönüşü Yok: Bir Babanın Güncesinde ve Kızının Belleğinde Ermeni Soykırımı*, by V. and J. Altounian, trans. R. Akman, 13–36, İstanbul: Aras Yayıncılık.

Altounian, V., and J. Altounian (2009), *Mémoires du génocide arménien: Héritage Traumatique et Travail Analytique*, Paris: Presses Universitaires de France – PUF.

Altunya, N. (2012), "Köy Enstitüsü Sistemi'ne Genel Bir Bakış/A General Overview of the Village Institute System," in E. Işın (ed.), *Düşünen Tohum, Konuşan Toprak: Cumhuriyet'in Köy Enstitüleri, 1940–1954/Mindful Seed, Speaking Soil: Village Institutes of the Republic, 1940–1954*, 82–108, İstanbul: İstanbul Araştırmaları Enstitüsü.

Anadolu Mavisi (1999), [Film] Dir. Orhan Tuncel, Cam. Haluk Cecan, Turkey: TRT.

Anagnostopulos, H. (2012), *Anavoles Ke Katifori (Süruncemeler—Yokuş Aşağı Gözü Kapalı)*, İstanbul: İstos Yayın.
Antalya'da Denizden Çıkanlar (2020), [Film] Dir. Alican Abacı, Turkey: Aw Film Production.
Apaydın, T. (1952), *Bozkırda Günler: Köy Notları*, İstanbul: Varlık Yayınları.
Aruoba, O. (1992), *Yürüme*, İstanbul: Metis Yayınları.
Aşıcı, A. A. (2015), "On the Sustainability of the Economic Growth Path of Turkey: 1995–2009," *Renewable and Sustainable Energy Review* 52: 1731–41.
Atasoy, E. (2016), "Utopia's Turkish Translations and Utopianism in Turkish Literature," *Utopian Studies* 27 (3): 558–68.
Atay, O. (1995), "Beyaz Mantolu Adam" [1st print 1973], in *Korkuyu Beklerken*, 11–26, İstanbul: İletişim Yayınları.
Atılgan, Y. (1959), *Aylak Adam*, İstanbul: Varlık Yayınları.
Avedikyan, S. (2021), *Retourner à Sölöz*, France: Saint-André-des-Arts.
Aydın, A. (2019), *Unwanted Guest*, Heybeliada, Ruhban Okulu, İstanbul. Available online: https://alperaydin.art/unwanted-guest (accessed September 12, 2022).
Baccolini, R., and T. Moylan (2003), "Introduction: Dystopia and Histories," in R. Baccolini and T. Moylan (eds.), *Dark Horizons: Science Fiction and the Dystopian Imagination*, 1–12, New York: Routledge.
Baird, D., A. Fairbairn, E. Jenkins, L. Martin, C. Middleton, J. Pearson, E. Asouti, Y. Edwards, C. Kabukcu, G. Mustafaoğlu, N. Russell, O. Bar-Yosef, G. Jacobsen, X. Wu, A. Baker, and S. Elliott (2018), "Agricultural Origins on the Anatolian Plateau," *Proceedings of the National Academy of Sciences* 115 (4): E3077–E3086.
Baker, Z., J. Ekstrom, and L. Bedsworth (2018), "Climate Information? Embedding Climate Futures within Temporalities of California Water Management," *Environmental Sociology* 4 (4): 419–33.
Baloğlu, A. (1999), *Sualtından Yansımalar*, İstanbul: İlke Basın Yayın.
Baloğlu, A. (2006), *İstanbul'un Sualtı Yaşamı*, İstanbul: İstanbul Büyükşehir Belediyesi Yayınları.
Baloğlu, A. (2010), *Bosphorus by the Sea/Denizden Boğaziçi*, İstanbul: A4 Ofset.
Barad, K. (2007), *Meeting the Universe Halfway: Quantum Physics and the Entanglement of Matter and Meaning*, Durham: Duke University Press.
Başaran, M. (1953), *Ahlat Ağacı*, İstanbul: Yücel Yayınevi.
Batur, P., and U. Özdağ (2019), "Novelist as Eco-Shaman: Buket Uzuner's *Water* [*Su*] as Requesting Spirits to Help the Earth in Crisis," in S. Slovic, S. Rangarajan and V. Sarveswaran (eds.), *The Routledge Handbook of Ecocriticism and Environmental Communication*, 326–38, Oxon/New York: Routledge.
Baydar, O. (1992), *Kedi Mektupları*, İstanbul: Can Yayınları.
Baydar, O. (2009), *Çöplüğün Generali*, İstanbul: Can Yayınları.
Baydar, O. (2019), *Köpekli Çocuklar Gecesi*, İstanbul: Can Yayınları.
Baydar, O. (2021), *80 Yaş Zor Zamanlar Günlükleri*, İstanbul: Can Yayınları.

Baykan, B. (2021), "Speculative Ecologies of Plastics in the Environmental Aesthetics of Pınar Yoldaş," in S. Oppermann and S. Akıllı (eds.), *Turkish Ecocriticism: From Neolithic to Contemporary Timescapes*, 245–66, Lanham: Lexington.

Baykurt, F. (1954), *Yılanların Öcü*, İstanbul: Literatür.

Baykurt, F. (1961), *Onuncu Köy*, İstanbul: Literatür.

Baykurt, F. (1967), *Kaplumbağalar*, İstanbul: Literatür.

Baykurt, F., K. Tahir, M. Makal, O. Kemal, and T. Apaydın (1960), *Beş Romancı Tartışıyor*, İstanbul: Düşün Yayınevi.

Baytop, A. (2009–10), "Hikmet Birand'ın (1904–1972) Anadolu Bitkileri Koleksiyonu," *Osmanlı Bilimi Araştırmaları* XI (1–2): 321–9.

Beledian, K. (2009), "Introduction," in *Accursed Years: My Exile and Return from Der Zor, 1914–1919*, by Y. Odyan, trans. A. S. Melkonian, ix–xxiii, London: Gomidas Institute.

Beledian, K. (2014), Footnotes to "Vahram Altounian'ın Güncesi," by V. Altounian, in *Geri Dönüşü Yok: Bir Babanın Güncesinde ve Kızının Belleğinde Ermeni Soykırımı*, trans. R. Akman, 13–36, İstanbul: Aras Yayıncılık.

Belge, M. (2006), "Mavi Anadolu Tezi ve Halikarnas Balıkçısı," *Birikim* 210, October. Available online: https://birikimdergisi.com/dergiler/birikim/1/sayi-210-ekim-2006-sayi-210-ekim-2006/2393/mavi-anadolu-tezi-ve-halikarnas-balikcisi/4876 (accessed October 3, 2019).

Benjamin, W. (2003), "On the Concept of History," in H. Eiland and M. W. Jennings (eds.), *Walter Benjamin: Selected Writings Volume 4, 1938–1940*, trans. E. Jephcott, 389–400, Cambridge, MA: Harvard University Press.

Benlisoy, F. (2013), "Rum Edebiyatından Bir Yazar Adı Söyleyebilir Miyiz?," interview by E. Gülcan, *Bianet*, March. Available online: https://m.bianet.org/biamag/kultur/145299-rum-edebiyatindan-bir-yazar-adi-soyleyebilir-miyiz (accessed March 1, 2020).

Bennett, J. (2005), "The Agency of Assemblages and the North American Blackout," *Public Culture* 17: 445–65.

Bennett, J. (2010), *Vibrant Matter: A Political Ecology of Things*, Durham: Duke University Press.

Berk, İ. (1982), *Günaydın Yeryüzü* [1st print 1952], İstanbul: Adam Yayınları.

Berk, İ. (1992), "İlhan Berk ile Söyleşi," interview by O. Koçak and İ. Savaşır, *Defter* 19: 135–50.

Berk, İ. (1994a), *Inferno*, İstanbul: Yapı Kredi Yayınları.

Berk, İ. (1994b), *Kanatlı At*, İstanbul: Yapı Kredi Yayınları.

Berk, İ. (1996), *Logos*, İstanbul: Yapı Kredi Yayınları.

Berk, İ. (1997), *Poetika*, İstanbul: Yapı Kredi Yayınları.

Berk, İ. (1998), "Artaud," in B. Keskin (ed.), *Kült Kitap*, 39–41, İstanbul: Yapı Kredi Yayınları.

Berk, İ. (2002), *Şeyler Kitabı*, İstanbul: Yapı Kredi Yayınları.

Berk, İ. (2005), *Kuşların Doğum Gününde Olacağım*, İstanbul: Yapı Kredi Yayınları.
Berk, İ. (2006a), *Adlandırılmayan Yoktur*, İstanbul: Yapı Kredi Yayınları.
Berk, İ. (2006b), *A Leaf About to Fall: Selected Poems*, trans. G. Messo, Cambridge: Salt Publishing.
Berk, İ. (2007a), *Akşama Doğru 1984–2005: Toplu Şiirler III*, ed. B. Keskin, İstanbul: Yapı Kredi Yayınları.
Berk, İ. (2007b), *Tümceler Geliyorum*, İstanbul: Yapı Kredi Yayınları.
Berk, İ. (2008), *Madrigals*, trans. G. Messo, London: Shearsman Books.
Berk, İ. (2009a), *The Book of Things*, trans. G. Messo, London: Salt Publishing.
Berk, İ. (2009b), "Ecology," in G. Messo (ed. and trans.), *İkinci Yeni: The Turkish Avant-Garde*, 44, Exeter: Shearsman Books.
Berk, İ. (2016), *New Selected Poems, 1947–2008*, trans. G. Messo, London: Shearsman Books.
Binder, T. (2023), "A Brief History of Sponge Diving in Bodrum," Bodrum Deniz Müzesi. Available online: https://bodrumdenizmuzesi.org/en/sponge-fishing/ (accessed October 16, 2023).
Bir Zamanlar Anadolu'da (2011), [Film] Dir. Nuri Bilge Ceylan, Turkey: Zeyno Film.
Birand, H. (1952), *Türkiye Bitkileri - Plantae Turcicae*, Ankara: Ankara Üniversitesi Fen Fakültesi Yayınları.
Birand, H. (1957), *Anadolu Manzaraları*, Ankara: TÜBİTAK Yayınları.
Black Sea Files (2005), [Film] Dir. Ursula Biemann, Switzerland.
Borges, J. L. (1964), "Inferno, 1, 32," in D. A. Yates and J. E. Irby (eds.), *Labyrinths: Selected Stories and Other Writings*, 237, New York: New Directions.
Brown, C. (2017), "Dystopia *Is* Realism: The Future Is Here If You Look Closely," *Lit Hub*, July 10. Available online: https://lithub.com/dystopia-is-realism-the-future-is-here-if-you-look-closely/ (accessed July 11, 2020).
Callaghan, P. (2015), "Myth as a Site of Ecocritical Inquiry: Disrupting Anthropocentrism," *Interdisciplinary Studies in Literature and Environment* 22 (1): 80–97.
Cassano, F. (2012), *Southern Thought and Other Essays on the Mediterranean*, trans. N. Bouchard and V. Ferme, New York: Fordham University Press.
Cecan, H. (2007), "Haluk Cecan ile 08 Mart 2006'da Yapılan Görüşme," interview by S. Çilingir, *Sadibey.com*, February. Available online: https://sadibey.com/2007/02/21/haluk-cecan-ile-08-mart-2006da-yapilan-gorusme/ (accessed December 8, 2019).
Clark, T. (1993), "By Heart: A Reading of Derrida's 'Che cos'è la poesia?' through Keats and Celan," *Oxford Literary Review* 15 (1): 43–80.
Clark, T. (2010), "Some Climate Change Ironies: Deconstruction, Environmental Politics and the Closure of Ecocriticism," *Oxford Literary Review* 32 (1): 131–49.
Clark, T. (2014), "Phenomenology," in G. Garrard (ed.), *The Oxford Handbook of Ecocriticism*, 276–90, Oxford: Oxford University Press.

Çolak, Y. (2021), "Döktüklerimizi Deniz Geri Verdi," *BirGün*, May 27. Available online: https://www.birgun.net/haber/doktuklerimizi-deniz-geri-verdi-346152 (accessed July 6, 2021).

Coole, D. (2010), "The Inertia of Matter and Generativity of Flesh," in D. Coole and S. Frost (eds.), *New Materialisms: Ontology, Agency, and Politics*, 92–115, Durham: Duke University Press.

Cooper, D. E. (1992), "The Idea of the Environment," in D. E. Cooper and J. A. Palmer (eds.), *The Environment in Question: Ethics and Global Issues*, 165–80, London: Routledge.

Çuhadar, B. (2019), "Böyle Bir Dönemde Ütopyalar Kuracak Halimiz Kalmadı," interview with Oya Baydar, *Hürriyet Kitap Sanat*, September 20. Available online: https://www.hurriyet.com.tr/kitap-sanat/boyle-bir-donemde-utopyalar-kuracak-halimiz-kalmadi-41334137 (accessed August 3, 2020).

Cumalı, N. (1962), *Susuz Yaz*, İstanbul: Ataç Kitabevi.

Dalton, A. (2013), "Introduction," in *& Silk & Love & Flame*, by B. Keskin, 13–17, London: Arc Publications.

De Amicis, E. (2005), *Constantinople*, London: Hesperus Press.

Debarbieux, B., and G. Rudaz (2015), *The Mountain: A Political History from the Enlightenment to the Present*, Chicago: University of Chicago Press.

DeLoughrey, E., and T. Flores (2020), "Submerged Bodies: The Tidalectics of Representability and the Sea in Caribbean Art," *Environmental Humanities* 12 (1): 132–66.

Derrida, J. (1978), *Writing and Difference*, trans. A. Bass, Chicago: University of Chicago Press.

Derrida, J. (1991), "'Eating Well,' or the Calculation of the Subject: An Interview with Jacques Derrida," in E. Cadava, P. Connor and J. L. Nancy (eds.), *Who Comes after the Subject?*, 96–119, New York: Routledge.

Derrida, J. (1995a), "*Che cos'è la poesia?*," in E. Weber (ed.), *Points … Interviews: 1974–1994*, trans. P. Kamuf & others, 288–99, Stanford: Stanford University Press.

Derrida, J. (1995b), "*Istrice 2: Ick bünn all hier*," in E. Weber (ed.), *Points… Interviews: 1974–1994*, trans. P. Kamuf & others, 300–26, Stanford: Stanford University Press.

Derrida, J. (2008), *The Animal That Therefore I Am*, trans. D. Wills, New York: Fordham University Press.

Derrida, J. (2009), "An Interview with Jacques Derrida on the Limits of Digestion," interview by D. Birnbaum and A. Olsson, *Journal #02*, January. Available online: https://www.e-flux.com/journal/02/68495/an-interview-with-jacques-derrida-on-the-limits-of-digestion/ (accessed May 12, 2019).

Deveciyan, K. (2006), *Türkiye'de Balık ve Balıkçılık* [1st print 1915], İstanbul: Aras Yayıncılık.

Dilovası (2016), [Film] Dir. Serdal Doğan, Turkey: Asi Film.

Dink, R. (2015), "Rakel Dink: Acı Acı Ağlıyorum," *T24*, April 2. Available online: https://t24.com.tr/haber/rakel-dink-aci-aci-agliyorum,294500 (accessed July 22, 2022).

Doğan, M. (2013), "Geçmişten Günümüze İstanbul'da Sanayileşme Süreci ve Son 10 Yıllık Gelişimi," *Marmara Coğrafya Dergisi* 27 (Ocak): 511–50.

Dolcerocca, Ö. N. (2017), "'Free Spirited Clocks': Modernism, Temporality and *The Time Regulation Institute*," *Middle Eastern Literatures* 20 (2): 177–97.

Driscoll, K. (2015), "The Sticky Temptation of Poetry," *Journal of Literary Theory* 9 (2): 212–29.

Duman, F. (1999), *Av Dönüşleri*, İstanbul: Can Yayınları.

Duman, F. (2012), *Ve Bir Pars, Hüzünle Kaybolur*, İstanbul: Can Yayınları.

Duman, F. (2014a), "Faruk Duman'ın Yeni Romanı *Köpekler İçin Gece Müziği*," interview by G. Akdemir, *Cumhuriyet Kitap Eki*, October 22. Available online: http://www.cumhuriyet.com.tr/haber/kitap/133125/Faruk_Duman_in_yeni_romani__Kopekler_icin_Gece_Muzigi_.html (accessed July 4, 2018).

Duman, F. (2014b), *Köpekler İçin Gece Müziği*, İstanbul: Can Yayınları.

Dündar, C. (2000), *Köy Enstitüleri*, İstanbul: İmge Kitabevi Yayınları.

Dündar, F. (2010), *Crime of Numbers: The Role of Statistics in the Armenian Question (1878–1918)*, New Brunswick: Transaction Publishers.

Eleonora, B. (2007), "*The Book of Dede Korkut*," *Journal of Graduate School of Social Sciences/Sosyal Bilimler Enstitüsü Dergisi* 9 (1): 135–48.

Erbil, L. (1989), *Tuhaf Bir Kadın* [1st print 1971], İstanbul: Can Yayınları.

Erbil, L. (2022), *A Strange Woman*, trans. N. Menemencioğlu and A. M. Spangler, Dallas/TX: Deep Vellum Publishing.

Erdi Lelandais, G. (2016), "Drought, Social Inequalities, Adaptation, and Farmers' Mobility in the Konya Plain of Turkey," in R. McLeman (ed.), *Environmental Migration and Social Inequality*, 91–102, Cham: Springer.

Ergin, M. (2017), *The Ecopoetics of Entanglement in Contemporary Turkish and American Literatures*, Cham: Palgrave Macmillan.

Ergülen, H. (2012), "Uzun Çocuk: İlhan Berk," *Sabitfikir*, August 23. Available online: http://www.sabitfikir.com/dosyalar/uzun-cocuk-ilhan-berk (accessed June 8, 2018).

Erhat, A. (1972), *Mitoloji Sözlüğü*, İstanbul: Remzi Kitabevi.

Erhat, A. (1977), "Giriş," in *Hesiodos: Eserleri ve Kaynakları*, by Hesiod, trans. S. Eyüboğlu and A. Erhat, 1–102, Ankara: Türk Tarih Kurumu Basımevi.

Erhat, A. (2018), *Mavi Yolculuk* [1st print 1962], İstanbul: Türkiye İş Bankası Kültür Yayınları.

Erhat, A. (2020), *Mavi Anadolu* [1st print 1960], İstanbul: Türkiye İş Bankası Kültür Yayınları.

Erhat, A., and C. Bektaş, trans. (1978), *Sappho Üzerine Konuşmalar ve Şiir Çevirileri*, by Sappho, İstanbul: Cem Yayınları.

"Erzurum Dağları Kar ile Boran" (2002), *Türkü Dostları*. Available online: https://www.turkudostlari.net/soz.asp?turku=448 (accessed July 30, 2023).

Evans, J. P. (2009), "21st Century Climate Change in the Middle East," *Climatic Change* 92: 417–32.

Fornaro, S. (2018), "A Sea of Metal Plates: Images of the Mediterranean from the Eighteenth Century until Post-modern Theatre," in R. R. Guardiola (ed.), *The Ancient Mediterranean Sea in Modern Visual and Performing Arts*, 109–20, London: Bloomsbury Academic.

Fortuny, K. (2019), *Animals and the Environment in Turkish Culture: Ecocriticism and Transnational Literature*, London: I.B. Tauris.

Garrard, G. (2014), "Ferality Tales," in G. Garrard (ed.), *The Oxford Handbook of Ecocriticism*, 241–59, New York: Oxford University Press.

Geçkin, A. (2003), *Kenarda*, İstanbul: Metis Yayınları.

Geçkin, A. (2015a), "Kim Bilir, Belki (İnsanlık Olarak) Henüz Konuşmaya Başlamadık," interview by H. Kesim, *IAN Edebiyat*, May. Available online: https://www.metiskitap.com/catalog/interview/36282 (accessed August 1, 2020).

Geçkin, A. (2015b), *Uzun Yürüyüş*, İstanbul: Metis Yayınları.

Gezgin, D. (2007a), *Bitki Mitosları*, İstanbul: Sel Yayıncılık.

Gezgin, D. (2007b), *Hayvan Mitosları*, İstanbul: Sel Yayıncılık.

Gezgin, D. (2009), *Su Mitosları*, İstanbul: Sel Yayıncılık.

Gezgin, D. (2012), *Ahraz*, İstanbul: Sel Yayıncılık.

Gezgin, D. (2015), "Ekoloji ve Yazın: Deniz Gezgin," *cin ayşe* 14: 30–1.

Gezgin, D. (2017a), "Deniz Gezgin: Yer Tutmadan Var Olmanın Yollarını Arıyordum," interview by H. Gökçe, *Sanatatak*, July 21. Available online: http://www.sanatatak.com/view/deniz-gezgin-yer-tutmadan-var-olmanin-yolunu-ariyordum (accessed October 12, 2019).

Gezgin, D. (2017b), "Tüm Bu Olan Biten, Kuş Bakışıyla, Yer Kavgası," interview by M. Kesmez, *K24*, July 6. Available online: https://t24.com.tr/k24/yazi/tum-bu-olan-biten-kus-bakisiyla-yer-kavgasi,1285 (accessed June 6, 2019).

Gezgin, D. (2017c), *YerKuşAğı*, İstanbul: Sel Yayıncılık.

Ghosh, A. (2016), *The Great Derangement: Climate Change and the Unthinkable*, Chicago: University of Chicago Press.

Ginn, F., M. Bastian, D. Farrier, and J. Kidwell (2018), "Introduction: Unexpected Encounters with Deep Time," *Environmental Humanities* 10 (1): 213–25.

Glover, L. (2006), *Postmodern Climate Change*, London: Routledge.

Göçmen, N. (2019), "Öğretmen ve Sanatçı Mehmet Türkçelik," *Önce Vatan*, February. Available online: https://www.oncevatan.com.tr/ogretmen-ve-sanatci-mehmet-turkceli (accessed November 1, 2021).

Gökalp, M. (2011a), *Türkiye Deniz Canlıları Rehberi*, İstanbul: İnkılap Kitabevi.

Gökalp, M. (2011b), "Ya Bakarken Görememişsek?," TEDxReset. Available online: http://tedxreset.com/content/ya-bakarken-gorememissek/ (accessed March 3, 2022).

Gökalp, M. (2022), *İstanbul'un Deniz Canlıları*, İstanbul: İstanbul Büyükşehir Belediyesi Yayınları.
Grimm, J., and W. Grimm (1812), "Rapunzel," in *Kinder- und Haus-Märchen*, v. 1, no. 12, Berlin: Realschulbuchhandlung.
Günday, H. (2013), *Daha*, İstanbul: Doğan Kitap.
Günday, H. (2016), *More*, trans. Z. Beler, New York: Arcade.
Güntekin, R. N. (1936), *Anadolu Notları*, İstanbul: Kanaat Kitabevi.
Gürbilek, N. (2020), *İkinci Hayat: Kaçmak, Kovulmak, Dönmek Üzerine Denemeler*, İstanbul: Metis Yayınları.
Gürçay, E. (2018), "[Babil'den Sonra] *Yeşil Gazete* 10 Yaşında," *Yeşil Gazete*, September 15. Available online: https://yesilgazete.org/blog/2018/09/15/babilden-sonra-yesil-gazete-10-yasinda/ (accessed April 10, 2019).
Gürdeniz, C. (2014), "Kanal İstanbul, Batı İstanbul Adası ve Jeopolitik Riskler," in M. Sarıkaya (ed.), *Çılgın Proje Kanal İstanbul*, 83–94, İstanbul: Kaynak Yayınları.
Gürses, H., and I. Ertuna Howison, eds. (2019), *Animals, Plants, and Landscapes: An Ecology of Turkish Literature and Film*, New York: Routledge.
Güven, D. (2011), "Riots against the Non-Muslims of Turkey: 6/7 September 1955 in the Context of Demographic Engineering," *European Journal of Turkish Studies* 12. Available online: http://journals.openedition.org/ejts/4538 (accessed March 11, 2022).
Hajib, Y. K. (1983), *Wisdom of Royal Glory (Kutadgu Bilig): A Turko-Islamic Mirror for Princes*, trans. R. Dankoff, Chicago: University of Chicago Press.
Halman, T. S. (1995), "Introduction: Fiction of a Flâneur," in T. S. Halman (ed.), *A Dot on the Map*, by S. F. Abasıyanık, 3–11, Bloomington: Indiana University Press.
Halman, T. S. (2004), "Preface," in T. S. Halman (ed.), *Sleeping in the Forest: Stories and Poems*, by S. F. Abasıyanık, vii–viii, New York: Syracuse University Press.
Hamelink, W. (2016), *The Sung Home: Narrative, Morality, and the Kurdish Nation*, Boston: Brill.
Hamzaoğlu, O., N. Etiler, C. I. Yavuz, and Ç. Çağlayan (2011), "The Causes of Deaths in an Industry-Dense Area: Example of Dilovası (Kocaeli)," *Turkish Journal of Medical Sciences* 41 (3): 369–75.
Hamzaoğlu, O., M. Yavuz, G. Türker, and H. Savlı (2014), "Air Pollution and Heavy Metal Concentration in Colostrum and Meconium in Two Different Districts of an Industrial City: A Preliminary Report," *International Medical Journal* 21 (1): 77–82.
Haraway, D. J. (1991), *Simians, Cyborgs, and Women: The Reinvention of Nature*, New York: Routledge.
Haraway, D. J. (2008), *When Species Meet*, Minneapolis: University of Minnesota.
Haraway, D. J. (2016), *Staying with the Trouble: Making Kin in the Chthulucene*, Durham and London: Duke University Press.
Heidegger, M. (2004), "The Animal Is Poor in World," in M. Calarco and P. Atterton (eds.), *Animal Philosophy: Essential Readings in Continental Thought*, 17, London: Continuum.

Helimişi, X. (2006), "Deniz ve Laz," trans. K. Aksoylu, *Evrensel*, February. Available online: https://www.evrensel.net/haber/169362/lazlarin-da-soyleyecekleri-var (accessed February 14, 2019).

Heske, F. (1952), *Türkiye'de Orman ve Ormancılık/Wald und forstwirtschaft in der Turkei*, trans. S. İnal, İstanbul: Hüsnütabiat Basımevi.

Heske, F. (1953), "Comment améliorer l'hydrologie de l'Anatolie grâce à la biologie et à l'écologie," in *Colloque D'Ankara Sur L'Hydrologie De La Zone Aride*, 268–71, Nevers-Paris: L'Imprimerie Fortin.

Hikmet, N. (1949), "Of Your Hands and Lies," trans. F. Engin, in M. Fuat (ed.), *NazımHikmetRan*. Available online: http://nazimhikmetran.biz/english/pages/siirl eri/ellerinize_ve_yalana.shtml (accessed February 2, 2023).

Hikmet, N. (2002), "Hasret" [1st print 1930], in G. Turan (ed.), *835 Satır – Şiirler 1*, 107, İstanbul: Yapı Kredi Yayınları.

Hikmet, N. (2007), "Nazım'ın İlk Kez Yayınlanan Şiiri: 'Dört Güvercin,'" *Bianet*, December 27. Available online: https://bianet.org/haber/nazim-in-ilk-kez-yayinla nan-siiri-dort-guvercin-103836 (accessed May 22, 2022).

Hobsbawm, E. (2001), *Bandits*, London: Weidenfeld & Nicholson.

Holt, E. (2019), "Net Food Importer Turkey Grapples with Challenges of Food Self-Sufficiency," *Inter Press Service*, November 18. Available online: http://www.ipsnews.net/2019/11/net-food-importer-turkey-grapples-challenges-food-self-sufficiency/ (accessed February 8, 2020).

Horden, P., and N. Purcell (2000), *The Corrupting Sea: A Study of Mediterranean History*, London: Blackwell Publishers.

Huebener, P. (2020), *Nature's Broken Clocks: Reimagining Time in the Face of the Environmental Crisis*, Regina: University of Regina Press.

Husserl, E. (2012), *Ideas: General Introduction to Pure Phenomenology*, trans. W. R. Boyce Gibson, London: Routledge.

Iğsız, A. (2018), *Humanism in Ruins: Entangled Legacies of the Greek-Turkish Population Exchange*, Stanford: Stanford University Press.

İklim Meselesi (2017), [Film] Dir. Altuğ Gültan, Turkey: Cornerman.

Ilgaz, R. (1999), *Yıldız Karayel* [1st print 1981], İstanbul: Çınar Yayınları.

İnalcık, H. (2014), "The Yörüks: Their Origins, Expansion and Economic Rule," *Cedrus II*: 467–95.

İnan, A. (2012), "Umay İlahesi Hakkında/Über die Göttin *umay*," trans. M. Kemaloğlu, *Alevilik-Bektaşilik Araştırmaları Dergisi* 6: 97–101. Available online: http://turkoloji.cu.edu.tr/pdf/inan_umay_ilahesi.pdf (accessed March 8, 2020).

Iovino, S. (2013), "Introduction: Mediterranean Ecocriticism, or, a Blueprint for Cultural Amphibians," *Ecozon@: European Journal of Literature, Culture and Environment* 4 (2): 1–14.

Iovino, S., and S. Oppermann, eds. (2014), *Material Ecocriticism*, Bloomington: Indiana University Press.

Işın, E. (2017), "Altın Çağından Sürgün Çağına Sokak Köpeklerinin Trajik Öyküsü," interview by N. Çelik, İstanbul Araştırmaları Enstitüsü Blog, March 20. Available online: https://blog.iae.org.tr/sergiler/altin-cagindan-surgun-cagina-sokak-kopek lerinin-trajik-oykusu (accessed March 22, 2019).

Islar, M. (2012), "Privatised Hydropower Development in Turkey: A Case of Water Grabbing?," *Water Alternatives* 5 (2): 376–91.

Johns-Putra, A. (2019), *Climate Change and the Contemporary Novel*, Cambridge: Cambridge University Press.

Jue, M. (2020), *Wild Blue Media: Thinking through Seawater*, Durham: Duke University Press.

Kabaağaçlı, C. Ş. (Halikarnas Balıkçısı) (1946), *Aganta Burina Burinata*, İstanbul: AKBA Kitabevi.

Kabaağaçlı, C. Ş. (Halikarnas Balıkçısı) (1947), "Ege'nin Öfkesi," in *Merhaba Akdeniz*, 100–4, İzmir: Doğanlar Basımevi.

Kabaağaçlı, C. Ş. (Halikarnas Balıkçısı) (1962), *Uluç Reis*, İstanbul: Remzi Kitabevi.

Kabaağaçlı, C. Ş. (Halikarnas Balıkçısı) (1966), *Turgut Reis*, İstanbul: Altın Kitaplar.

Kabaağaçlı, C. Ş. (Halikarnas Balıkçısı) (1969), *Deniz Gurbetçileri*, Ankara: Bilgi Yayınevi.

Kabaağaçlı, C. Ş. (Halikarnas Balıkçısı) (1971), *Anadolu'nun Sesi*, İstanbul: Yeditepe Yayınları.

Kabaağaçlı, C. Ş. (Halikarnas Balıkçısı) (2017), *Mavi Sürgün* [1st print 1961], İstanbul: Remzi Kitabevi.

Kabaağaçlı, C. Ş. (Halikarnas Balıkçısı) (2018), *Aganta! Burina! Burinata!*, trans. G. Key, İstanbul: Ege Yayınları/Provezza Sailing Team.

Kadirbeyoğlu, Z. (2010), "In the Land of Ostriches: Developmentalism, Environmental Degradation and Forced Migration in Turkey," in T. Afifi and J. Jager (eds.), *Environment, Forced Migration, and Social Vulnerability*, 223–34, Cham: Springer.

Kanık, O. V. (2005), "Ayrılış" [1st print 1949], in O. Tapınç (ed.), *Bütün Şiirleri*, 123, İstanbul: Yapı Kredi Yayınları.

Kara Atlas (2015), [Film] Dir. Umut Vedat, Turkey.

Karabulut, T. (1971), *Çepel Dünya*, İstanbul: Ararat Yayınevi.

Karakatsanis, L. (2014), *Turkish-Greek Relations: Rapprochement, Civil Society and the Politics of Friendship*, London: Routledge.

Karaosmanoğlu, Y. K. (1932), *Yaban*, İstanbul: Muallim Ahmet Halit Kütüphanesi.

Karasu, B. (1979), *Göçmüş Kediler Bahçesi*, İstanbul: Milliyet Yayınları.

Karasu, B. (1991), *Kısmet Büfesi* [1st print 1982], İstanbul: Metis Yayınları.

Karasu, B. (1994a), "Bir Hayvanla Yaşamak," in S. Dolanoğlu (ed.), *Ne Kitapsız Ne Kedisiz (Denemeler I)*, 59–67, İstanbul: Metis Yayınları.

Karasu, B. (1994b) "Cinayetin Azı Çoğu," in S. Dolanoğlu (ed.), *Ne Kitapsız Ne Kedisiz (Denemeler I)*, 51–8, İstanbul: Metis Yayınları.

Karasu, B. (1994c), *Night*, trans. G. Gün, Baton Rouge: Louisiana State University Press.

Karasu, B. (2003), *The Garden of Departed Cats*, trans. A. Aji, New York: New Directions.
Kasaba, R. (2013), "Nomads and Tribes in the Ottoman Empire," in C. Woodhead (ed.), *The Ottoman World*, 11–24, London: Routledge.
Kelley, C. P., S. Mohtadi, M. A. Cane, R. Seager, and Y. Kushnir (2015), "Climate Change in the Fertile Crescent and Implications of the Recent Syrian Drought," *Proceedings of the National Academy of Sciences of the United States of America* 112 (11): 3241–6.
Kemal, O. (1952), *Murtaza*, İstanbul: Varlık Yayınları.
Kemal, Y. (1955), *İnce Memed 1*, İstanbul: Çağlayan Yayınevi.
Kemal, Y. (1961), *Memed, My Hawk*, trans. E. Roditi, London: Collins and Harvill Press.
Kemal, Y. (1970), *Ağrıdağı Efsanesi*, İstanbul: Cem Yayınevi.
Kemal, Y. (1971) "Yanan Ormanlarda Elli Gün" [1st print 1955], in *Bu Diyar Baştan Başa*, 337–423, İstanbul: Cem Yayınevi.
Kemal, Y. (1975), *The Legend of Ararat*, trans. H. Kemal, ill. A. Dino, London: Collins and Harvill Press.
Kemal, Y. (1976), *The Legend of the Thousand Bulls*, trans. T. Kemal, London: Collins and Harvill Press.
Kemal, Y. (1978), *Deniz Küstü*, İstanbul: Milliyet Yayınları.
Kemal, Y. (1984), *İnce Memed 3*, İstanbul: Toros Yayınları.
Kemal, Y. (1985a), "Denizler Kurudu," in *Denizler Kurudu*, 129–208, İstanbul: Toros Yayınları.
Kemal, Y. (1985b), *The Sea-Crossed Fisherman*, trans. T. Kemal, New York: George Braziller.
Kemal, Y. (1993), *Binboğalar Efsanesi* [1st print 1971], İstanbul: Toros Yayınları.
Kemal, Y. (1994), *İnce Memed 4* [1st print 1987], İstanbul: Görsel Yayınlar.
Kemal, Y. (1995), *Zulmün Artsın*, İstanbul: Can Yayınları.
Kemal, Y. (1999), *Yaşar Kemal on His Life and Art*, interview by A. Bosquet, trans. E. L. Hébert and B. Tharaud, New York: Syracuse University Press.
Kemal, Y. (2000), *Yaşar Kemal: Bir Geçiş Dönemi Romancısı*, interview by N. Gürsel, İstanbul: Everest Yayınları.
Kemal, Y. (2004a), "Bebek," in A. Sezen and T. Erdoğan (eds.), *Sarı Sıcak* [1st print 1952], 17–43, İstanbul: Yapı Kredi Yayınları.
Kemal, Y. (2004b), "Ekin," in A. Sezen and T. Erdoğan (eds.), *Sarı Sıcak* [1st print 1952], 159–62, İstanbul: Yapı Kredi Yayınları.
Kemal, Y. (2009), *Binbir Çiçekli Bahçe*, İstanbul: Yapı Kredi Yayınları.
Kemal, Y. (2011), "Anadolu Babamızın Çiftliği Değil," *Radikal*, April 13. Available online: http://www.radikal.com.tr/hayat/anadolu-babamizin-ciftligi-degil-1045959/ (accessed August 8, 2019).
Keskin, B. (2002), "Yeryüzü Karşısında Konuşmak Ne Zor!," interview by P. Özer, *Cumhuriyet Kitap*, April 30. Available online: https://www.metiskitap.com/catalog/interview/2934 (accessed July 4, 2018).

Keskin, B. (2005), *Yeryüzü Halleri* [1st print 2002], in *Kim Bağışlayacak Beni*, 7–40, İstanbul: Metis Yayınları.
Keskin, B. (2006), "Tıpkı Hayat Gibi İşte," interview by P. Özer, *Kitap-lık* 96: 34–9.
Keskin, B. (2013), *& Silk & Love & Flame*, trans. G. Messo, London: Arc Publications.
Kıyafet, H. (1969), *Gominis İmam*, Ankara: İmece Yayınları.
Koray, Y. (1962), *Deniz Ağacı*, İstanbul: Remzi Kitabevi.
Köse, M. (2010), *Mükellefiyet*, İstanbul: Doğan Kitap.
Köse, M. (2012), *Göl Dağı*, İstanbul: Doğan Kitap.
Köse, M. (2014), *Büyük Yürüyüş*, İstanbul: Doğan Kitap.
Koyuncu, K. (2020), "'Atın Beni Denizlere,' 'Hey Gidi Karadeniz,'" *Kazım Koyuncu Şarkı Sözleri*, KuzeyMavi. Available online: https://kuzeymavi.com/kazim-koyuncu-sarki-sozleri/ (accessed March 1, 2021).
Kristeva, J. (1982), *Powers of Horror: An Essay on Abjection*, New York: Columbia University Press.
Kudret, C. (1976), "Mavi Sürgün Olayı," in *Nesin Vakfı Edebiyat Yıllığı 1976*, 567–92, İstanbul: Tekin Yayınları.
Kurnaz, L. (2011), "Nükleer Santral Gerçekten Gerekli Mi?," *T24*, March 17. Available online: https://t24.com.tr/yazarlar/bilinmeyen/nukleer-santral-gercekten-gerekli-mi (accessed July 4, 2020).
Kurnaz, L. (2019), "Çernobil ve Yeni Enerji Kaynakları: Ne Nükleer Ne Termik, Çare Rüzgar ve Güneş!," interview by D. Kaynak, *Tarih*, July. Available online: https://tarihdergi.com/cernobil-ve-yeni-enerji-kaynaklari/ (accessed August 4, 2021).
Leopold, A. (1949), *A Sand County Almanac*, Oxford: Oxford University Press.
Librandi, M. (2018), *Writing by Ear: Clarice Lispector and the Aural Novel*, Toronto: University of Toronto Press.
Livaneli, Z. (2008), *Son Ada*, İstanbul: Doğan Kitap.
Livaneli, Z. (2022), *The Last Island*, trans. A. A. Şahin, New York: Other Press.
Lüfer-Boğaz'ın Prensi/Bluefish-Prince of Bosphorus (2017), [Film] Dir. Mert Gökalp, Turkey.
Maden (1978), [Film] Dir. Yavuz Özkan, Turkey: Maden Film.
Mahşerin Atlıları (2000), [Film] Dir. and Cam. Haluk Cecan, Turkey: TRT.
Makal, M. (1950), *Bizim Köy*, İstanbul: Varlık Yayınları.
Makal, M. (1979), *Köy Enstitüleri ve Ötesi*, İstanbul: Çağdaş Yayınları.
Malay, M. (2018), *The Figure of the Animal in Modern and Contemporary Poetry*, New York: Palgrave.
Margosyan, M. (1992), *Gavur Mahallesi*, İstanbul: Aras Yayınları.
Margosyan, M. (2006), *Tespih Taneleri*, İstanbul: Aras Yayınları.
Margosyan, M. (2011), *Kirveme Mektuplar* [1st print 2006], İstanbul: Aras Yayınları.
"Marmara Ölürse, Karadeniz de Ölür" (2021), *Yeşil Gazete*, June 4. Available online: https://yesilgazete.org/tbmm-iklim-arastirmalari-komisyonu-marmara-olurse-karadeniz-de-olur/ (accessed August 4, 2023).
Martinelli, M. (2010), *Rumore di Acque*, Spoleto (PG): Editoria e Spettacolo.

Matur, B. (2015), *Son Dağ*, İstanbul: Everest Yayınları.
Matvejević, P. (1999), *Mediterranean: A Cultural Landscape*, trans. M. Heim, Los Angeles: University of California Press.
McHugh, S. (2009), "Animal Farm's Lessons for Literary (and) Animal Studies," *Humanimalia: A Journal of Human-Animal Interface Studies* 1 (1): 24–39.
Messo, G. (2009), "Introduction: Cartography of the Turkish Avant-Garde: Mapping the *İkinci Yeni*," in G. Messo (ed. and trans.), *İkinci Yeni: The Turkish Avant-Garde*, 10–15, Exeter: Shearsman Books.
Millas, H. (2005), *Türk ve Yunan Romanlarında "Öteki" ve Kimlik*, İstanbul: İletişim Yayınları.
Miraç, Y. (1988), *Karadeniz Hırçın Kız*, İstanbul: Yeni Türkü Şiir Yayınları.
Miraç, Y. (2015), *Kömürkirchen*, İstanbul: Ayrıntı Yayınları.
Mirzabaev, A., J. Wu, J. Evans, F. Garcia-Oliva, I. A. G. Hussein, M. H. Iqbal, J. Kimutai, T. Knowles, F. Meza, D. Nedjraoui, F. Tena, M. Türkeş, R. J. Vazquez, and M. Veltz (2019), "Desertification," in *Climate Change and Land*, Special Report by the Intergovernmental Panel on Climate Change (IPCC), August. Available online: https://www.ipcc.ch/srccl/chapter/chapter-3/ (accessed January 26, 2023).
Moe, A. M. (2013), "Toward Zoopoetics: Rethinking Whitman's 'Original Energy,'" *Walt Whitman Quarterly Review* 31: 1–7.
Moe, A. M. (2014), *Zoopoetics: Animals and the Making of Poetry*, Lanham: Lexington.
Monani, S., and J. Adamson (2017), "Introduction: Cosmovisions, Ecocriticism and Indigenous Studies," in S. Monani and J. Adamson (eds.), *Ecocriticism and Indigenous Studies: Conversations from Earth to Cosmos*, 1–19, New York: Routledge.
Montaigne, M. de (1957), "An Apology for Raymond Sebond," in *The Complete Works of Montaigne*, trans. D. M. Frame, bk. 2, chap. 12, 331, Stanford: Stanford University Press.
Moran, B. (2003), *Türk Romanına Eleştirel Bir Bakış 2: Sabahattin Ali'den Yusuf Atılgan'a*, İstanbul: İletişim Yayınları.
Morton, T. (2007), *Ecology without Nature: Rethinking Environmental Aesthetics*, Cambridge, MA: Harvard University Press.
Morton, T. (2013), *Hyperobjects: Philosophy and Ecology After the End of the World*, Minneapolis: University of Minnesota Press.
Morton, T. (2016), *Dark Ecology*, New York: Columbia University Press.
Muammer, A. (2015), *İstanbul Balık Kültürü*, İstanbul: Küre Yayınları.
Mungan, M. (1992), "Kadırga," in *Yaz Geçer*, 51–69, İstanbul: Metis Yayınları.
Nesin, A. (1957), "Boğaziçi Hastalığı," in *Deliler Boşandı*, 36–41, İstanbul: Nesin Yayınevi.
Nietzsche, F. (1999), *Thus Spake Zarathustra*, trans. T. Common, New York: Dover Publications, Inc.
1915 Tehcir Yolu (2015), [Film] Dir. Nazım Alpman, Turkey.
Nixon, R. (2013), *Slow Violence and the Environmentalism of the Poor*, Cambridge, MA: University of Harvard Press.

Notti, E., and M. Treu (2018), "Sailors on Board, Heroes *en Route*: From the Aegean World to Modern Stage," in R. R. Guardiola (ed.), *The Ancient Mediterranean Sea in Modern Visual and Performing Arts*, 121–43, London: Bloomsbury Academic.

Odman, A. (2019), "Asbest Tehlike Haritası: 'Ortalık Toz Duman,'" *Beyond İstanbul*, November. Available online: https://beyond.istanbul/asbest-tehlike-haritası-orta lık-toz-duman-d1fc2af8bb13#_ftn12 (accessed October 3, 2019).

Odyan, Y. (1919), "Anidzyal Dariner," *Jamanak*, İstanbul.

Odyan, Y. (2009), *Accursed Years: My Exile and Return from Der Zor, 1914–1919*, trans. A. S. Melkonian, London: Gomidas Institute.

Odyan, Y. (2022), *Lanetli Yıllar: İstanbul'dan Der Zor'a Sürgün ve Geri Dönüş Hikayem 1914–1919*, trans. S. Malhasyan and K. Taşkıran, İstanbul: Aras Yayıncılık and Kor Kitap.

Öğüt Yazıcıoğlu, Ö. (2022), *Shamanism in the Contemporary Novel: Stories Beyond Nature-Culture Divide*, Lanham: Lexington.

Öğüt Yazıcıoğlu, Ö., and E. Hamzaçebi (2019), "Writing Beyond the Species Boundary: Bilge Karasu's *The Garden of Departed Cats* and Sema Kaygusuz's *Wine and Gold*," in H. Gürses and I. E. Howison (eds.), *Animals, Plants, and Landscapes: An Ecology of Turkish Literature and Film*, 127–56, New York: Routledge.

Only One World Left (2019), [Film] Dir. Alican Abacı, Turkey: Aw Film Production.

Oppermann, S., ed. (2012), *Ekoeleştiri: Çevre ve Edebiyat*, Ankara: Phoenix.

Oppermann, S. (2019), "Storied Seas and Living Metaphors in the Blue Humanities," *Configurations* 27 (4): 443–61.

Oppermann, S., U. Özdağ, N. Özkan, and S. Slovic, eds. (2011), *The Future of Ecocriticism: New Horizons*, Newcastle Upon Tyne: Cambridge Scholars.

Oppermann, S., and S. Akıllı, eds. (2021), *Turkish Ecocriticism: From Neolithic to Contemporary Timescapes*, Lanham: Lexington.

Orfoz 'Resifin Efesi' (2021), [Film] Dir. Mert Gökalp, Turkey.

Orwell, G. (1945), *Animal Farm: A Fairy Story*, London: Secker & Warburg.

Öymen, O. (2014), "Kanal İstanbul Projesinin Dış Politika ve Uluslararası Hukuk Boyutu," in M. Sarıkaya (ed.), *Çılgın Proje Kanal İstanbul*, 55–73, İstanbul: Kaynak Yayınları.

Özdağ, U. (2008), "Reading Yaşar Kemal's *The Sea-Crossed Fisherman* in the Year of the Dolphin," *Concentric: Literary and Cultural Studies* 34 (1): 45–74.

Özdağ, U. (2009), "An Essay on Ecocriticism in 'the Century of Restoring the Earth,'" *Journal of American Studies of Turkey* 30: 125–42.

Özdağ, U. (2014), *Çevreci Eleştiriye Giriş: Doğa, Kültür, Edebiyat*, Ankara: Ürün Yayınları.

Özdağ, U., and G. Alpaslan, eds. (2019), *Anadolu Turnaları: Biyoloji, Kültür, Koruma/ Anatolian Cranes: Biology, Culture, Conservation*, Ankara: Ürün Yayınları.

Özdemir, U. (2017), "Alevilerin Dışavurumu: Müzik ve Kimlik," interview by U. Tol, *Sivil Sayfalar*, March 12. Available online: https://www.sivilsayfalar.org/2017/03/12/ alevilerin-disavurumu-muzik-kimlik/ (accessed August 16, 2021).

Özsoy, D. (2012), "Bir *Flâneuse*ün Portresi: George Sand," in H. Köse (ed.), *Flanör Düşünce*, 303–20, İstanbul: Ayrıntı Yayınları.

Özveren, E. (2015), "Writing with the Mediterranean in the Twentieth Century: The Advent of the Fisherman of Halicarnassus," *Mediterranean Studies* 23 (2): 195–222.

Pamuk, O. (1998), *Benim Adım Kırmızı*, İstanbul: İletişim Yayınları.

Pamuk, O. (2002a), *Kar*, İstanbul: İletişim Yayınları.

Pamuk, O. (2002b), *My Name Is Red*, trans. E. M. Göknar, New York: Vintage.

Pamuk, O. (2004), *Snow*, trans. M. Freely, New York: Vintage International.

Pekin, F., and B. Dinç (2004), *Efsanevi Başkent İstanbul*, İstanbul: İş Bankası Kültür Yayınları.

Perec, G. (1990), "A Man Asleep," in *Things: A Story of the Sixties and A Man Asleep*, trans. D. Bellos and A. Leak, 127–224, Boston: David R. Godine.

Perker, A. (2018), "Günübirlikçiler," in K. Kutlukhan and A. Tohumcu (eds.), *İstanbul 2099*, 15–35, İstanbul: Doğan Egmont Yayıncılık.

Picchione, J. (2016), *The New Avant-Garde in Italy: Theoretical Debate and Poetic Practices*, Toronto: University of Toronto Press.

Rancière, J. (2010), *Dissensus: On Politics and Aesthetics*, trans. S. Corcoran, London: Continuum.

Rasim, A. (1954), "Vay Lüfer Vay," *Balık ve Balıkçılık* 2 (1): 18.

Remlinger, P. (1932), "Les chiens de Constantinople, leur vie, leur mort," *Mercure de France* 817 (43e-237): 24–70.

Rigby, K. (2004), *Topographies of the Sacred: The Poetics of Place in European Romanticism*, Charlottesville: University of Virginia Press.

Rowland, L. (2019), "Indigenous Temporality and Climate Change in Alexis Wright's *Carpentaria* (2006)," *Journal of Postcolonial Writing* 55 (4): 541–54.

Sabuncuoğlu, K. (2021), *Sessiz Çığlık*, photograph. Available online: https://kerimsabuncuoglu.com/ (accessed February 3, 2019).

Şahin, Ü. (2016), "Warming a Frozen Policy: Challenges to Turkey's Climate Politics After Paris," *Turkish Policy Quarterly*, September 23. Available online: http://turkishpolicy.com/article/818/warming-a-frozen-policy-challenges-to-turkeys-climate-politics-after-paris (accessed May 5, 2020).

Şahin, Ü. (2019), "Oya Baydar'dan Huzursuz Edici Bir Gelecek Öngörüsü: *Köpekli Çocuklar Gecesi*," *Yeşil Gazete*, November 8. Available online: https://yesilgazete.org/oya-baydardan-huzursuz-edici-bir-gelecek-ongorusu-kopekli-cocuklar-gecesi/ (accessed March 22, 2020).

Şahin, Ü. (2020), "The Politics of Environment and Climate Change," in A. Özerdem and M. Whiting (eds.), *The Routledge Handbook of Turkish Politics*, 177–89, London: Routledge.

Şahin, Ü. (2022), "[COP27] Ümit Şahin: Türkiye'nin Açıkladığı, Azaltım Değil Artış Hedefi," interview by B. Ünlü, *Yeşil Gazete*, November 15. Available online: https://yesilgazete.org/cop27-umit-sahin-turkiyenin-acikladigi-azaltim-degil-artis-hedefi/ (accessed December 1, 2022).

Sargent, L. T. (2001), "US Eutopias in the 1980s and 1990s: Self-fashioning in a World of Multiple Identities," in P. Spinozzi (ed.), *Utopianism/Literary Utopias and National Cultural Identities: A Comparative Perspective*, 221–32, Cotepra/U of Bologna.

Şatıroğlu, Â. V. (1971), "Kara Toprak," in Ü. Y. Oğuzcan (ed.), *Dostlar Beni Hatırlasın*, 145–7, İstanbul: Türkiye İş Bankası Kültür Yayınları.

Sayar, A. (1970), *Yılkı Atı*, İstanbul: E Yayınları.

Saydam, C. (2014), "Çılgın Proje Nedir, Neden Olmaz?," in M. Sarıkaya (ed.), *Çılgın Proje Kanal İstanbul*, 13–54, İstanbul: Kaynak Yayınları.

Schick, I. C. (2010), "İstanbul'da 1910'da Gerçekleşen Büyük Köpek İtlafı: Bir Mekan Üzerinde Çekişme Vakası," *Toplumsal Tarih* 200: 22–33.

Schlegel, F. (1971), "Athenaeum Fragments," in *Friedrich Schlegel's Lucinde and Fragments*, trans. P. Firchow, 161–240, Minneapolis: University of Minnesota Press.

Schwartzstein, P. (2016), "The Black Sea Is Dying, and War Might Push It Over the Edge," *Smithsonian Magazine*, May. Available online: https://www.smithsonianmag.com/science-nature/black-sea-dying-and-war-might-push-it-over-edge-180959053/ (accessed October 3, 2019).

Şen, Ö. L. (2013), *A Holistic View of Climate Change and Its Impacts in Turkey*, İstanbul: İstanbul Policy Center-Sabancı University-Stiftung Mercator Initiative. Available online: http://ipc.sabanciuniv.edu/en/wp-content/uploads/2012/09/A-Holistic-View-of-Climate-Change-and-Its-Impacts-in-Turkey.pdf (accessed February 14, 2018).

Sessiz Dünyada Gezintiler (1991), [Film] Dir. Orhan Tuncel, Cam. Haluk Cecan, Turkey: TRT.

Seventh National Communication of Turkey Under the UNFCCC (2018), Republic of Turkey Ministry of Environment and Urbanization. Available online: https://unfccc.int/sites/default/files/resource/496715_Turkey-NC7-1-7th%20National%20Communication%20of%20Turkey.pdf (accessed April 1, 2019).

Seyfettin, Ö. (1918), *Yalnız Efe*, İstanbul: Altın Kitaplar Yayınevi.

Seyir Günlüğü (1988), [Film] Dir. Orhan Tuncel, Cam. Haluk Cecan, Turkey: TRT.

Sezer, S. (1999), "Köy Kökenli Emekçilerin Yazarı," *Varlık* 1106: 37–44.

Sharpe, K. B. (2018), "Hellenism without Greeks: The Use (and Abuse) of Classical Antiquity in Turkish Nationalist Literature," *Journal of the Ottoman and Turkish Studies Association* 5 (1): 169–90.

Şık, B. (2018), "Açlık Sorunu Nereye Gidiyor, Biz Nerede Duruyoruz?," *Gazete Duvar*, October 16. Available online: https://www.gazeteduvar.com.tr/yazarlar/2018/10/16/549299/ (accessed February 2, 2019).

Sofuoğlu, M. (2019), "How Istanbul's Wounded Golden Horn Became Turkey's Success Story," *TRT World News Magazine*, March. Available online: https://www.trtworld.com/magazine/how-istanbul-s-wounded-golden-horn-became-turkey-s-success-story-24597 (accessed August 22, 2020).

Sofya, E. (2014), *Dik Âlâ*, İstanbul: Yapı Kredi Yayınları.

Sofya, E. (2015), "Ekoloji ve Yazın: Elif Sofya," *cin ayşe* 14: 31.
Soysal, S. (1970), *Yürümek*, Ankara: Doğan Yayınevi.
Steinberg, P., and K. Peters (2015), "Wet Ontologies, Fluid Spaces: Giving Depth to Volume through Oceanic Thinking," *Environment and Planning D: Society and Space* 33 (2): 247–64.
Streit-Bianchi, M., M. Cimadevila, and W. Trettnak, eds. (2020), *Mare Plasticum – The Plastic Sea: Combatting Plastic Pollution Through Science and Art*, Cham: Springer.
Suny, R. G. (2015), *"They Can Live in the Desert but Nowhere Else:" A History of the Armenian Genocide*, Princeton: Princeton University Press.
Susuz Yaz (1963), [Film] Dir. Metin Erksan, Prod. Metin Erksan and Ulvi Doğan, Turkey.
Tanpınar, A. H. (1949), *Huzur*, İstanbul: Remzi Kitabevi.
Tanpınar, A. H. (1961), *Saatleri Ayarlama Enstitüsü*, İstanbul: Remzi Kitabevi.
Tanpınar, A. H. (2008), *A Mind at Peace*, trans. E. Göknar, Brooklyn: Archipelago.
Tanpınar, A. H. (2013), *The Time Regulation Institute*, trans. M. Freely and A. Dawe, New York: Penguin.
Tekin, L. (1984), *Berci Kristin Çöp Masalları*, İstanbul: Adam Yayıncılık.
Tekin, L. (1993), *Berji Kristin: Tales from the Garbage Hills*, trans. R. Christie and S. Paker, New York: Marion Boyars.
Tekin, L. (2004), *Unutma Bahçesi*, İstanbul: Everest Yayınları.
Tekin, L. (2009), *Rüyalar ve Uyanışlar Defteri*, İstanbul: Doğan Egmont Yayıncılık.
Tekin, L. (2014), "Yazara Dil Gerekmez," interview by H. A. Toptaş, *Egoist Okur*, January 5. Available online: http://egoistokur.com/ latife-tekin-ve-hasan-ali-toptas-bulusmasi-yazara-dil-gerekmez/ (accessed March 3, 2018).
Temelkuran, E. (2008), *'Ağrı'nın Derinliği*, İstanbul: Everest Yayınları.
Tharaud, B. (1999), "Introduction," in *Yaşar Kemal on His Life and Art*, by Y. Kemal, trans. E. L. Hébert and B. Tharaud, xiii–xxv, New York: Syracuse University Press.
Tharaud, B. (2012), "Yaşar Kemal, Son of Homer," *Texas Studies in Literature and Language* 54 (4): 563–90.
The Book of Dede Korkut (1974), trans. G. Lewis, Harmondsworth: Penguin Books.
Timperley, J. (2018), "The Carbon Brief Profile: Turkey," *Carbon Brief*, May 3. Available on: https://www.carbonbrief.org/carbon-brief-profile-turkey (accessed May 3, 2019).
Tohum/Seeds (2018), [Film] Dir. Sevinç Baloğlu, Turkey: SUFİLM.
Tonguç, İ. H. (1939), *Canlandırılacak Köy*, İstanbul: Remzi Kitabevi.
Tsanov, R., ed. (2007), *Economic Development and Security in the Black Sea Region*, CSIS New European Democracies Project Report, Washington, D.C. Available online: https://csis-website-prod.s3.amazonaws.com/s3fs-public/legacy_files/files/media/csis/pubs/070103_blacksea.pdf (accessed July 1, 2020).
"Turkey: Main Destination for EU's Waste" (2020), *Eurostat*, April. Available online: https://ec.europa.eu/eurostat/web/products-eurostat-news/-/DDN-20200 416-1 (accessed December 8, 2022).

"Türkiye" (2023), *Climate Action Tracker*. Available online: https://climateactiontracker.org/countries/turkey/ (accessed May 8, 2023).

Uğur, Z. (2016), Review of *Mémoires du génocide arménien: Héritage Traumatique et Travail Analytique*, by V. and J. Altounian, *Journal of the Ottoman and Turkish Studies Association* 3 (1): 208–10.

Uğurtaş, S. (2020), "Why Turkey Became Europe's Garbage Dump," *Politico*, September. Available online: https://www.politico.eu/article/why-turkey-became-europes-garbage-dump/ (accessed December 8, 2019).

Ukray, M. (2021), *Çöl Gezegen*, E-Kitap Yayıncılık.

Ünal, E. (2019), "Nereden Çıktı Bu İklim Aktivistleri?," *Açık Radyo*, November 1. Available online: https://acikradyo.com.tr/iklimacil/nereden-cikti-bu-iklim-aktivistleri (accessed December 17, 2019).

Ünaydın, R. E. (1938), *Boğaziçi: Yakından*, İstanbul: Çituri Biraderler Basımevi.

Uzuner, B. (2012), *Uyumsuz Defne Kaman'ın Maceraları: Su*, İstanbul: Everest Yayınları.

Uzuner, B. (2014), *The Adventures of Misfit Defne Kaman: Water*, trans. C. Frost and A. Dawe, İstanbul: Everest Yayınları.

Uzuner, B. (2015), *Uyumsuz Defne Kaman'ın Maceraları: Toprak*, İstanbul: Everest Yayınları.

Uzuner, B. (2018a), *The Adventures of Misfit Defne Kaman: Earth*, trans. A. Boord, İstanbul: Everest Yayınları.

Uzuner, B. (2018b), *Uyumsuz Defne Kaman'ın Maceraları: Hava*, İstanbul: Everest Yayınları.

Uzuner, B. (2020), *The Adventures of Misfit Defne Kaman: Air*, trans. P. Arıner, İstanbul: Everest Yayınları.

Uzuner, B. (2021), "As the Climate and World Change: Climate Fiction in Literature," *Bianet*, August 19. Available online: https://bianet.org/5/101/248987-climate-fiction-in-the-literature (accessed December 22, 2022).

Uzuner, B. (2023), *Uyumsuz Defne Kaman'ın Maceraları: Ateş*, İstanbul: Everest Yayınları.

Varol, K. (2014a), *Haw*, İstanbul: İletişim Yayınları.

Varol, K. (2014b), "Roman ve Toplumsal Sorunlar," Cevdet Kudret Edebiyat Ödül Töreni, November 8. Available online: http://www.cevdetkudretodulleri.com/arsiv/2014-2/ (accessed October 3, 2018).

Varol, K. (2019), *Wûf*, trans. D. Rogers, Austin: University of Texas Press.

Vassaf, G. (2014), *İstanbul'da Kedi*, İstanbul: Yapı Kredi Yayınları.

Vlastos, Y. (2013), *Baba Konuşabilir Miyim?* İstanbul: İstos Yayın.

Walker, W. (1992), "Triple-Tiered Migration in *The Book of Dede Korkut*," in J. Whitlark and W. Aycock (eds.), *The Literature of Emigration and Exile*, 23–32, Texas: Texas Tech University Press.

Weiwei, A. (2016), "Odyssey," *Ai Weiwei On Porcelain*, Sabancı University Sakıp Sabancı Museum, 2018, İstanbul.

Weyler, R. (2017), "The Ocean Plastic Crisis," *Greenpeace International*, October 15. Available online: https://www.greenpeace.org/international/story/11871/the-ocean-plastic-crisis/ (accessed March 6, 2022).

"What's GAP?" (2015), Southeastern Anatolia Project Regional Development Administration, Republic of Turkey Ministry of Industry and Technology. Available online: http://www.gap.gov.tr/en/ (accessed July 2, 2018).

Wolfe, C. (2003), *Animal Rites: American Culture, The Discourse of Species, and Posthumanist Theory*, Chicago: University of Chicago Press.

Wolfe, C., L. Cole, D. Landry, B. Boeher, R. Nash, E. Fudge, and R. Markley (2011), "Speciecism, Identity Politics, and Ecocriticism: A Conversation with Humanists and Posthumanists," *The Eighteenth Century* 52 (1): 87–106.

Wright, A. (2001), "A Family Document," in M. Halligan (ed.), *Storykeepers*, 223–40, Potts Point: Duffy & Snellgrove.

Yazıcı, N. (2011), "Halikarnas Balıkçı'sının Yazınsal Eserlerinde Türk Kimliğine Dair Söylemler," *Türkbilig* 22: 163–70.

Yılanların Öcü (1962), [Film] Dir. Metin Erksan, Prod. Nusret İkbal, Turkey.

Yıldırım, M. (2019), "Şiddet ile İhtimam Arasında: *Dört Ayaklı Şehir* ve İstanbul'un Köpeksizleştirilmesi," interview by İ. Oranlı, *Cogito* 93: 220–37.

Yol (1982), [Film] Writ. Yılmaz Güney, Dir. Şerif Gören, Prod. Edi Hubschmid and K. L. Puldi, Turkey and Switzerland: Güney Film and Cactus Film A.G.

Yoldaş, P. (2015), "Ecosystems of Excess," in H. Davis and E. Turpin (eds.), *Art in the Anthropocene: Encounters among Aesthetics, Politics, Environments and Epistemologies*, 359–70, London: Open Humanities Press. Available online: http://openhumanitiespress.org/books/download/Davis-Turpin_2015_Art-in-the-Anthropocene.pdf (accessed March 1, 2020).

Index

Abacı, Alican 39, 44 n.37
Abasıyanık, Sait Faik 9, 11, 32–4
Abdal-é-Zeyniki 101. *See also dengbêj*
abjection 141–2. *See also* Kristeva, Julia
absent referent 129. *See also* Adams, Carol J.
Açık Radyo (Open Radio) 55–6
activism
   climate 55–6, 59, 68, 70–6
   environmental 55–6, 59
   political 49
   youth 47, 70–7
Adalet ve Kalkınma Partisi (Justice and Development Party) 21, 55–7
Adams, Carol J. 129. *See also* absent referent
Adana 111, 113
Aegean
   Region 58
   Sea 1–4, 7–9, 13, 22, 25–35, 43 n.23, 115–17
Agamben, Giorgio 137
Ağaoğlu, Adalet 120 n.3
agency
   animal 67, 132, 136, 139–40, 145
   human 15, 37, 90, 133, 139–40
   of matter 12, 17, 35–6
   of the natural world 65, 67
agriculture 48–52, 59, 63, 69, 71
   history of 48, 62, 68–9
   soilless 68
Akçam, Taner 108
Alaimo, Stacy 14–16, 36, 39–40. *See also* transcorporeality
Ali, Sabahattin 99
allegory 45, 131–4
Altounian, Vahram 90, 107, 112–14
analogy 51, 104, 146
Anatolia 1, 4, 25, 28–32, 46–54, 59–69, 81, 89–93, 99–101, 104, 107, 110, 114, 117–19, 130, 134
   Central 48, 52–3, 58, 91, 100, 107, 110
   Eastern 52, 90–1, 106–7, 109–11
   Northern 58, 62, 99
   Southern 16, 27, 90, 100, 110
   Southeastern 58, 61, 91, 94, 97, 106, 110, 130
Anatolian Humanism 28. *See also* Blue Anatolianism
ancestral wisdom 47, 62
Anday, Melih Cevdet 28, 43 n.26
animal
   allegory 131–4
   alterity 5, 126–8, 135–7, 139–44, 154, 159, 161–2
   gaze 135–6, 147, 161
   human-animal 4, 5, 13, 126–7, 137, 151, 161
   humanimal 5, 127, 139, 142, 154, 156, 161
   life 3, 5, 127, 129, 131, 134, 156
   marine 36–8, 61
   representation 5, 127, 132, 136
   rights 75, 130, 153
   slaughter 128–9, 155
   sounds 131–2, 149–50, 156–61
   street 5, 128–33
animism 64, 67
animot 126. *See also* Derrida, Jacques
Ankara 56, 82 n.2, 125
Antep 105, 113
Anthropocene 37–8, 73, 78
anthropocentrism 37, 65–7, 125–7
Apaydın, Talip 49, 83 n.7
apocalypticism 78
Ararat, Mount 91, 97, 99, 101, 106–7, 114, 123 n.23, 123 n.24
archeology 27–30, 41 n.11, 48, 61–9
Armenians 3, 4, 16, 32, 61
   deportation of 90–1, 106–14
   1915 narratives 90, 108–14
   tehcir 107, 110, 123 n.27
art 10, 37–9, 124 n.40, 141
   bioart 3, 9, 37–8

Aruoba, Oruç 95
asbestos 42 n.13
Asia Minor 28–9
âşık 48, 100–1, 122 n.16
　bard 64, 101
　folk poetry/music 3, 48, 82 n.3, 92, 99–102, 106
　itinerant poet-singers 4, 89–90, 100–1, 106, 120
Atatürk Dam 59
Atay, Oğuz 121 n.11
Atılgan, Yusuf 99, 120 n.3
aurality 127, 157
　aural novel 157
　See also Librandi, Marilia
autobiography 4, 25–6, 33, 90, 107, 125, 153
　heterobiography 153
Aydın, Alper 38–9
Aziz, Nesin 11

Baccolini, Raffaella
　and Tom Moylan 71
Baloğlu, Alptekin 16–17, 42 n.12
Barad, Karen 12, 15
Başaran, Hatun Birsen 49
Başaran, Mehmet 49
Baydar, Oya 47, 54, 60, 69–82, 86, 131
Baykurt, Fakir 46, 49–54, 59, 62, 81, 83
belatedness 4
　of climate action 45–7, 54, 59, 69–70, 72–7, 79, 81
　and Turkish modernity 45–6
　See also temporality
Beledian, Krikor 110–14, 124
Belge, Murat 31
Bennett, Jane 37, 39
Bergama 56
Berk, İlhan 127, 143–50, 155, 164–5
Biemann, Ursula 22
biodiversity 35, 48, 52, 69
　marine 7, 9, 13–17, 57
Birand, Hikmet 48, 82 n.2
black comedy 132
Black Sea 1–4, 5 n.1, 7–18, 20–3, 40, 47, 56
　Region 12, 38, 57, 59, 61

Blue Anatolianism 9, 25–32, 34–5. See also Anatolian Humanism
bluefish 10–11, 16
Blue Humanities 14–15
Bodrum 16, 25–7, 41 n.11
　Castle 25–6
body
　animal 19, 36–7, 140, 156
　corporeality 140, 154, 160
　embodiment 5, 15, 127, 142, 146, 149–54, 157, 160, 162
　humanimal 127
　queer 139, 142
　unnameable 127, 139, 142, 144, 154
　See also transcorporeality
Borges, Jorge Luis 136–7
Bosphorus 1, 10–1, 16–22, 34, 42 n.20, 115–6
brigand 101–6, 111
　bandit 90, 101, 104
　eşkiya 104
　outlaw 4, 89–93, 100–3, 120
Bursa 91, 108, 112–13, 129
Büyük Anadolu Yürüyüşü (The Great Anatolian March) 56

Canal İstanbul 21–3, 55
Cassano, Franco 35
Cecan, Haluk 14
Ceylan, Nuri Bilge 48
Chernobyl 57, 84 n.22. See also nuclear
Clark, Timothy 79–81, 126, 148, 162 n.2
climate
　change 45–7, 49, 52, 54–61, 68–72, 77–82
　contributing factors to 56–8
　crisis 4, 46, 54–61, 65, 68, 72, 74, 76–9, 81–2
　disaster 61, 70–3, 80–2
　fiction 4, 45–7, 50, 54, 59–61, 66, 70, 73, 76, 81–2
　impact 51, 54, 58–63, 69, 71–4, 77, 81–2
　politics 46, 54–6
　skepticism 69
Climate Action Tracker 55
coal 55–6
　-fired power plant 55–6, 58
　mining 57

Conference of the Parties (COP) 55
Çukurova 52, 92, 100–6
Cumalı, Necati 46, 49–52, 54

Dadaloğlu 92
Dardanelles 1
dark ecology 140. *See also* Morton, Timothy
decarbonization 58
DeLoughrey, Elizabeth
  and Tatiana Flores 15–16
Derrida, Jacques 126–7, 135–7, 162 n.2, 163 n.12, 165 n.23. *See also animot*
Der Zor 110–13. *See also* desert
desert 4, 24, 52, 75, 89–90, 107, 115, 120, 124 n.36
  agricultural 52, 69
  desertification 4, 50–4, 58, 68, 82
  Syrian 108–13
  See also Der Zor
Deveciyan, Karekin 16
diffraction 15
Dilovası 18
diving 14–16, 39
  sponge 25, 27, 31, 41 n.11
  See also underwater
Diyarbakır 108–9, 112, 130–1
Dolcerocca, Özen Nergis 45
drought 2, 51–61, 71, 76–8, 86 n.43
  in Syria 72, 86 n.43
Duman, Faruk 127, 130, 134–7, 142–4, 163
Dündar, Fuat 107–8
dystopia 38, 47, 60, 69, 77, 79
  climate and 47, 60, 69–71
  critical 70–1
  eco- 70, 81
  political 70

earth ethic 64, 67, 69
earthquake 2, 58, 71
eating 36, 117, 129, 138–41, 158, 164 n.17
ecocentrism, ecocentric 47, 60, 66
ecofeminism 85 n.28
economy 59
  carbon-dependent 66
  global 91, 115–16
elegy 97, 109, 133

energy 22, 46, 55–8, 61, 69
entanglement
  human-animal 137–42, 158–62
  land-sea 17, 23, 39
  natural-cultural 8, 89–90
  temporal 78–9, 81
entomology 143
environment, environmental
  degradation 4, 5, 47, 54, 60, 64, 69–71, 73, 76
  health 19
  marine 7–18, 36–9
  mobilization 46, 55–6, 59, 61, 63, 67
  and politics 4, 23, 89–91, 116
  epic 62, 74, 101
    Greek 28–9
    Kyrgyz 64–6
    Turkic 64–6
epistemology 15, 67, 145
Erbil, Leyla 121 n.3
Erhat, Azra 28–30, 43 n.25
erosion 52–3
Euphrates River 91, 111–13
extinction 5
  Rebellion 56, 74
  species 2, 13–14, 130
Eyüboğlu, Sabahattin 28

fable 125–7, 130–8
feudalism 49, 105
  landlords (*Agha*s) 102–5
film 9, 39, 48, 56–7, 68, 78, 94, 114
Fisherman of Halicarnassus 25–6, 43 n.21. *See also* Kabağaçlı
fishing 7, 9–17, 25–7, 32, 109
flood 59, 61, 69–81
food security 58, 69
forest 1, 48, 83, 91, 96–7, 102–4, 115–17, 134–6, 152
  deforestation 21, 52–4, 84 n.16
  fires 2, 52–4, 59, 61
fossil fuel 55, 57
future, futuristic 37–8, 47, 52, 54, 57–62, 68–9, 71–82

Gabudikyan, Silva 114
Garip poets 43 n.26
Garrard, Greg 127

Geçgin, Ayhan 89–99, 121 n.12
geopolitics 22, 40, 91, 114–20
Gezgin, Deniz 127, 156–61, 166
Gezi Park 55, 95–9, 121 n.7
GHG emissions 54–7
Gökalp, Mert 14–16
Golden Horn 17–20
Greece 23–31, 34–5
  Greek Orthodox Christians 30–4 (*see also* Rum)
  Turkish-Greek population exchange 31
Greenpeace 35, 55
Günday, Hakan 91, 115–20
Güney, Yılmaz 94
Günyol, Vedat 28
Gürbilek, Nurdan 95

Halkların İklim Yürüyüşü (People's Climate March) 55
Hamzaoğlu, Onur 18
Haraway, Donna 8, 139
Heidegger, Martin 165 n.26
Hesiod 28–9
Heske, Franz 53–4
Hikmet, Nazım 40 n.3, 105, 122 n.21
Hittite Empire 30, 47, 62
Hobsbawm, Eric 104
Homer 27–9
human smuggling 91, 115–19. *See also* migration
hunting 13, 61, 127, 130, 135–6, 138, 157–8
Husserl, Martin 143, 147, 165 n.26
hydroelectricity 56–7, 61, 96, 155

İkinci Yeni (The Second New) 143
İklim Haber (Climate News) 56
Ilgaz, Rıfat 12
illegibility, illegible 5, 127, 137, 142, 144, 162. *See under* poetics
Indigenous 67–8, 80
infrastructure 9, 21–3, 55, 57, 155
intergenerational
  accountability 4, 45, 77, 82
  conflict 70
  dialogue 47, 60, 64, 76
  justice 75
Intergovernmental Panel on Climate Change 58

Ionia 28–9
Iovino, Serenella 3, 24
island 13, 21, 29, 30–4, 36, 60, 70, 128
Islar, Mine 57
İstanbul 10–13, 16–23, 25, 27, 30–4, 53, 55, 60, 89, 91, 94–5, 107–8, 110, 112–13, 128–9

Jue, Melody 15

Kabaağaçlı, Cevat Şakir 25–32. *See also* Fisherman of Halicarnassus
Karakatsanis, Leonidas 31
Karasu, Bilge 125–9, 137–42, 144, 154, 158–9, 163–4
Kaş 16, 39
Kemal, Yaşar 7, 13–14, 18–20, 22–3, 46, 48–9, 51–4, 56, 59, 62, 69, 81, 90–3, 100–6
Keskin, Birhan 127, 150–4, 161
Kévorkian, Raymond H. 112
kirve 108, 123 n.29
Konya 59, 111, 113
Koray, Yaman 13
Köse, Metin 56–7
köy edebiyatı (village literature) 49, 59
köy enstitüleri (village institutes) 48–9
Kristeva, Julia 142. *See also* abjection
Kurds, Kurdish 3, 4, 33, 72, 91, 100, 106
  dengbêj 100–1, 106 (*see also* Abdal-é-Zeyniki)
  elegy 109
  language 72, 108, 131
  -Turkish conflict 97–9, 130–3
Küresel Eylem Grubu (Global Action Group) 55
Kurnaz, Levent 58
Kuzey Ormanları Savunması (Northern Forests Defense) 55
Kyoto Protocol 54

Lausanne Treaty 31
Laz 3, 12, 41 n.8
legend 65–6, 92–3, 101–2, 105–6, 136
Librandi, Marilia 157, 159. *See also* aurality; poetics
liminality 5, 127, 137, 139, 142, 144, 162

Livaneli, Zülfü 70
logos 127, 144

magic tragic 131. *See also* McHugh, Susan
Malay, Michael 143
Makal, Mahmut 49
map, mapping 1, 2, 4, 7, 30, 90–1, 107, 110, 112–13, 118–20
Mardin 61
Margosyan, Mıgırdiç 90, 107–10, 114
marine
 ecosystem 7–8, 12–20, 23, 39
 habitat 7, 9, 14, 16, 39
 life 11–20, 22–3, 27–9, 39–40
 pollution 4, 9, 14, 17–23, 35–9
 preservation 8, 9
 species 12–17, 38
Marmara
 Region 19
 Sea of 1, 4, 7–13, 17–23, 30, 32
materiality, material 64, 97, 120, 130, 152, 160
 cultural and 4, 8, 152
 and discursive 24, 155
 ecocriticism 3
 flows 9, 18, 36
 of seawater 7, 8, 11, 12, 15, 17, 22, 27–8, 40
 of waste 19, 35–9
 See also new materialism
matter
 agency of 12
 inert 17
 mobility of 39
 toxic 19, 23, 37
 waste 9, 35, 38
Matur, Bejan 97
Matvejević, Predrag 12, 24–5, 35
Mavi Yolculuk (Blue Voyage) 28–9
McHugh, Susan 131, 137. *See also* magic tragic
mecbur 105
Mediterranean
 Garbage Patch 36
 history 23–7, 31, 34
 identity 23–6
 pollution 35–40
 Region 29, 58–9
 Sea 1, 7–9, 14, 16, 23–30, 34–5, 47, 91, 102, 114–19
memoir 25, 108, 110–11, 124
metafiction 125
metamorphosis 26, 140, 142, 154, 157, 159, 161
Middle East 4, 64, 71, 91, 114, 116, 119–20
migration
 of animals 13, 16
 environmental 2, 46, 59, 73
 forced 73, 76
 internal 18, 90
 in the Mediterranean 8, 24, 114–15
 to/via Turkey 61, 91, 115–20
 undocumented 91, 115
 See also human smuggling
military 33, 92, 98, 107, 112, 134
 animals 130–2
 coups 49
 impact on the sea 35, 39, 42 n.18
 presence in the Black Sea 22
 zone 97
Ministry of Environment, Urbanization and Climate Change 54
Miraç, Yaşar 12, 57
mobility, human 89–93, 100–1, 110, 114, 118. *See also* movement
modernity 24, 27, 45–6, 73, 75, 82 n.1
Moe, Aaron 146, 150, 152. *See also* poetics
Monani, Salma
 and Joni Adamson 68
Montreux Convention 22, 42 n.17
Moran, Berna 104
more-than-human
 beings 38, 66–7, 136, 143, 154
 bodies 36
 nature 131, 144, 157
 others 16, 128
 sounds 127
 world 5, 126, 137, 142, 144, 148, 156, 162
Morton, Timothy 79–80, 89, 120, 140. *See also* dark ecology
mountain 1, 3, 4, 24, 48, 53, 56–7, 64, 76, 89–107, 111–17, 119–20, 132–4, 140, 142, 148, 152–6, 158

movement
  animal 125–6, 146, 152
  human 4, 12, 15, 39, 89–93, 95, 97–8, 100–1, 118–20 (*see also* mobility)
Muammer, Asaf 10
mucilage 20–1
Mungan, Murathan 40 n.1
Müze Gazhane (Gazhane Museum) 56, 84 n.20
mythology, mythical 8, 23, 27–9, 47, 61–7, 74, 135–6, 138–9, 156, 161

naming 142–4
  politics of 143, 155
  the unnameable 127, 139–40, 144, 154
nationalism 3, 8–9, 30–5
  transnationalism 9, 35, 116
neoliberalism 3, 47, 60, 62, 67, 69, 72
new materialism 9, 12, 39. *See also* matter
Nietzsche, Friedrich 94, 162
Nixon, Rob 72
nomadism 4, 53, 64, 68, 89–93, 100, 103
  sedentary life 64, 92–3
Northern Anatolian Mountains 1, 99
novella 134–7, 142
nuclear
  anti- 56
  Bureau of Nuclear Energy 57
  power plant 57–8, 61
  waste 58
  See also Chernobyl

Odyan, Yervant 90, 107–8, 110–12
Oghuz Turks 64, 91
Öğüt Yazıcıoğlu, Özlem 3, 63–4, 67
  and Ezgi Hamzaçebi 140–1
oil
  discharge 23, 35, 158, 160
  transit 22
onomatopoeia 131
ontology, ontological 9, 15, 138–9
Oppermann, Serpil 2, 3, 27
Ottoman Empire 30, 45, 47, 90–2, 106–8
Özdağ, Ufuk 2, 41 n.10
Özkan, Yavuz 56

palimpsest 35
Pamuk, Orhan 122 n.22, 128
pandemic 77, 81

Paris Agreement 54
pathetic fallacy 153
pharmakon 76
phenomenology 143, 147–8
  bracketing (*epoché*) 147–8, 150
plastic 8, 9, 35–40, 133
  plastisphere 36, 40
plateau 1, 48, 91, 100, 103, 106–7
poetics 5, 143, 152–3
  bodily *poiesis* 146, 149, 151 (*see also* Moe, Aaron)
  echopoetics 127, 157, 159 (*see also* Librandi, Marilia)
  of illegibility 127, 142–4, 147–8, 150
  mythopoesis 47, 62, 65
poetry 12, 57, 64, 97, 99, 126, 129, 131, 137, 143–56
pollution 4, 8, 9, 14–23, 35, 38–9, 55, 61
posthumanism, posthuman 37

Rasim, Ahmet 10
reading
  absolute 126, 143
  animals 127, 131, 143–5
  misreading 126, 153
relationality 139–40, 142
Rigby, Kate 150
river 7, 21, 57, 91, 106–7, 109, 111–13, 135, 155
Rum 3, 30–4. *See under* Greece

Sabuncuoğlu, Kerim 16
Şahin, Ümit 52, 54–8, 77
Sappho 29
Sargent, Lyman Tower 70–1
Şatıroğlu, Âşık Veysel 48, 122 n.16
Sayar, Abbas 130
Saydam, Cemal 21–2
Schick, Irvin Cemil 128
science fiction 69, 77, 78, 86 n.40
semantic
  economy 144
  extra- 157
  indeterminacy 143
  value 149
September Events (1955) 31, 33
shamanism, shamanic 47, 60–9
short story 11, 27, 51–2, 93
slow violence 72

social realism 49
Sofya, Elif 127, 131, 154–6, 159, 161
Soysal, Sevgi 32–4, 99, 121 n.3
speciesism, speciesist 127, 142, 153, 156, 162
  interspecies 14, 162
  multispecies 152, 158
speculative biology 4, 37
Suny, Ronald Grigor 107–8, 110

Tanpınar, Ahmet Hamdi 10–11, 45–6
Taurus Mountains 1, 53, 56, 90–3, 99–102, 104–6, 113
Tekin, Latife 5, 18–19, 23, 49, 54, 60, 70, 127, 148
temporality
  climate and 4, 45, 47, 70, 72–3, 77–82
  ecological clocks 73, 79, 81
  generational time 70, 75
  irregular 46, 73, 78–9, 81–2
  narrative 70, 77
  timescale 70, 80
  and uncertainty 47, 70, 77
  See also belatedness
Tengriism 62
text
  ancient 27
  ecological 145
  second 148
  world- 143
Tharaud, Barry Charles 105
Thoreau, Henry David 94
Thrace 1, 21, 84 n.22
Tigris River 109–10
Tonguç, İsmail Hakkı 48
tourism 8, 14, 28, 30
toxicity, toxic 19, 23, 37, 39–40, 71, 158
transcorporeality 36, 39. *See also* Alaimo, Stacy; body
transfiguration 127, 142, 151–6, 161
Turcoman 91–2, 100
Türkçelik, Mehmet 38–9

Ünaydın, Ruşen Eşref 11
underwater
  environment 7, 9, 17, 38, 12–14
  life 35–6, 39

photography/videography 3, 9, 14–17, 39
  submersion 14–17, 39, 74
  See also diving
United Nations Framework Convention on Climate Change 54, 84 n.17
urban
  centers 11, 59, 90–1, 110
  development 9, 21, 23, 128
  sprawl 18, 21
  transformation 20–1, 23, 55–6
Uzuner, Buket 47, 54, 60–9, 76, 82

valley 4, 57, 89, 97, 107, 109, 117, 119–20
Van 100–1, 106, 114
Varol, Kemal 127, 130–4
Veli, Orhan 40 n.2
Vlastos, Yani 9, 32–5

walking 25, 33, 51, 63, 108–11, 133, 142, 155–8, 162
  narratives 90, 93–4, 120 n.3
  rural 4, 89–91, 93–9, 120, 121 n.4, 134
  urban 93, 99, 120 n.3
  See also Yoruk
war 25, 31, 61, 71–3, 76–7, 97–9, 104–7, 117, 120, 127, 130–4
waste 39–40, 79
  domestic 20–1, 35
  imported 35–6
  industrial 18–21, 35
water
  bodies of 4, 7–8, 15, 21, 40
  grabbing 57
  scarcity 4, 46, 50–4, 58–60
  toxic 18–20
wilderness 96, 98, 102, 135
Wolfe, Cary 131, 137, 144
Wordsworth, William 94
Wright, Alexis 80

Yerevan 106, 114
yersiz yurtsuz 93, 95
Yervant, Odyan 90, 107, 110–12
Yeşil Düşünce Derneği (Green Thought Association) 56

Yeşil Gazete (Green Newspaper) 56
Yeşiller Partisi (Green Party) 56
yokyer 157–61, 166 n.37
Yoldaş, Pınar 37–9

Yoruk 68, 90–3. *See also* walking
Yücel, Hasan Ali 43 n.25, 82 n.4

zoopoiesis 152

www.ingramcontent.com/pod-product-compliance
Lightning Source LLC
Chambersburg PA
CBHW052117300426
44116CB00010B/1699